HARVARD EAST ASIAN MONOGRAPHS

57

GOVERNMENT CONTROL OF THE PRESS
IN MODERN CHINA
1900-1949

GOVERNMENT CONTROL OF THE PRESS

IN MODERN CHINA

1900-1949

by

Lee-hsia Hsu Ting

Published by

East Asian Research Center

Harvard University

Distributed by

Harvard University Press

Cambridge, Mass.

1974

The East Asian Research Center at Harvard University
administers research projects designed to further
scholarly understanding of China, Japan, Korea,
Vietnam, Inner Asia, and adjacent areas. These studies
have been assisted by grants from the Ford Foundation.

Z
658
C6
T5
1974

Library of Congress No. 74-79850
SBN 674-35820-1

To
MY FATHER
and
the Loving Memory of
MY MOTHER

FOREWORD

Who can print *what?* That is a major unresolved issue in every country. This monograph presents detailed data on how the issue was treated during the first half of the twentieth century in China, specifically on how government intervention affected the publishing world.

The author, Lee-hsia Ting, was born and grew up in China and was graduated from the National Central University at Chungking in 1944 with an A.B. degree in English. She then attended Mount Holyoke College, where she took a master's degree in English literature in 1948. As an undergraduate in wartime Chungking she had edited a monthly, *Hsüeh-sheng chih yu* (The Students' Friend), published by her father, and after returning to China in 1948, she had further experience as an assistant professor at the University of Nanking (1948-51), as an assistant officer to the British Council in Nanking (1949-51), and as an editor in the United States Information Service in Hong Kong (1952-53), where she also published a number of Chinese translations of English works. In the 1960s Mrs. Ting became a professional librarian, taking a master's degree in library science at the University of Texas at Austin in 1964 and a Ph.D. in library science at the University of Chicago in 1969, where the present study began as a doctoral thesis. She is now assistant professor at Northern Illinois University at DeKalb.

Mrs. Ting's careful and painstaking exhumation of cases, incidents, and policies in Chinese publishing from 1900 to 1949 provides an unique basis for further work on this politically disputed but academically neglected field.

East Asian Research Center

CONTENTS

ACKNOWLEDGMENTS

Few American books on modern China do not owe a debt in one way or another to Professor John K. Fairbank. This one is no exception. It is a privilege to begin the acknowledgments by expressing my heartfelt gratitude to this distinguished scholar and great friend of China, whose encouragement and assistance have made the publication of this book possible. I am deeply indebted also to Dean Howard W. Winger, whose patient guidance and profound knowledge of the history of printing have been a constant source of inspiration to me; to Professor T. H. Tsien, who first suggested this investigation and helped me in various ways; and to Professor Philip Kuhn for his invaluable advice. I am grateful to the curators and staff of the University of Chicago Far Eastern Library, Library of Congress Orientalia Division, Harvard-Yenching Library, University of California (Berkeley) East Asiatic Library, and Hoover Institution Library, without whose kind permission to allow me to use their stacks, this study could not have been completed. I wish also to thank Mrs. Anne T. Stevens and Mrs. Florence Trefethen for their expert editing, Miss Sheila Merwin for checking romanizations, and Mrs. Suzanne Mayer for reading my manuscript.

INTRODUCTION

Political control over communications, including censorship and other kinds of restrictions, is not a problem peculiar to China. It has existed in every land in varying degrees in one form or another for many centuries. The censorship and other devices for political control that were employed in China during the first half of the twentieth century, however, had certain unusual features. Although China evolved during this period from an ancient empire into a young republic, the country was practically a "sub-colony" dominated by many foreign powers. Political upheaval and social unrest, oriented toward many alien ideologies including democracy and communism, caused varied and complex problems. The widespread use of Western printing methods toward the end of the nineteenth century had also brought with it a revolution in the publishing world and produced a rapid increase in the number and variety of publications, especially of newspapers and magazines. Writers and publishers, under the influence of the Western democratic tradition, began to clamor for freedom of speech and of the press. The conflict between regimes determined to suppress publications supposedly detrimental to them and writers bent on expressing their views reached a feverish pitch.

Because of the dominance of political problems throughout the entire period, emphasis on the suppression of dissenting political opinions, rather than allegedly wrong views on religion or ethics, was from the very beginning a most important objective of censorship, and it became increasingly important as the years went by. The control of the state was tighter over newspapers and magazines—especially those that dealt with current affairs and social, economic, or political ideas—than over books or other types of publications. The various constitutions promulgated in this period all guaranteed freedom of speech, writing, and publication, and yet the publication laws and regulations in one way or another always curtailed these constitutional rights of the people.

How did the political situation at the time help shape the

many publication laws and regulations in China? How were they put into practice? Did the censors faithfully carry out their duties? How did the government obtain control of some reputable newspapers and presses, and thereby exert its direct influence on their editorial or publishing policies? What were the reactions of the people in general, and the writers and publishers in particular, to governmental control? Did it achieve its goals, or did it only help bring about the downfall of the various regimes? Did the government authorities learn anything from their, or others', experience? Is there any truth in the theory that the censorship imposed by the Kuomintang government did not succeed in stopping the well-organized and persistent efforts of the Chinese Communists to spread their ideology and literature, but succeeded splendidly, on the other hand, in destroying the individual, feeble attempts of dissenting liberals? What effect did these policies have on the publishing world and publications in the country? What influence did they have on the intellectual history of China during this period? These are some of the interesting, but puzzling, questions.

Although a most fascinating problem, government control of the press in China during this period has never received a comprehensive and thorough investigation in any language. The purpose of this study is to fill the gap by tracing the development of the publication laws and regulations, presenting the many censorship cases, and discussing such various aspects of the problem as those listed above. Wherever space permits, brief references will also be made to the similarities and differences in method and theory between censorship in China during this period and that in the Western world.

This study concerns chiefly books, newspapers, and magazines —particularly those that dealt with current affairs and social, economic, and political ideas—published in China or by Chinese revolutionaries overseas from 1900, when there were growing demands for a constitutional government, to 1949, when the Chinese Communists took over the mainland and the state began to control almost all publications. Emphasis will be placed on the suppression of "dangerous" publications during those years when

China was under the rule of the Kuomintang. Communist-held or Japanese-occupied areas will only be mentioned briefly, since the Kuomintang regime was universally recognized as the only legitimate government of China at that time. Some important incidents, however, involved foreign authorities in the International Settlement at Shanghai, and these incidents will be treated. Other means of mass communication, such as movies, radio, and the stage, will not be included.

As is true with any investigation of unexplored subjects, the collecting of data for this study has been a major problem. Since the usual victims of suppression before 1911 were the revolutionary publications, many censorship cases have been described in books on the 1911 Revolution. Some writers have also reported on such cases which took place in the warlord years. Materials on government control when China was under the Kuomintang, however, are hard to find. Some journalists, for instance, wrote in great detail about their arrests by the warlords but, for obvious reasons, barely mentioned their arrests by the Kuomintang authorities. Except for those which happened in the foreign settlements in Shanghai, few censorship cases ever went to the court, and information on postal bans, persecution of writers, and so on, was seldom released officially. The nature of this study has precluded any possible assistance from the Kuomintang government in Taiwan. Information in published bibliographies and indexes is scarce and fragmentary, and even tables of contents of magazines are not entirely reliable. It has thus been necessary for me to glean information from all types of obscure nooks and crannies in Chinese magazines, newspapers, and government documents published during these years, including seemingly irrelevant essays, notes by editors, letters to and from the editors, authors' biographies, and so on. Valuable information on specific cases may sometimes turn up in unexpected places, such as editors' publication schedules and brief announcements, advertisements, and news stories from various towns and cities.

Although this study covers books, newspapers, and magazines alike, it has obtained most of its information from Chinese periodical literature published during this period. Liberal magazines have supplied more materials for the study than conservative, radical, and Communist publications, but these have also been consulted. Chinese periodical literature in this period enjoyed a unique position. For various reasons, periodical publishing flourished more than the publication of books. Many important works appeared in magazines before they appeared in book form, and some can be found only in magazines. A few periodicals, such as *Hsin ch'ing-nien (La Jeunesse)*, exerted a tremendous influence on Chinese intellectual history. Over 15,000 magazines, one may add, saw the light during this period in China.[1] Few of them survived more than a few years; some might have had only one or two issues. Not many of these magazines have found their way into American libraries. Even when a library has the title, it rarely has all the issues. There were occasions when I had to look for different issues of one and the same magazine in all of the five libraries listed above in the Acknowledgments. I have combed carefully through shelf after shelf of magazines in these libraries, which have the largest Chinese collections in this country. Though I do not claim exhaustiveness, I feel that the materials covered in this book constitute a representative cross section of all available sources and can thus present a reliable picture.

Political affiliations in China were extremely tangled and complex throughout this period. One has to have an intimate knowledge of the conditions prevailing there at the time to evaluate and interpret properly the often confusing and conflicting information. I have consulted many books in modern Chinese history, and have made every possible attempt to give an objective and impartial account, based on the data I have collected. When there is more than one version of a story, the other versions are often given in the notes, if not in the text itself.

Any study of censorship can be made from different angles. Since the principal target of government control in China was political dissension, it is natural to present the materials grouped chronologically according to the various political eras in Chinese history: namely, the last years of the Ch'ing dynasty (1900-1911),

the first fifteen years of the new republic (1912-1927), the prewar
years under the Kuomintang (1927-1937), the war of resistance
(1937-1945), and the postwar years (1945-1949). The first chapter,
however, will be devoted to the development of the publication
laws and the important regulations for the press in order to provide
a general background, especially for those who are interested in a
comparative study of similar practices in various countries.[2]
Experts on China who are familiar with Chinese laws and regulations
may ignore it.

The extensive use of Chinese sources and references to Chinese
publications has made it necessary to include a number of romanized
Chinese names, although I have tried to keep them to a minimum.
When a Chinese publication is mentioned for the first time, its title
in romanized form is used, together with its English title if it has
one. The English title, if better known in this country, will then be
used consistently in the text. For those publications that do not
have English titles, translated titles are often supplied, also in
parentheses, but not italicized. Some frequently used terms in
romanization which will not be translated are *pao* (newspaper),
jih-pao (daily), *wan-pao* (evening paper), *chou-k'an* or *chou-pao*
(weekly), *yueh-k'an* (monthly), and *tsa-chih* (magazine). Except
for a few names well known in the West, personal names are
romanized according to the Wade-Giles system, with the surname
given first in accordance with the Chinese custom. The conventional
form of geographical names is used. The city that served as the
capital of China during the last three imperial dynasties is called
Peking except for the chapters dealing with the years 1927-1949,
when it was called Peiping. Translated forms are used, however, for
all government offices, laws, and regulations. To save space, the
Kuomintang (Nationalist Party)[3] will be referred to as the KMT or
simply the Party as it was often called during its reign on mainland
China, and the Chinese Communist Party, the CCP. Although the
word "press" is used to represent all printed matter in this study,
the term "press law" (*hsin-wen fa*) means only a law designed to
govern newspapers and magazines. It should not be confused with
the term "publication law" (*ch'u-pan fa*), which covers all types of

publications. Because of the large number of journal articles cited, the bibliography lists only books, journals, and newspapers, but not specific titles of articles. Sources of information and further references are, however, carefully indicated in the notes at the end of the book.

One last word of caution: Western readers who live in countries where there is a clear distinction between the powers of the executive, legislative, and judicial branches of the government may find it difficult to understand the nature of the authorities responsible for the suppression of publications in China during this period. In the imperial and warlord days, the emperors' words or the warlords' wishes could be the law, and whether a written law was applied or disregarded depended on whether it suited their purposes. For the most part of the second quarter of the present century, China was under the dictatorship of the KMT, and the range and scope of the Party's authority was similar to that of a Communist party in a Communist country. The national government was responsible to the KMT National Congress. The Party's Central Executive Committee decided on the guidelines for lawmaking; it often took upon itself the duties of a judge and meted out punishments to offending publishers as well as editors. The Party's headquarters, central as well as local, together with the Ministry of the Interior and local governments, were invested by law with the authority to regulate the press. However, military personnel and, in the later years, the secret agents and San-min-chu-i Youth Corps (the Youth Corps of the Three People's Principles, hereafter referred to as the Youth Corps) also often took the law into their own hands. On many occasions, as this work will show, even the victimized publishers and editors did not know for sure who or which agency had authorized the closing of their publications or the arrest of their persons. I have tried to describe such cases with the utmost clarity; for the instances where this has been impossible I must beg the indulgence of my readers.

Chapter I

PUBLICATION LAWS AND REGULATIONS
IN MODERN CHINA

China, like all countries where books have been produced and read, has had a long history of attempts by nervous officials to censor, repress, or in some way control them. As in other countries, too, official concern has mounted whenever books have been made more easily available to wider groups of readers. This became apparent with the spread of printing in China, which began as early as the eighth century. In 1090, Su Ch'e, an official who had returned from a mission in the northern provinces, made a report to the Che Tsung Emperor which contained specific references to the possibly harmful effects of unauthorized books. He wrote:

> People of this dynasty [i.e., country] make blocks for print-
> ing . . . Many of the printed books are circulating there [i.e.,
> in the North] . . . Ignorant common people have been printing
> even obscene literature in order to make a profit. If books
> were allowed to spread freely to the North, they might either
> reveal national secrets or arouse the barbarians' contempt and
> disgust. Either would be bad.[1]

These are familiar strictures. Su, like many officials all over the world throughout the history of printing, recommended a system of censorship and control so that no books offensive to the imperial government could be printed and the offensive ones already in print could be destroyed. His recommendations were accepted, for the Board of Rites, in its memorial to the emperor shortly afterwards, acknowledged them and mentioned the types of books that should not be published, the procedures for censorship, and the punish-ments for offenders.[2]

Small commercial papers, predecessors of modern newspapers, were also in circulation in the Sung dynasty (A.D. 960-1280). As the fear of foreign invasion bred rumors, the government took measures to regulate these papers too. One of the first references to such attempts was recorded in 1193.[3] Items usually prohibited in publication laws all over the world, such as those revealing government or military secrets, spreading rumors, printing obscene literature, and the like, were outlawed during those days in the criminal code of the Sung dynasty or by imperial proclamations.[4]

One of the old statutes concerning publications that deserves our special attention is "Tsao yao-shu yao-yen" (Prohibition of devilish books and talks), since it was by this law that the notorious *Su pao* case was supposed to be tried in 1903. Included in one of the sections on "Thieves and Robbers" in the Penal Code, it was promulgated first in the T'ang dynasty (A.D. 718-906) to prohibit witches, wizards, and other kinds of sorcerers from exploiting and cheating ignorant people, and to prescribe punishments for makers and distributors of such writings.[5] It seems to have had at first no political implications, nor was it directed specifically at printed works.[6] Subsequent dynasties continued to make use of the law for controlling the press after slight revisions.[7] Not until the Ch'ing dynasty, however, did the nature of the law begin to change. The K'ang-hsi Emperor expanded it in 1677, 1679, and 1714 to include three provisions which specifically forbade pornography and dangerous writings, and the Yung-cheng Emperor in 1725 made the three provisions into bylaws and added a fourth one, which forbade people to spread "wicked ideas" or "rumors" by speech, song, or writing, to circulate obscene literature, or to seek confidential information. The statute was revised slightly several times thereafter and remained in effect until the first decade of this century.[8] The significance of the prohibition of "devilish" books is obvious. Ordinances of this kind were issued and frequently reissued, especially during periods of social disorder, as may be seen in the Veritable Records of the nineteenth century.

Although the first publication law did not come into effect until 1906, the idea of having a set of laws designed specifically for the press had been contemplated before then. Western influence began to flood into China after the ending of the Opium War in 1842. The

Manchu government, because of its inefficiency and corruption, yielded many of China's sovereign rights and territories to the Western powers. The defeat of the Chinese Imperial Navy in the Sino-Japanese War of 1895 made Chinese scholars clamor for reforms to save the nation. Inspired by high ideals of patriotism and aided by the introduction of Western methods of printing, Chinese newspapers and magazines began to proliferate. The Kuang-hsü Emperor, though overshadowed and often cowed by the conservative Empress Dowager Tz'u-hsi, was anxious to introduce reforms to rejuvenate the nation. In 1898, he endorsed Grand Councillor Sun Chia-nai's recommendation to appoint K'ang Yu-wei the editor-in-chief of *Shih-wu pao* (*Chinese Progress*), a progressive paper in Shanghai. Sun's suggestion that the editor-in-chief be held responsible for what was to be printed in the paper made K'ang, whose reform program had incurred the jealousy and hatred of many powerful conservative elements, very uneasy. He was afraid that he might be persecuted some day for an imaginary crime, because at this time, as he put it, "the progressive and the conservative elements are in conflict, and there is no definite idea about what is right or wrong, black or white." A written press law, he seemed to believe, could protect him. Thus, on August 9 of that year, Sun presented K'ang's plan to the emperor and mentioned for the first time in an official Chinese document the term "press law":

> As for the press law, K'ang Yu-wei will collect and translate the laws and regulations of various countries and transmit them to me for submission to the judgment of your Imperial Majesty.

The emperor immediately accepted Sun's recommendation and ordered K'ang to draft a press law.[9] With the failure of the Reform Movement of 1898 a little over a month later, however, the Empress Dowager obtained control of the country again. K'ang fled from China, and that was the end of his chance to write an enlightened law to protect the press.

In August 1906, the Special Statute of the Great Ch'ing

Dynasty Governing Publications, drafted jointly by the Ministry of Commerce, the Ministry of Police, and the Ministry of Education, was promulgated.[10] Besides having the distinction of being the first formal publication law in China, it is noteworthy because of the following features, some or all of which may also be found in the publication laws enforced later in that country:

(1) For the first time, a special bureau, the Bureau for the Registration of Publications, was set up in Peking to regulate the registration of all printers, publishers, and printed matter.

(2) In order to preserve the dignity of the imperial household, the law meted out severe punishment for all who had a part in libelous publications—the author, printer, owners and managers of bookstores, and even salesmen.

(3) The local police was formally given the power to deal with publications. All printers and publishers were required to apply for registration at their local police offices and submit copies of the publication to the police and the Bureau for the Registration of Publications. All printed matter had to bear the name and address of the printer, who was required to keep a detailed record of everything he had printed for the inspection of the police.

(4) The post office was officially employed as a means of indirect control, as it was forbidden to deliver the "recorded materials" printed or published by anyone who had been convicted once of sedition or twice of libel or blackmail.

Soon afterwards, the Ministry of Police announced the Nine Regulations Governing Newspapers, which specified that every new newspaper, before it began publication, had to apply for registration and obtain approval from the Bureau for the Registration of Publications. Among the things that a newspaper must not print were comments on "government policies and measures," or "information about diplomatic or domestic affairs" forbidden specifically by responsible authorities. At that time, newspapers often appeared in the same format as magazines, and the distinction between the two was not very clear. The regulations were thus designed for the control of both newspapers and magazines. They supplemented the first publication law, and were rescinded when the Press Law of the Great Ch'ing Dynasty came into effect in 1908.

The first press law, consisting of forty-five articles, was drafted by the Ministry of Commerce and modeled after an obsolescent Japanese press law. It was later slightly modified in 1910. With a few exceptions, such as publications devoted only to scholarly research, the arts, and such matters, all newspapers (i.e., newspapers and magazines) were required to register and their publishers to post a bond with the local government, which would then report to the Executive Board via the governor of the province. They also had to be submitted to the police for examination before their publication (Article 7). The introduction of the bond system and the insistence on prepublication censorship certainly instituted severe restrictions. The most interesting feature, however, was Article 40, which empowered the customs authorities to prohibit the importation of undesirable periodical literature printed in foreign countries. At that time, one may add, the revolutionary magazines were chiefly published in Japan and then imported into China.

In spite of the strenuous efforts of the imperial government to control publishing, revolutionary ideas flourished. In 1911, the revolution led by Dr. Sun Yat-sen overthrew the Manchu dynasty. A provisional government was set up in Nanking, and Dr. Sun took his oath as the provisional president on January 1, 1912. China became a republic.

On March 11, 1912, the Provisional Constitution was adopted. This was not the first constitution known to the Chinese people in those tumultuous months,[11] but it did exert lasting influence on later Chinese constitutions. Chapter II, Article 6.4, for instance, promised to give the people, for the first time in Chinese history, freedom of speech, writing, and publication, though Article 15 specified that these rights might be curtailed by laws enacted to improve the public well-being or to maintain peace during any emergency.

Since the new government did not endorse the publication

law and the press law of the Ch'ing dynasty, the Ministry of the Interior put into effect, in March 1912, a Provisional Press Law, which required publishers and editors of newspapers and magazines to register with the Ministry by April 1 of that year. The law was soon rescinded by Dr. Sun upon the request of the National Press Association, because it had not been enacted by the legislative body in accordance with the Constitution, and the Parliament was expected to draft a publication law which would make a separate law for newspapers and magazines unnecessary.

The provisional government, unfortunately, was short-lived. On March 10, the day before the Senate in Nanking proclaimed the Provisional Constitution, Yuan Shih-k'ai was formally installed in Peking as the provisional president of the new republic. In his effort to further his personal gains and fulfill his ambitions, Yuan made the Nanking government move to Peking. His Constitutional Compact, which reshaped the government and substantially strengthened the powers of the president, was put into effect on May 1, 1914. Hoping to become an emperor, Yuan could not tolerate any civil liberties for the people. Nevertheless, the constitutional articles guaranteeing freedom of speech, writing, and publication were retained with the qualifying clause "within the scope of laws and ordinances" (Chapter II, Article 5.4).

Shortly before the appearance of the Constitutional Compact, a set of newspaper regulations, thirty-five in number, was promulgated on April 2, 1914, and revised a year later. The rules were quite similar to those in the Press Law of 1908. Newspaper and periodical publishers had to apply for licenses from the police. The bond system was retained. Advance censorship and indirect control through the post office and customs service were not mentioned. These regulations were abrogated in 1916 by Li Yuan-hung, who succeeded Yuan as president.

More important than these regulations, however, was Yuan's publication law, which followed in essence the Publication Law of 1906. Containing twenty-three articles, it was promulgated on December 4, 1914, and was retained long after Yuan's death.

Among the articles which were to be invoked time and again was Article 3, which stipulated that the publisher's name, address, date of birth, native town, and the date of publication had to be clearly printed. The most famous article was Article 11, which forbade the publication of "any writing, drawing or picture" if it "aims at a change in the form of the government," "is harmful to the public peace," "tends to impair public morals," or "reveals any secret" documents of "a military, diplomatic or any other official organ" without authorization. In case of violations, the proper police authority might confiscate the publication and its type form, and the author and the publisher were to be punished with a fine or imprisonment.

For more than a decade after Yuan came into power in 1912, China was in chaos. The warlords, who occupied different parts of China, constantly attacked and harassed one another. From 1915 onward, China's intellectuals searched feverishly for new solutions to the nation's problems. They were inspired by one of the most potent forces in the modern world, nationalism, and their indignation was often directed at those who, they felt, had betrayed the country to foreign interests. National Peking University, situated at the capital and nerve center of China, became a hotbed for agitators and started the May Fourth Movement—a movement now regarded by the Chinese Communists as marking the beginning of contemporary revolutionary nationalism in China. The Russian Revolution of 1917 gave further impetus to the Chinese intellectuals, since it led to the overthrow of the dynastic order and reminded them of the Chinese Revolution of 1911. Marxism came flooding into China. The Chinese Communist Party was formally established on July 1, 1921, and leftist periodicals kept appearing in the market.

On October 10, 1923, the Substantive or "Permanent" Constitution of the Republic of China was promulgated to replace the Provisional Constitution of 1912, which had again become effective after Li Yuan-hung had repealed Yuan's Constitutional Compact in 1916. Freedom of speech, authorship, and publication was again guaranteed, but belied by a qualifying clause: "Such freedom shall not be restricted except in accordance with the law" (Chapter IV, Article 11).

The Publication Law of 1914, which had aroused great indignation among the Chinese public, practically fell into disuse after Yuan's death. Foreign authorities of the International Settlement in Shanghai, however, repeatedly employed the law to prosecute publishers and editors from 1923 to January 1926, when Tuan Ch'i-jui, the provisional chief executive, finally rescinded it under heavy public pressure.

A year before the repeal of Yuan's publication law, Chu Shen, the commissioner of the Peking Municipal Police, had promulgated the Regulations Governing the Press, ten in number. For the first time, every publisher of newspapers and magazines was required to have a reliable firm as his guarantor and permission from the landlord of the premises he was to use. Also for the first time, news agencies (which had just begun to develop in China) were mentioned separately in Chinese laws or regulations governing the press, and a distinction was drawn between newspapers and magazines. It is interesting to note that, because of the liberal ideas then in vogue, periodicals concerned with "academic research" were specifically singled out and placed under control too.

When the warlords were fighting with one another in the other parts of China, the KMT completed its reorganization in Canton in July 1924, and allowed individual Chinese Communists to join it. In April 1927, Chiang Kai-shek and other KMT leaders went to Nanking and declared it the capital of China. The Northern Expedition led by Chiang was a success, but the Great Purge ousting the Communist elements from the KMT soon began. On October 10, 1928, the national government established by the KMT in Nanking became the central government of China. The Organic Law for the Republic of China, promulgated by the KMT Central Executive Committee on October 4, 1928, declared its adherence to Dr. Sun Yat-sen's Three People's Principles and provided for a system of "political tutelage" for a period of six years, during which time the national government would administer national affairs under the direction and supervision of the KMT. Meanwhile the Communists maintained a separate army and an independent soviet government over several provinces in Central China, with their capital in Juikin. The suppression of communism was thus one of the most important domestic problems confronting the KMT. Besides the five large-scale military "bandit suppression" campaigns launched by the KMT between 1931 and 1933, this policy was also clearly reflected in the publication laws and regulations promulgated by the regime.

In 1929, the KMT Central Political Committee passed the six guiding principles for setting up laws to regulate publications. For the first time, acknowledgment was officially made that a publication law was to be enacted to "safeguard the freedom of the press," though the second part of the same principle, "to prevent the circulation of improper publications," tended to cancel out what was promised in the first part of the sentence. Registration and censorship of all publications would be handled by authorities under the national government. Publications "to propagate reactionary ideas" were specifically mentioned among those which might not be registered.

In accordance with these principles, a new publication law, containing forty-four articles in six chapters, was promulgated on December 16, 1930. Its principal provisions were as follows:

(1) The publisher of a newspaper or periodical had to register, fifteen days before the publication of its first issue, with the Ministry of the Interior through the provincial government (or special municipal government under the direct jurisdiction of the Executive Yuan, such as Shanghai) and, if the publication should deal with matters that concerned the principles or affairs of the KMT, also with the KMT Central Publicity Department through the Party's provincial (or municipal) headquarters.

(2) Copies of the publication had to be submitted to certain government agencies, and some publications also to the KMT Central Publicity Department.

(3) Publications were forbidden to contain items designed "to undermine the KMT or violate the Three People's Principles," or "to overthrow the National Government or to damage the

interests of the Republic of China." Article 21 enjoined that

> In war, emergency or time of necessity under special circum-
> stances, publications shall be forbidden or restricted, in
> accordance with the orders of the National Government, from
> carrying items dealing with political, military, and foreign
> affairs.

(4) Violators were punishable by the prohibition of circulation,
the detention or seizure of the publications, the destruction of the
type forms, fines, and prison terms. Offensive publications printed
in foreign countries might be banned or seized at the time of their
entry.

(5) Certain types of persons whom the government deemed
undesirable would not be allowed to serve as publishers or editors
of newspapers or periodicals. Publishers, however, were not required
to deposit a bond.

A set of twenty-five regulations entitled Regulations Governing
the Application of the Publication Law was drafted jointly by the
Ministry of the Interior and the KMT Central Publicity Department,
and was enforced in 1931. All publications and pictures that had
anything to do with the principles of the KMT or the implementation of its programs or policies were required to register with the
Central Publicity Department. Since the KMT was in control of the
country, any publication that discussed current affairs could thus
be interpreted as belonging to this category. The author or publisher
of every book was required to submit the manuscript first to the
Ministry of the Interior (or the Central Publicity Department
whenever applicable), together with its application for a permit for
publication, even though the Publication Law did not require the
submission of manuscripts for approval. Any book published
without a permit would be confiscated and the author or publisher
punished.

To control the distribution of publications, the government
regulated bookstores and compiled lists of prohibited books and
magazines, which often included many seemingly nonpolitical

books already approved by, and registered with, the authorities in accordance with the Publication Law. Apparently, manuscripts submitted to the government agencies were not always examined, although publishers always had to suffer the consequences. The latter, therefore, requested uniform prepublication censorship. The result was the establishment of the Censorship Commission in Shanghai, which was placed under the KMT Central Publicity Department, and the promulgation of the Rules for Censoring Books and Periodicals in 1934. According to the Organization Charter of the Censorship Commission of Books and Periodicals, which was approved by a standing committee of the KMT Central Executive Committee, the purpose of the commission was to "carefully suppress [undesirable] publications, increase the efficiency of censorship, and [thus] reduce possible [financial] losses to publishers and authors." Manuscripts of all books and magazines in the fields of literature and social sciences were to be censored before publication. However, "books and periodicals which are connected with the local Party or government organizations" and "periodicals which have been published for over a year, demonstrated their correctness in thought, and never contravened the Standards for Censoring Propaganda Materials or the Publication Law" could apply for a censorship exemption permit from the Central Publicity Department. The censorship permit (or censorship exemption permit) number had to be printed on the back cover of the publication.[12]

The period of "political tutelage" by the KMT was supposed to end in 1935. In 1936, a Draft Constitution of the Republic of China was promulgated, and a People's Congress was scheduled to meet, on November 12, 1937, to adopt the constitution and to organize a new national government responsible to it, instead of the KMT National Congress. Like the Provisional Constitution promulgated in 1931, freedom of speech, writing, and publication was again solemnly promised in the Draft Constitution, with the qualifying clause: "Such freedom shall not be restricted except in accordance with the law" (Chapter II, Article 13).

Since the KMT presumably was to relinquish its one-party

control soon, the Revised Publication Law, which contained fifty-four articles in six chapters, was promulgated on July 8, 1937,[13] and the new Regulations about its application on July 28. The new law was in the main the same as the Publication Law of 1930. All articles hitherto regarded as objectionable by scholars and writers were preserved without any change. As in the Publication Law of 1930, publications still could not contain items "designed to undermine the KMT or violate the Three People's Principles." Two types of publications were specified as punishable: seditious literature (Article 21) and obscene literature (Article 22). The punishment was to be much more severe for allegedly seditious literature than for obscene and indecent literature. A newspaper or periodical could be closed down permanently if it violated Article 21, but a violator of Article 22 would be penalized with nothing worse than temporary suspension or a fine.

Provisions were made for even tighter control of publications. In the Publication Law of 1930, publishers of newspapers and periodicals were required only to register with the Ministry of the Interior or the Central Publicity Department through provincial (or municipal) authorities. There was no mention of approval or rejection of the application. Now, publishers had to apply for registration, prior to the publication of the first issue, with the responsible local authorities, who were to forward the application within fifteen days to the provincial (or municipal) government for approval. Publication could begin after obtaining this approval. Under normal circumstances, the law said, the provincial (or municipal) government was to decide on the application within twenty-eight days and, if found acceptable, forward it to the Ministry of the Interior for a registration card. Local authorities might send officials to investigate the organization, circulation, and other activities of the news agencies, suspend the sales and circulation of publications which violated the law, temporarily seize the copies, and report the case, through the provincial (or municipal) government, to the Ministry of the Interior for instruction. The introduction of the licensing system deserves special attention, as it was to play a very important role in suppressing undesirable publications, especially during the postwar years.

Other major changes in the new law were verbal rather than substantial: the KMT Central Publicity Department was now called the Ministry of Information, and the Party organs at various levels were no longer mentioned as regulating agencies. The Revised Publication Law seemed to assign a relatively minor role to the Ministry of Information, which ostensibly was only to receive a copy of the application form from the Ministry of the Interior after the latter issued the registration card, and then get one copy of every publication as several other government agencies did. In fact, it continued to be the most powerful agency for press control.

On the day before the promulgation of the Revised Publication Law, a far more important event took place. For several decades, Japan had been engaged in carrying out her plan of aggression, and creating one incident after another in China as pretexts for the eventual conquest of the entire country. In September 1931, the Japanese invaded Manchuria and soon afterwards established the puppet state of "Manchoukuo." In April 1933, Japanese forces penetrated the province of Hopei. Although popular demand raged for the cessation of the civil war and for resistance to the foreign invaders, the KMT government was more interested in its so-called "bandit suppression" campaigns. The CCP, the object of these campaigns, suggested a united front against Japan. On February 10, 1937, its Central Committee offered to suspend all hostile activities against the national government, change the title of the Chinese Soviet Government to the Special Area Government of the Republic of China and that of the Red Army to the Chinese National Revolutionary Army, and place the latter under the command of the national government in Nanking. To forestall strong resistance, the Japanese struck hard and fast. With the Marco Polo Bridge Incident on July 7, the Chinese war for national survival began.

In September 1937, after lengthy negotiations between Chiang Kai-shek and Chou En-lai, came the formal announcement of the formation of the second KMT-CCP united front. Though both parties were in nominal accord regarding their objectives and paid lip service to the Three People's Principles, they interpreted Sun Yat-sen's theories in very different ways and remained strange bedfellows.

On November 20, 1937, the national government announced the removal of its seat from Nanking to Chungking. All plans to convene the People's Congress were interrupted, so the people were told, and China remained in the period of "political tutelage" under the KMT. The KMT Extraordinary National Congress adopted, on April 1, 1938, the Program of Armed Resistance and National Reconstruction, which declared:

> The freedom of speech, the freedom of the press, and the freedom of assembly shall be *fully* protected by law in the course of the war, provided they do not contravene the Three People's Principles which are the nation's highest principles, and provided they are within the scope of laws and ordinances.[14]

Nevertheless, the Revised Standard for Censoring Wartime Books and Periodicals, directed clearly at opposition parties—especially the CCP—was promulgated in the same year. Since the Revised Standard was admittedly to be used as the source of guiding principles in censorship during the war years, its two parts will be translated in full.

I. Erroneous utterances [are those which]
   A. distort, misunderstand, or twist out of context the principles, declarations, political platforms, policies, and resolutions of the Kuomintang;
   B. record incorrectly the revolutionary history and administrative programs of the central government with the purpose of confusing readers;
   C. express views from a selfish partisan standpoint incompatible with the principle of placing the interest of the nation above everything else;
   D. spread opinions inconsistent with the need of our war of resistance and harmful to the future conduct of the war of resistance;

E. deliberately express pessimistic opinions or exaggerate the strength of the enemy, and may tend to weaken the people's conviction in our ultimate victory;

F. undermine the morals and good customs of our country, or give vent to other decadent utterances which may dampen the people's zeal for the war of resistance or exert bad influence on society;

G. contain prejudicial, radical, and bigoted statements that may arouse the ill feelings of friendly nations and become detrimental to our international relations.

II. Reactionary utterances [are those which]

A. maliciously slander or contravene the Three People's Principles and the declarations, political platforms, and policies of the central government;

B. maliciously attack the Kuomintang, slander the government, calumniate the leader or any current programs of the central government;

C. disclose secret military or diplomatic information or plans of national defense without the approval of the authorities;

D. conduct propaganda for the enemy, puppet organizations, or traitors;

E. foment prejudicial and radical ideas stressing class opposition, and may thus undermine our sacred mission to unite all forces for the war of resistance and the reconstruction of the nation;

F. agitate for the establishment of any puppet organizations other than the National Government in China, any puppet bandit armies other than the National Revolutionary Army, and all other reactionary actions which may disrupt national unity;

G. provoke hostilities between the national and local governments, or cause misunderstanding between the Kuomintang, the Government, the military, and the people, with a view to impairing the unity of the entire nation;

H. spread and fabricate rumors in order to disturb and confuse the people.

In 1939, the Revised Wartime Press Censorship Regulations, consisting of fifty-five regulations in five chapters, were approved by the National Military Council.[15] Among the types of information listed as censorable were reports prejudicial to the KMT. The Wartime Press Censorship Bureau was established under the supervision of both the National Military Council and the Ministry of Information. The Bureau was to be the highest wartime press censorship organization. Under its direct control, there would be a censorship department in each province or special municipality, and a censorship office in each important district.

In 1940, the Regulations for Censoring the Manuscripts of Wartime Books and Periodicals, containing nineteen regulations, came into effect. "To satisfy the needs of the wartime," a Central Commission for the Censoring of Books and Periodicals (hereafter to be called the Central Censorship Commission) was to be organized as the central organ for the censorship of wartime books and periodicals, with the provincial, municipal, or district censorship bureaus (hereafter to be called censorship offices) taking charge of censorship duties in their respective localities. The relationship between the Central Censorship Commission and the censorship offices was similar to that between the Wartime Press Censorship Bureau and the local press censorship offices as described above.

Books and magazines could not be published (nor could those published before the regulations came into effect be distributed) without a censor permit number displayed on the cover, except for works dealing with the natural and applied sciences, or textbooks approved by the Ministry of Education. Two copies of each book or periodical, upon its publication, were to be sent to the censorship office for rechecking to assure that no undesirable material had found its way into the publication after initial examination of the manuscript. Any part of a manuscript containing statements repugnant to the government would be suppressed unless the necessary deletions or revisions required by the censorship office had been made.

By this time, the deterioration in the KMT-CCP alliance had

become apparent. Patriotism had gradually yielded to partisan interests, and mutual distrust had developed into outright hostility. In January 1941, the "New Fourth Army Incident," in which the Communist New Fourth Army was almost completely wiped out by the KMT troops, brought the conflict into the open. As relationships between the two parties worsened, the control of the press became much more severe, and more rules and regulations were put into effect.

In 1941, the Rules for Submitting Periodicals for Censorship were announced. The editor or publisher of a periodical was required to furnish, besides other items, a detailed table of contents each time a manuscript was submitted for censorship. All manuscripts had to be published as permitted, without further changes or uncensored materials. Periodicals could not reveal the titles of articles deleted by the order of the censorship office. Editors could not make any explanation to the readers, either in the editor's postscript or the editor's note, as to the passages or articles that had been deleted; nor could they make any notation in the article suggesting the dictates of the censors, such as "the above has been omitted," "what comes in between has been omitted," "the following has been omitted," or use any other means to indicate deletions or revisions by the order of the censorship office (Rule no. 7).[16] All periodical covers, illustrations, editor's postscripts, editor's notes, and short supplementary notes to fill up small blank spaces between articles also had to be examined. Dr. Sun Yat-sen's teachings or Generalissimo Chiang Kai-shek's speeches "respectfully" reprinted to fill out such blank spaces would be exempt from censorship (Rule no. 8). The censor permit number was to be printed on the upper left corner of the back cover, but in no other place. What was covered in Rules no. 7 and 8, one may add, had actually been in practice for some time. Aware of its claim to being a free, democratic government, the KMT did not want any trace of censorship shown in any publications.

The Rules for Submitting Books for Censorship were announced in 1942. The first part of this set of rules concerned the censoring of the manuscripts of books, and was about the same as the rules for periodicals. Its second part, which dealt with books published earlier, between July 1937 and September 1940, specified that such books might not be sold until they had been censored and listed in the "Books Permitted for Circulation." Publishers or authors were required to submit manuscripts for censorship if they intended to issue a new edition or a reprint of these books. Strict control was thus placed on those books published during the honeymoon period of the union between the KMT and the CCP.

In the same year, the National General Mobilization Act came into effect. Though this act was not designed exclusively for the press, two of its articles did have important bearing and will be quoted here:

> Article 22. Upon enforcement of this law, the Government may, whenever necessary, impose restrictions on or discontinue a newspaper or news agency, restrictions on a statement published in a newspaper, news correspondence or other printed matter, or may require the newspapers to publish a specific statement.
> Article 23. Upon enforcement of this law, the Government may, whenever necessary, impose restrictions on the people's freedom of speech, publication, writing, correspondence, assembly, and association.[17]

Two years later, in 1944, two new sets of regulations were promulgated. One was called the Regulations for the Censorship of Wartime Publications and Standards for Censorable Information, and the other was the Regulations for Censorship of Wartime Books and Periodicals. As compared with the previous rules and regulations, the two somewhat similar new sets seemed a little more liberal.

Regulation no. 1 of the first set declared that, in order "to protect national defense secrets and to maintain social order, the National Government exercises the right of censorship over wartime publications." It then went on to list under twelve headings the standards by which writings might be censored. Besides following the provisions in Chapter 4 of the Revised Publication Law, the censors were also to suppress information "contradicting the highest

principles on which the Government of this country is founded."
The Three People's Principles had always been held as the "highest
principles of this country," as the Program of Armed Resistance
and National Reconstruction had reaffirmed in 1938. According to
the explanation following these regulations, any writing could be
construed as contradicting the "highest principles" of the nation if
it should

(1) incite contention, alienate, and disrupt the unity of the
people in the country;
(2) advocate the principle of aggression;
(3) propagate Fascism or class dictatorship;
(4) propagate private monopoly;
(5) propagate class struggle.

The important difference between these two sets of regulations
and the previous ones lay in the distinction between censorship in
advance (censoring of manuscripts) and censorship after publication
(censoring of printed matter). All newspapers, plays, and motion
pictures still had to be censored in manuscript form. Authors and
publishers of certain types of materials not primarily concerned
with military, political, or foreign affairs could now have a choice
between having their works censored in manuscript form or in
printed form. Those who "voluntarily" submitted manuscripts for
censorship were to be absolved from blame for writings approved
by the censors. This was a welcome change, since there had been
at least one very famous case in which a publisher-editor was
punished for publishing an article already approved by the censors.[18]
One regulation stipulated that "explanations of the Standards
of Censorable Information shall be forwarded from time to time by
the Central Censorship Commission to the publishers of books and
periodicals." The meaning of this regulation seems to have been
that the explanations of the Standards might vary from time to
time, and that the authors and publishers had to watch always for
the varying interpretations in order not to offend the censors.
After the Sino-Japanese War ended in 1945, the national
government moved back to Nanking. China did not enjoy peace,

though, because the civil war was waged on an even larger scale. On December 25, 1947, the Constitution of the Republic of China became effective. Needless to add, the people's "freedom of speech, teaching, writing, and publication" was once again most solemnly guaranteed, and then negated by a qualifying clause that such freedoms might not be restricted by law unless under certain circumstances (Chapter II, Articles 11 and 23). China finally had a "constitutional" government, at least in name. Many wartime laws and regulations had been rescinded soon after the war. The Revised Publication Law nevertheless remained in effect, and was often invoked along with other special laws, such as the Martial Law (revised in 1948, and again in 1949), the National General Mobilization Act, Provisional Measures for Punishing the Violation of the National General Mobilization Act (promulgated in 1942 and revised in 1949), and Measures for Punishing Treason and Rebellion (1949).[19]

In 1949, the Chinese Communists took over the mainland, and the KMT government fled to Taiwan. Under the Communist rule, government control of the press has been complete. Although there has not been any law specifically entitled "publication law," many regulations and administrative orders have been issued to control publications and their distribution, such as the Provisional Regulations Governing Publishers, Printers and Distributors, the Provisional Regulations Governing the Registration of Periodicals (both promulgated on August 16, 1952), and Provisional Regulations for the Control of the Stalls Renting Books and Periodicals (promulgated on July 20, 1955). In Taiwan, the Revised Publication Law of 1937 was replaced, on April 9, 1952, by a new publication law. Six years later, on June 28, 1958, a more stringent publication law was adopted in spite of protests from many quarters alleging that the new law might abridge freedom of the press. Several other special laws have also been in effect there. Since these laws and regulations lie beyond the scope of this study, they will not be discussed here.

Chapter II

THE TWILIGHT OF THE CH'ING DYNASTY, 1900–1911

Although China has had a long history of journalism, modern newspapers as they are known today did not come into existence there until the nineteenth century, when the foreign missionaries, in order to facilitate the propagation of the Gospel, introduced Western typography. After China's humiliating defeat in the war with Japan in 1895, progressive Chinese officials, sensing the urgency of the time, began to build modern schools and, for a short while, encouraged newspapers.[1] Most newspapers and magazines at the turn of the century were run by reformers who sought political reform within the Confucian framework. Gradually, new schools, publishing houses, and newspapers began to advocate doctrines quite heretical by Confucian standards. Japan's victory over imperial Russia in 1905 convinced the Chinese of the superiority of Western science and technology, and Chinese students went abroad, especially to Japan, in increasing numbers.[2] Japan thus became the rendezvous for fervid young nationalists thinking along revolutionary lines.

Reformist and Revolutionary Newspapers Published Abroad

Among the Chinese leaders in Japan were two of the reformers of 1898, K'ang Yu-wei and Liang Ch'i-ch'ao, who remained royalists striving to achieve constitutional monarchy. Liang began editing in 1898 *Ch'ing-i pao* (*China Discussion*), issued three times a month in Yokohama, which discussed Chinese politics but concentrated its attacks on the Empress Dowager and her favorites. In 1902, Liang founded in Yokohama *Hsin-min ts'ung-pao* (New citizen), a semi-monthly, to help spread his ideas on the ways to create a new culture through the study of the systems of other nations. This news magazine—though called a newspaper at that time—emphasized news reporting, comments on current affairs in China, and articles on "new knowledge," especially Western political ideas. It immediately became a favorite among the Chinese students, and exercised tremendous influence on young people in China. Liang was very skillful in translation. Through him, Chinese youth became acquainted with such Western thinkers as Aristotle, Francis Bacon, Descartes, Darwin, Montesquieu, and Rousseau.

The Empress Dowager's hatred for the reformers is well known. In an imperial edict dated October 9, 1898 outlawing *Shih-wu pao,* a newspaper edited by Liang before his flight to Japan, she had called the editors "polite rascals who know no modesty or shame." After *Ch'ing-i pao* came out, the court hated K'ang and Liang even more. The imperial edict of February 14, 1900 offered a reward of 10,000 silver taels for their arrest, ordered the burning of their books, and threatened severe punishment for those who bought or read the newspapers Liang edited. "If nobody buys them," reasoned the Empress Dowager, "the rebels will find no way to work their harm."[3] As *Su pao* reported in 1903, Grand Councillor Chang Chih-tung ordered local authorities to suppress publications which spread the new ideas of freedom and democracy, known in China at that time as the "new" books and magazines. Government agents found in two bookstores in Shanghai some copies of *Hsin-min ts'ung-pao* and "stock certificates" held by the prepublication subscribers to the reprint edition of *Ch'ing-i pao.* They arrested two clerks on this evidence, but had to release them later as the clerks were Christians and therefore protected by foreign missionaries. All who had subscribed to these magazines, except for a few officials, were blackmailed by the agents.[4] Suppression of the magazines obviously boosted their sales. In advertising the reprint edition of *Ch'ing-i pao,* *Hsin-min ts'ung-pao* proudly announced that the paper had been "repeatedly suppressed" by the Manchu government.[5]

Not satisfied with the mild proposals of the reformers led by K'ang and Liang, Chinese students of a more revolutionary bent gathered under the banner of Hu Han-min, Wang Ching-wei, Sung Chiao-jen, Huang Hsing, and Dr. Sun Yat-sen, and began to preach revolutionary ideas in 1899-1900. In 1903, the Russian army occupied Manchuria and every power wanted a slice of the China melon. Chinese students stepped up their efforts in their publications to introduce new ideas and arouse nationalism. A few of these magazines will now be discussed.

Hu-pei hsueh-sheng chieh (Students of Hupei), a monthly, was founded early in 1903 by students coming from Hupei, and edited by Lan T'ien-wei and others. According to a report in *Su pao* on February 28, 1903, people in China regarded the magazine as students' rhetorical exercises and few paid any attention to it. Then Chang Chih-tung instructed the Superintendent of Chinese Students in Japan to prohibit its publication. Many people were surprised by this move, and scores of readers hurriedly subscribed. As a result, the first issue had to be reprinted. "How could journalists elsewhere find a Grand Councillor to promote their publications?" *Su pao* commented satirically.

When the Russo-Japanese War broke out in that year, Chinese students in Tokyo organized a volunteer corps under Lan's leadership and planned to return to China to defend their country from foreign domination. The magazine changed its name to *Han-sheng* (The voice of China).[6] Although it was said that *Hu-pei hsueh-sheng chieh* ceased publication because Viceroy Tuan Fang had given the Hupei Students Association 26,000 taels, there was actually no truth to this report. However, "because of the interference of the Chinese officials and Japanese police," scholarship students, threatened with the loss of government subsidies, had to resign from *Han-sheng*'s editorial board.[7]

In 1905, Dr. Sun Yat-sen went to Japan and organized the T'ung Meng Hui (Revolutionary Alliance), which sponsored the publication of *Min pao* (*The Minpao Magazine*), edited successively by Ch'en T'ien-hua, Chang Chi, and Chang Ping-lin. This influential magazine was a successor to *Erh-shih shih-chi chih Chih-na* (China in the twentieth century), which was founded by Sung Chiao-jen, T'ien T'ung, and others in June of that year to advocate nationalism. In the second issue of *Erh-shih shih-chi chih Chih-na*, Ts'ai Hui-tung wrote an article criticizing the Japanese invasion of China. The issue was confiscated and the magazine was banned. Sung and T'ien barely escaped arrest.[8]

The first issue of *Min pao* came out on November 26, 1905,

with a foreword written by Dr. Sun. In its third issue, Hu Han-min expounded the six principles supported by the paper, among which were the establishment of a republic of China and the regulation of land ownership. The Revolutionary Alliance's Manifesto of 1905 and Hu's article marked the beginning of Sun's interest in social and economic problems. His revolutionary ideas on such issues as land tenure and the "people's livelihood" naturally clashed with Liang's conservatism. From its fourth issue, *Min pao* became engaged with *Hsin-min ts'ung-pao* in an ideological war until the latter ceased publication in 1907. Hu Han-min and Wang Ching-wei were the chief theoreticians for the paper and developed much of the party's revolutionary thought. Chinese students in Japan drifted steadily away from the moderation of the monarchists K'ang and Liang toward the radicalism of Sun and his associates.

With the magazine's aim so clearly stated, its tone was understandably radical. In 1908, T'ang Shao-i, Envoy Extraordinary of the Manchu government, was in Japan on his way to the United States, reportedly to seek a Sino-American alliance. Chang Ping-lin wrote a short editorial to attack this plan, and enraged the mandarin. The Japanese government, at the request of the Chinese Minister in Japan, banned the magazine on the pretext that T'ang Tseng-pi's article "The Psychology of Revolution" in its issue no. 24 advocated anarchy and assassination and disturbed the peace. The issue was confiscated.[9]

Another casualty among Chinese student magazines caused by T'ang's trip was *Ssu-ch'uan tsa-chih* (Szechwan magazine), founded in Tokyo in August 1907 by students from Szechwan. Edited by Wu Yü-chang, it focused its attacks on foreign aggression and the Manchu government, and advocated revolution. It became engaged also in organizing revolutionary activities and secret societies. In 1908, because of an article on the "Red Flag Incident" in its fourth issue, the magazine was outlawed. Wu was fined 100 yuan and given a six-month suspended sentence by the Japanese authorities who acted, Wu believed, on T'ang's request.[10]

Chinese women students were very active too. In 1907 they founded *Chung-kuo hsin nü chieh* (New Chinese women) in Tokyo, one of the first women students' magazines. Publication of the article "Women Should Carry on the Revolution by Means of Assassination" in its sixth issue brought about its demise.[11]

Most of the student papers in Japan in this period were run by groups of students coming from the same province and intended for youths in their home province. Besides the two magazines run by the Hupei and Szechwan students mentioned above, there were also several others, such as *Che-chiang ch'ao* (Tides of Chekiang), *Chiang-su* (Kiangsu), and *Yun-nan* (Yunnan). Magazines were numerous, but few survived more than a few issues. Some died a natural death from financial difficulties;[12] others met the axe because they were too radical or advocated assassination.

Revolutionary enthusiasm was widespread among the Chinese in other parts of the world as well. The first Chinese revolutionary newspaper published anywhere in the world was perhaps *Chung-kuo jih-pao* (*China*). Dr. Sun Yat-sen, realizing the importance of propaganda work, sent Ch'en Shao-pai to Hong Kong in 1899 to start a party paper, and the first issue of the daily came out in December of that year. There was also an edition issued once every ten days. Uncertain about British policy toward the Chinese, the paper dared not publicly advocate revolution at first, but its tone became more radical after a few months. In 1905, Viceroy Ts'en Ch'un-hsuan forbade the paper's importation into Kwangtung, its principal market, because of its stand on a dispute over his plan to nationalize the Canton-Hankow Railway. It was ironical indeed that the paper was prohibited in China not because of its advocacy of revolution, but because of its involvement in a relatively minor issue.[13]

The premises of *Chung-kuo jih-pao* served also as a center of revolutionary activities and a store to sell other revolutionary magazines and pamphlets banned by the Manchu government to overseas Chinese. In June 1907, it distributed *T'ien t'ao* (Heaven's punishment), a supplement to *Min pao,* which carried an illustration showing the Kuang-hsü Emperor with his head broken. The Hong Kong Department of Chinese Affairs charged that this cartoon was instigating assassination, and the pamphlet was seized by the police.

Two months later, the Hong Kong Legislative Council, at the request of the Manchu government, passed a law prohibiting inflammatory publications. Since the law prohibited only such words as "anti-Manchu" or "revolution," however, *Chung-kuo jih-pao* could successfully evade it by using terms such as "nationalism" or "restoration."[14]

In 1908, Chü Cheng, a revolutionary who had fled from China, set up in Rangoon *Kuang-hua jih-pao*. It was financed by Chinese merchants coming from Fukien and Kwangtung. When the paper printed a couplet by Lü Chih-i which seemingly alluded to the Chinese consul's skill in squeezing money from Chinese businessmen, the enraged mandarin, who had been sent there to keep an eye on "subversive activities," threatened to confiscate the seven stockholders' properties in their home towns in China. Six of the seven yielded to pressure. The paper had to be sold at auction to moderate reformers, who changed its name to *Shang-wu pao*. But members of the Revolutionary Alliance raised more money and resumed publication of *Kuang-hua pao* in the same year. Chü Cheng and Lü Chih-i remained editors and started a literary dual with *Shang-wu pao*, which soon folded up of its own initiative.

In 1910, the moderate reformers collaborated with the Chinese consul to bring about the downfall of *Kuang-hua pao*. At the consul's advice, the Chinese Foreign Office through diplomatic channels requested the British authorities in Rangoon to close it down and expel its responsible officers on the ground that the paper spoke for anarchism. As a result, Chü and the business manager of the paper were deported. Its employees fled, and *Kuang-hua pao* was moved to Penang. A month after Chü's deportation, Lü and others tried their hands again at publishing *Chin-hua pao* in Rangoon. Because of heavy pressure from the police, the paper survived only eight months.[15]

The Chinese consul in Rangoon was not the only Chinese diplomat who forbade Chinese merchants abroad from financing radical papers. Stockholders of *Tzu-yu hsin pao* in Honolulu had the same experience. This was a paper founded by Lu Hsin in 1907, published three times a week. Sun Fo, Dr. Sun Yat-sen's only son, was employed as a translator. The editors were fortunate enough at first to have a free hand in running the paper, but the stockholders soon became wary of the danger of losing their properties in China. Because of its sympathy for the revolutionaries, its importation into China was prohibited by the Manchu government.[16]

Revolutionary Newspapers in China

Meanwhile, in China, nationalism was reaching a high pitch, and students were restless. Revolutionary organizations, newspapers, and magazines mushroomed. The Manchu government naturally tried its best to stamp out these activities. It was under these circumstances that many censorship cases occurred, the most famous and important of which was the Shanghai Sedition Case, commonly known as the *Su pao* case. It received unprecedented attention in foreign capitals and was brought up in the British House of Lords and the Belgian Senate. Since this case has been amply covered elsewhere,[17] we shall deal with it but briefly, emphasizing its unique features and those of its implications that have important bearing on our discussion later in this book.

Su pao, a newspaper published in the International Settlement in Shanghai, was owned by Ch'en Fan, who was at first a monarchist reformer. Early in 1903, inflammatory articles began to appear in the paper and its tone became more and more radical. It appealed powerfully to many patriotic Chinese youths agog for revolution. Among the many anti-Manchu articles, it published on June 9 a recommendation and a review of Tsou Jung's *Ko-ming chün* (The revolutionary army), a pamphlet advocating violent revolution, influenced by the ideas of Rousseau, Mill, Carlyle, and the American Constitution.[18] On June 29, it carried excerpts of Chang Ping-lin's rebuttal of K'ang Yu-wei's moderate political views. Chang called the emperor by his personal name and labeled him a "petty thief," "who cannot distinguish millet from wheat."[19] At the request of Yuan Shu-hsün, the Chinese intendant of Shanghai, six men, including Chang and Tsou, were arrested by the Shanghai Municipal Police and the paper was closed on July 7. The Shanghai Municipal Council, however, refused to surrender the prisoners to Chinese jurisdiction. The foreign diplomats' opinions were at first divided in regard to the disposal of the six defendants.[20] After the brutal execution of Shen Chin, a journalist, on July 31 in Peking,[21] all concerned foreign governments agreed that the prisoners must not be given up for punishment outside the Settlement,[22] and therefore the accused were tried in the Mixed Court. In May 1904, four of them were released. Chang and Tsou were sentenced to three and two years respectively at hard labor and banishment from the Settlement upon their release from prison. On April 3, 1905, Tsou died in prison at the age of twenty.

There is no doubt that many passages in the two pamphlets and the newspaper were intended to incite the overthrow of the alien Manchu dynasty by force, and that, even by American standards, they would be regarded as posing a "clear and present danger" to the existing regime.[23] At a time of so much unrest, perhaps even such a staunch defender of freedom of speech and of the press as J. S. Mill would have demurred at protecting the two writers.[24] They admitted that they had written the pamphlets, which "were of a most violent and incendiary description," as Lord Lansdowne told the British House of Lords.[25] The defendants were Chinese, and they had committed a crime on Chinese territory against their sovereign and his government, and Tsou had even preached wholesale slaughter of an entire race.

At that time, the law that governed seditious libel in China was still the old statute, the Prohibition of Devilish Books and Talks. Any free thought regarding the monarchical form of government in China or even the slightest criticism of its functions could be interpreted as lese majesty, and the unfortunate editor or author was liable to the death penalty. The Manchu government was most anxious to have the defendants delivered at once to Nanking; it was afraid that foreign authorities would impose a light sentence on them and that Shanghai would then become a hotbed for the dissemination of revolutionary ideas. In fact, an imperial edict had already been issued to order the summary decapitation of the defendants.[26] The Shanghai Municipal Council, however, refused to surrender them on the ground that the Chinese law was too harsh

and barbarous. For humanitarian reasons, its position was hailed
by many observers in China as well as abroad. Nevertheless, the
case would not have achieved such notoriety had it not been for
the unique position of the foreign settlements in China and the
struggle for power between foreign authorities and the Manchu
government.

The foreign settlements owed their origin to the treaties the
foreign powers had signed with China as a result of their successful
invasions of China starting in the 1840s. These settlements had
been expanded through the so-called "precedents" and "established
usages," by which the foreigners had gradually extended their
power far beyond the limits set in the treaties. This was done with
the connivance of ignorant Manchu government officials, who
regarded such infractions as of no importance. According to the
treaties, the Shanghai Municipal Council had no *locus standi* in
jurisdiction over the Chinese. By 1903, however, the Council,
elected by the foreign land-renters and representing the foreign
businessmen's interests, had already become the supreme governing
body in the International Settlement. The Mixed Court with a
Chinese magistrate and a foreign assessor on the bench had extended
jurisdiction not only to cases of a "mixed nature," but also to cases
in which no foreign interests were involved. The Chinese authorities
could only arrest a Chinese citizen in the Settlement with a warrant
issued by the Mixed Court, countersigned by the Senior Consul,
and executed by the Municipal Police.[27] As Kotenev maintained,
foreigners in China felt that it was "an immutable law of logic which
has forced the Chinese nation to give up a part of its sovereign right
in favor of more progressive ideas." With the growth of the
economic strength of the foreign community, the Municipal Council
felt increasingly obliged to "protect the native residents against the
deficiency of the old Chinese administration of justice."[28] While
seeking to curb the power of the Chinese magistrate and to replace
the Mixed Court with its own police court, it was interested
principally in the jurisdiction of civil and commercial matters
involving money. Yuan Shu-hsün's agreement to allow the defendants
to be tried and punished in the Settlement, which had been made

before the arrests of the six defendants, would establish an
important precedent for foreign jurisdiction in purely Chinese
cases. Furthermore, the pretext of forestalling offensive seditious
publications in the Settlement could give the Municipal Council
the right to supervise and control the native papers, and subject
them to local legislation with a view to licensing them.[29]

The trial itself was indeed bizarre. No one seemed certain
what kind of court the Mixed Court was. The following dialogue
in the court shows the divergence of opinions:

> Mr. White-Cooper [prosecutor on behalf of the Manchu
> government]: This is a Chinese court.
> The Assessor: It is a Mixed Court.
> Mr. Ellis [defense counsel]: A Chinese Mixed Court.[30]

According to the treaties, the case should have been tried under
Chinese law. Yet no one can be sure under the law of which
country the trial was conducted.[31] The legal niceties were in fact
not relevant. As all events during the trial showed, the attitude and
decision of many foreign governments had indeed less to do with
justice than with political considerations. Although the case and
trial lasted only one year, their effects were to be felt in China for
many years to come.

There were several reasons for the case's significance. First,
it proved the contention of the "Old China Hands" that, as long
as they stood firm, they could always wrest more privileges from
the Manchu government. The case created very important precedents in regard to the status of the assessors and the jurisdiction of
the Mixed Court, which helped bring about such later developments
as the Municipal Council's refusal to surrender political offenders
to the Chinese authority and its assumption of complete control
over the Mixed Court in November 1911. For almost a decade
before the Mixed Court was returned to China in January 1927, it
was employed as a major instrument to suppress Chinese nationalism
in the Settlement; this will be discussed in the next chapter.

Second, the case showed clearly the incompetence and

ignorance of the Manchu government officials. The government
had a strong case, but it blundered all along. One cannot help
wondering why, after months of investigation and with the whole
machinery of the government behind them, the officials in charge
of the case should arrest four persons irrelevant to it while ignoring
more important culprits such as the paper's editors-in-chief. The
intendant of Shanghai seemed to have had no knowledge of the
treaty provisions, the methods the Settlement authorities used to
expand their influence, and the mentality and motives of the
foreigners with whom he had to deal.[32] The government wanted
only vengeance, and its apparent barbaric desire for vendetta
alienated world opinion and finally forced it to rubber-stamp the
assessor's judgment. For the first time, the Chinese imperial
government had to sue Chinese subjects on Chinese territory
according to non-Chinese laws and abide by the decision of a
foreign vice-consul. The defeat the government suffered in this
case gave a considerable boost to the revolutionary forces and
inspired several unsuccessful uprisings by the revolutionaries in
the next few years.

Third, this case gave the revolutionary pamphlets and articles
much free publicity and made them more popular than they might
otherwise have been.[33] In order to prove the crime of the defendants,
Yuan Shu-hsün ordered the objectionable passages translated and
published in the *North China Daily News,* a British semiofficial
newspaper in the Settlement in Shanghai, and its Sunday edition,
the *North China Herald.* These passages were repeatedly cited and
argued about within and without the court, and some of them
found their way to newspapers abroad. There is a certain truth in
the defense counsel's argument:

> Had these prisoners never been charged or brought before the
> court, their writings would have sunk into oblivion and never
> been heard of.[34]

The notoriety of the trial, Tsou's surrendering himself, his
untimely death in prison, and the ban the government imposed on

the *Ko-ming chün,* ironically, made the pamphlet a "best seller" of the time. When the first edition came off the press, only one book-seller dared to sell it. After Tsou's arrest and subsequent death, over twenty editions were issued in such places as San Francisco, Singapore, Hong Kong, and Yokohama. To avoid postal or customs inspections, the pamphlet appeared under several different titles. It was claimed that "over a million copies" were sold or otherwise distributed. Though the figure was obviously inflated, the influence of the pamphlet in stirring up the revolution cannot be denied.[35]

Fourth, the outcome of the case gave the foreign authorities in the Settlement a reputation as champions of freedom of the press, capable of sheltering seditious writers. It encouraged the mushrooming of more revolutionary newspapers and magazines in the Settlement, and contributed greatly to the development of Shanghai into the nation's publishing center.[36] Feng Tzu-yu, a KMT historian, claimed that 155 such newspapers and magazines sprang up after the trial.[37] What the Manchu government had feared now came to pass. Like Japan, the settlements in Shanghai became the hotbed of revolutionary ideas and activities. Having learned a bitter lesson, the Manchu government never attempted again to seek the extradition of Chinese writers or publishers in the settle-ments, but merely tried to forbid the circulation of their publi-cations outside their borders.

One case in point was that of *Kuo-min jih-jih pao* (*China National Gazette*), which was partially responsible for an important event in the history of Chinese press laws. This newspaper published its first issue in August 1903 in Shanghai, when the six *Su pao* defendants were still awaiting their trial. In order to obtain the protection of the foreign authorities, the paper followed the current practice of having itself registered in the name of a foreigner, A. Somoll. Run by the former staff of *Su pao* and inheriting from *Su pao* its editorial policy, it emphasized news of schools, new political parties, and "new" books, and attacked corrupt govern-ment officials. Such a paper naturally provoked the Manchu government. Chary of involving foreign settlement authorities, the government tried early in October to prevent people along the

Yangtze River from reading the paper. The Chinese Foreign Office requested the Chinese Maritime Customs, then under the control of the British, to order the Imperial Post Office not to deliver the paper. The Customs agreed that it would instruct the postal service to stop delivering copies clearly marked on the cover as *China National Gazette,* but suggested that a more effective means would be to outlaw the paper.[38] A censor thus memorialized the throne in mid-October to enact a press law to regulate the newspapers and magazines. On October 28, *Shen pao (Shun pao)*, a moderate paper in Shanghai, commenting on the ineffectiveness of such a ban, pleaded also for a press law to protect the conformist papers. These proposals led eventually to the enactment of China's first press law in 1908.[39]

Among the other revolutionary papers published in the Settlement in Shanghai, the following are most illustrative of their nature and their fate.

O-shih ching-wen (Alarming reports on Russian invasion), founded in 1904 by Ts'ai Yuan-p'ei, aimed primarily at informing the Chinese people about the Russian aggression in Manchuria and attacking the Manchus for giving away Chinese territory. It soon increased its size and coverage, and changed its name into *Ching-chung jih-pao* (Tocsin daily news). One of its editors, Lin Pai-shui, set up *Chung-kuo pai-hua pao,* using colloquial Chinese to reach the masses. Another editor, Ch'en Ch'ü-ping, founded *Erh-shih shih-chi ta wu-t'ai tsa-chih* (Twentieth-century events). All three pleaded for revolution. On March 23, 1905, *Ching-chung jih-pao* carried a letter critical of the corruption of a high Manchu official. At the instigation of the Manchu government, the German consul in Shanghai requested the Mixed Court to arrest the paper's editor-in-chief and its manager. Both of them had already escaped, but an agent selling the paper was imprisoned for one and a half years, and a proofreader for six months. The printing press was confiscated, and the paper was closed by the authorities. The other two papers soon came also to their inevitable end.[40]

On May 15, 1909, Yü Yu-jen started *Min-hu pao* in Shanghai. Taking a lesson from the tragic fortunes of the *Su pao* and the

China National Gazette, Min-hu pao did not publicly discuss the racial problem between the Chinese and the Manchus. However, it was more radical in its comments on current affairs and its attacks on the corruption of officials. At that time, a relief association to raise funds for the famine in Shensi was housed on the premises of the paper, with Yü as one of its members. In July, the intendant of Shanghai, instructed by the Viceroy of Shensi and Kansu, charged *Min-hu pao* with the misappropriation of the relief fund. Yü and a staff member were arrested, and the paper was banned. Meanwhile, the paper got involved also in three other lawsuits. A railway company official and an army officer accused it of slander, and the son of a former intendant of Shanghai accused it of defaming his late father. Yü argued that the paper had merely printed the facts and was therefore not guilty of libel. An attorney for the plaintiff raised the question whether a paper had the right to reveal all the shortcomings of officialdom without reservation. The fourteen court hearings in connection with these four cases took more than a month while Yü was kept in jail. In spite of evidence that proved the defendants' innocence, Yü was found guilty of libel and was expelled from the foreign settlement. His staff member was bonded over for good behavior. Contemporary public opinion maintained that the Manchu officials merely used these cases as pretexts for suppressing the paper, which lasted less than three months.[41]

On September 27, an advertisement appeared in the paper in Shanghai: *Min-hu pao* announced the sale of all its machinery and property to *Min-hsü pao*. A new paper was thus born on the same premises, edited by Yü in fact, if not in name. Its tone was even more radical than that of its predecessor. The only paper at that time which dared to publish any anti-Japanese writings, it exposed a narcotic traffic ring run by Japanese ronins in Shantung, called the Japanese "leaders of bandits and vagrants," and condemned the barbarous conduct of Japanese imperialism in the Far East. On November 19, the Japanese consul in Shanghai protested to the intendant of Shanghai. By order of the Mixed Court, the premises of the paper were sealed off. The Japanese consul cited sixty-two passages as evidence that the paper was guilty of undermining friendly relations between China and Japan, including Yü's articles "Crisis of China" and "Chinchow-Tsitsihar Railway and the Peace in the Far East," published respectively on November 16 and 17. Both the Japanese consul and vice-consul refused to appear as plaintiffs, but sat as assessors in the Mixed Court. Without any hearing of the facts, this irregularly constituted court gave its judgment on December 29: The paper was permanently outlawed and the presses used to print it were not allowed to produce another newspaper. The paper lasted only forty-two days. This "outrage to justice," as the *North China Herald* called it, aroused much criticism from many quarters in China.[42]

In October 1910, Yü set up still another paper on a much larger scale—*Min-li pao*. It employed many of the best minds of the time, including among its editors Chang Chi-luan and Ma Chün-wu, who were to become famous journalists in China, and Yeh Ch'u-ts'ang, who was to be made the head of the Central Publicity Department in the KMT regime. Among its reporters were such revolutionary leaders as Sung Chiao-jen and Ch'en Ch'i-mei. Wu Chung-hsin was its manager, and Yü its director and editor-in-chief. It had correspondents in various cities in Asia and Europe, and served in fact as headquarters for revolutionary activities. The paper was founded at a time when the Manchu government had yielded to popular demands to start preparations for a constitutional monarchy, and a little more freedom of speech was allowed. After the successful 1911 Revolution, all its important staff members became high government officials. It was closed in 1913 under the pressure of Yuan Shih-k'ai's henchmen.[43]

Newspapers in other Chinese cities were subjected to more persecution. In North China, *Kuo-wen pao* of Tientsin was founded in 1897 by Yen Fu, a pioneer translator who introduced Western thought into China. In 1900, it printed in three installments a memorial written by Shen P'eng, a member of the Hanlin Academy, to impeach two of the Empress Dowager's favorites, which no one dared to present to the throne. The Manchu officials ordered Shen's arrest and prohibited people from buying or reading the paper.[44]

In 1904, Hang Hsin-chai founded in Peking the *Ching-hua jih-pao,* which used the colloquial style. Four months later, P'eng I-chung had his *Chung-hua pao* published in the same city in classical Chinese. In October 1906, both papers were suspended, and P'eng and Hang arrested because they "discussed government affairs recklessly" and offended the authorities. As a contemporary magazine, *Han-chih* (The Chinese flag) commented, the incident helped only in making two unknown journalists idols of other Chinese.[45]

In Wuchang, *Wu-ch'ang pai-hua pao,* a colloquial paper supported by the Ch'ün chih hsueh she (Society for the Study of Popular Government), was founded in 1908. The paper died after Manchu officials forbade its principal contributor, Li Ya-tung, who was then in jail in Hanyang, from communicating with the outside world.[46]

The founders of the Society for the Study of Popular Government then started another paper, *Shang-wu pao,* in Hankow in the winter of 1909, and put it under the charge of Chan Ta-pei. It was closed in 1910 by the authorities because of its opposition to the government's plan to borrow foreign capital for the construction of the Canton-Hankow-Chengtu Railway.[47]

Chan Ta-pei soon founded *Ta-chiang jih-pao,* also in Hankow, and became its editor-in-chief with Ho Hai-ming as his assistant. It published reports on the corruptions and mismanagement of the officials in that area and agitated for revolution in its editorials. When the uprising at Canton on March 29, 1910 failed, it printed articles and letters written by the seventy-two martyrs who died on the occasion and distributed them with the paper. The Manchu government was very angry about this, but the last straw came when the paper printed an article entitled "Utter Confusion Is the Wonder Drug to Save China," written by Huang K'an, a member of the Revolutionary Alliance. Chan and Ho were brought to the local court, but they refused to reveal the author's identity. The chief judge, being a progressive man, gave them the choice of a one-year prison term or a fine. Failing to pay the fine, they stayed in prison until released by their comrades during the uprising of 1911.[48]

With the help of revolutionaries, *K'o pao* was founded in Canton in 1911 by Ch'en Chiung-ming and other members of the Legislative Council of Kwangtung, who opposed legalized gambling. Its account of the assassination of a Manchu general by a Chinese revolutionary led the authorities to close it down.[49] For the same reason, *Chung-hua hsin pao* in Swatow met the same fate.[50]

Occasionally, clever revolutionary papers could avoid any penalty. One example was *Ts'ui-hsin pao*, founded by Chang Kung and other patriots in Kinhwa, Chekiang. Because of its unfavorable comments on the government, the intendant obtained permission from the governor of Chekiang to close it. Chang got wind of the order and averted the closing by hurriedly changing the signs and furniture on the premises.[51]

Revolutionary Pamphlets

Besides newspapers and magazines, there were also many anti-Manchu and revolutionary pamphlets. Partly because of the *Su pao* case, revolutionary ideas reached a high tide in Shanghai in 1903-1904.[52] Ming scholars' accounts of the atrocities of Manchu soldiers in their brutal conquest of China, such as *Yang-chou shih-jih chi* (Ten days in Yangchow) and *Chia-ting t'u-ch'eng chi* (The massacre in Kiating), though prohibited for over two centuries, could still be found in private libraries. These works were reprinted by revolutionary societies and bookstores and sold openly or distributed secretly.

Of the many pamphlets written by contemporary authors, Ch'en T'ien-hua's *Ching-shih chung* (The tocsin) and *Meng hui-t'ou* (Sudden awakening), both aiming at arousing the masses to action, were second only to *Ko-ming chün* in popularity. They circulated along the Yangtze River in spite of the government's ban. Besides those smuggled into China from Japan, many copies were secretly printed and distributed by revolutionaries in China, and exerted great influence among them. By that time, many secret revolutionary societies had already been established. The Jih chih hui (Society for Daily Improvement) in Wuchang, for instance, had a reading room, providing new publications, including *Hsin-ming ts'ung-pao*, for the public. Ch'en's two pamphlets were of course avidly sought and read. In the New Army, they were often found on the soldiers' beds. In 1903, a student brought back from Tokyo 7,000 copies of *Meng hui-t'ou* and left them at a school. They were burned by the school's trustees.[53] In 1906, Ts'ao A-kou of Kinhwa, Chekiang, an admittedly avid reader of *Meng hui-t'ou,* was beheaded by the Manchu intendant after the Han Chinese magistrate delayed for months in reaching a decision. The intendant's subsequent threat to mete out similar punishment for any other readers served only to draw the people's attention to these pamphlets, as a KMT historian reported. Even uneducated country folk, who had begun to be excited by the idea of revolution, tried by various means to obtain copies from Shanghai.[54]

Another case which happened also in Chekiang in 1906 involved Ch'en Meng-hsiung, who was accused as a member of a subversive secret society. Presented as evidence was Ao Chia-hsiung's *Hsin shan-ko* (New rustic songs), a volume of songs to spread the ideas of revolution, which Ch'en had distributed in a girls' school in Yotsing. Ch'en, having received advance warning, fled to Japan, but Ao was arrested. To spare his friend, Ch'en returned to China and surrendered himself. Through the inter-cession of influential country squires, the governor of Chekiang, in 1907, instead punished the informant for false accusations and dismissed the magistrate in charge of the case.[55]

Methods and Effects of Control

The case of Ch'en Meng-hsiung, however, was most unusual. More common occurrences were temporary or permanent suspension of newspapers, arrests, imprisoning or fining of their editors, and smashing of their properties for offending the authorities.[56] Besides punitive measures, the Manchu government also tried to prevent undesirable writings from being printed. A publication law was promulgated in 1906 and a press law in 1908, but they do not seem to have been effectively carried out. In August 1909, for instance, the Chinese press in Peking threatened to cease publication altogether and to call on all other Chinese newspapers in the country to do the same if the Ministry of the Interior insisted on enforcing Article 7 of the Press Law, which required every paper to submit its proofs to the police authorities before publication. A censor, fearing that the suspension of the publication of all newspapers in the country would make the government a butt of ridicule throughout the world, advised the government not to impose this rule. The Prince Regent intervened, and the matter was amicably settled in the press's favor.[57] In spite of the laws and regulations, there was no "prior censorship, no tax, no license, or even registration" in this era, as Roswell S. Britton observed.[58] At any rate, the government had no way to enforce its laws in the foreign settlements or in Japan, where the revolutionaries found refuge.

Occasionally, instead of force, government officials would try bribery. In 1900, a high official advised the throne to award official positions to the owners and editors of conservative papers that had attacked the Reform Movement.[59] To please Chang Chih-tung, who disliked *Han-k'ou jih-pao,* the intendant of Wuchang in 1903 bought the foreign-protected paper, which became henceforth an official publication.[60] When the *Su-pao* case was pending, Tuan Fang advised Wei Kuang-t'ao to take over the paper and maintain good relations with other publications.[61] But the proposal was obviously not adopted. Government-subsidized papers in China probably began in 1908, when Ts'ai Nai-huang, intendant of Shanghai, with the approval of Viceroy Tuan Fang and the Chinese Foreign Office, bought with public funds some Shanghai newspapers (including *Chung-wai jih-pao*) that he considered not quite under his thumb, and operated them under the guise of private journals.[62] The government could, of course, set up its own papers to compete with their revolutionary rivals.[63] This more clever method was not very successful because the government could not buy off all papers it frowned upon, as Viceroy Chang Jen-chün found out in 1910, when he was ordered by the throne to investigate "the official management of newspapers and the private use of public funds therefor" in Kiangsu, and more particularly in Shanghai, after a censor had impeached Ts'ai Nai-huang for wasting funds on buying these newspapers.[64] There was, however, still no monopoly in printing during these years.[65]

Neither harsh punishments nor lucrative briberies succeeded in restraining fanatic revolutionaries, who valued their ideals more than their lives. An examination of some better-known publications of this period cannot fail to impress the reader with their audacity, unsurpassed in Chinese history. Even passages openly encouraging political assassinations and idolizing assassins appeared in print. Failing to control the making of books and newspapers, the Manchu government concentrated on controlling their distribution. The Empress Dowager stupidly felt that she could eradicate publications not to her liking by prohibiting their circulation, as her predecessors had done during the manuscript or block-printing days. The government's principal device to minimize the threat posed by inflammatory Chinese publications in Japan was to prevent their importation into China. However, ingenious students could still find ways of smuggling them in. Students from Hupei, for instance, organized the Ch'ang Ming Company as a front to transport revolutionary publications into their native province.[66] One student made his Manchu friend, who enjoyed the privilege of passing through Chinese customs without having his luggage examined, an unwitting carrier of *Min pao*. Students from Shensi bound the prohibited magazine into large volumes, labeled them "Psychology," and thus eluded the watchful eyes of the customs inspectors.[67]

The government also tried hard to hamper the circulation of revolutionary books and newspapers published in Shanghai and elsewhere. Long lists of banned books and papers were published, and people were warned in no uncertain terms against reading them.[68] Since revolutionary ideas were supposed to appeal most to young people, the government set up special regulations for the schools. Students were not allowed to "express their preposterous [i.e., revolutionary] ideas," to write books or articles or have them published, to work as editors or reporters for newspapers, or to buy or read novels or rebellious books. Books which were not required for subjects offered in the schools were not allowed on campus, and schools could not buy such books without the approval of the Board of Education. Students who violated the rules would be expelled and punished, while superintendents of schools who did not take necessary precautionary measures to enforce them would be given demerits or dismissed. Furthermore, students were forbidden to give speeches or receive visitors without the approval of school authorities; even their correspondence was censored.[69] Though such a policy achieved some success in certain schools,[70] it often irked students to such an extent that they withdrew from the schools en masse.[71] Oftentimes, it even whetted their appetite for the banned publications, which otherwise they might not have read.[72]

With the public at large, repressive policies had varying degrees of temporary success. Among the bookstores established by 1903, some were truly revolutionary, but most aimed only at profit.[73] The measures adopted by the Manchu government were designed primarily to intimidate the profit-minded booksellers and some overcautious readers.[74] Revolutionary booksellers, especially those in Shanghai, however, steadfastly maintained their position. Reading clubs were established in small towns in the interior, which subscribed to "new" publications from Shanghai and Japan. Many of these clubs were like the subscription libraries in the Western world.[75] Revolutionary societies, besides, were effective in secretly importing, reprinting, and distributing revolutionary writings.[76]

In short, in its efforts to muffle dissent, the Manchu government was much less effective than some modern European governments have been. The Chinese scholars working for the moribund dynasty could not find precedents to follow in Chinese history, because several new factors had been introduced. First was the introduction of Western typography into China during the nineteenth century, which made possible the mass reproduction of reading materials for the public. Second, the presence of foreign powers and settlements, whose interests did not always agree with those of the Manchu government, seriously hampered the government's efforts at suppression. Third, Chinese hatred for the

Manchus, which had never died out, began to grow apace with the increasing deterioration of the national economy and the importation of Western concepts of nationalism, freedom, and democracy. Many Chinese officials secretly sympathized with progressive ideas and the revolutionaries' cause. There were instances in which the Han Chinese officials dragged their feet concerning the so-called rebellious publications. The ceaseless invasions by Western powers and the imminent danger of China's totally losing her semblance of independence perhaps impelled all Chinese to clamor for changes. Even in the West, when kings and their governments had faced much less serious obstacles, as, for example, in Tudor England, suppression of publications printed in territories beyond governmental control had not been successful.[77] The severe but crude policies of the Manchu government were formulated by people who could not even understand the forces they were fighting against and the problems confronting them. Such policies were doomed to, and did, end in miserable failure.

Chapter III

THE GROWING PAINS OF THE NEW REPUBLIC, 1912-1927

On January 1, 1912, the Republic of China was born in Nanking. The success of the 1911 Revolution, as historians have pointed out, owed more to the press than to the military.[1] Unfortunately, the compromise plan Dr. Sun Yat-sen accepted, though preventing more bloodshed and possible foreign intervention, stopped the revolution short and transferred the authority to Yuan Shih-k'ai in Peking. Yuan, an autocrat at heart, regarded Sun's KMT program, which was based upon the three general concepts of nationalism, democracy, and the "people's livelihood," as dangerous radicalism. In November 1913, he declared the KMT illegal and ousted the party's representatives from the Parliament. On January 10, 1914, he dissolved the Parliament itself and proceeded with his plans to make himself emperor.

The Press Under Yuan Shih-k'ai
Apprehensive of possible disapproval by the press, Yuan directed his blows first at the newspapers, more than one hundred of which had appeared in Peking alone.[2] His government, therefore, promulgated the Martial Law on December 15, 1912, Police Regulations on March 2, 1914, and Publication Law later in the same year. Commanders in the curfew areas could thus suppress any newspapers, magazines, or books suspected of hostility to the government. No newspapers could use secret codes in sending news dispatches. Special agents were posted in the telegraph offices in Shanghai, and all telegrams commenting on current affairs were detained. Special agents were sent to the editorial offices of many newspapers of questionable loyalty to inspect the galley proofs.[3] Journalists were arrested and newspapers suppressed with no reasons given.[4] Publications by the KMT or its sympathizers were closed by government orders. In Kaifeng, Honan, the KMT-

affiliated newspaper *Min-li pao* was closed in 1913. Several staff members and typesetters were killed.[5]

As for hostile publications printed in areas beyond his control, Yuan, following the example set by the Ch'ing emperors, simply forbade the post office to deliver them and enjoined the public not to read them.[6] Occasionally, with the cooperation of the authorities in the foreign settlements, he could get hostile journalists arrested and their papers closed. The KMT paper *Chen-tan min pao* in the French Concession in Hankow, for instance, was closed by the French authorities in 1913 at Yuan's request for publishing a pictorial supplement that contained cartoons allegedly directed against Yuan and his vice-president Li Yuan-hung. Two editors and the artist were arrested and sent to the Chinese authorities in Wuchang. One editor and the artist were executed, and the other died in prison.[7]

Yuan's monarchical ambitions found an advocate when, in 1915, Frank J. Goodnow, a professor of Columbia University and Yuan's constitutional adviser, suggested the restoration of monarchy in China. Soon Yuan's supporters organized the Ch'ou an hui (Peace Planning Society) to campaign for their leader, and adopted measures to show that public opinion was on their side. *T'ien-min pao* in Peking was closed down because it refuted some of the arguments advanced by the Peace Planning Society.[8] No one was allowed to discuss the pros and cons of different forms of government except to uphold monarchism.

Numerous attempts were made to bribe or intimidate influential thinkers and journalists. Before Liang Ch'i-ch'ao's famous "Strange, the So-Called Form of Government Question" appeared in *Ta Chung-hua* monthly (*The Great Chung Hwa Magazine*) in Shanghai, for instance, Yuan tried to bribe him with a huge sum of money to withhold its publication, but Liang refused.[9] Chang Ping-lin was placed under house arrest in Peking in 1914, but was treated very well because Yuan realized that "an essay of Chang's may be worth several divisions of soldiers." Although he was allowed to read and write as he pleased, his writings on current affairs were carefully

destroyed by his guards.[10] To manipulate public opinion, Yuan
spent large sums of money to win over journalists of a lesser
caliber and was generally quite successful.[11] When money failed,
force followed.[12] As a result, no paper, except a few in the foreign
settlements, dared antagonize him.[13] An edition of the *Ya-hsi-ya
pao* (Asiatic daily news), his own mouthpiece, was published for a
few months in 1915 in Shanghai, where it could not find readers
or distributors, and was twice threatened with bombs. Those in
charge of the paper, though, did not seem to worry. As long as
they could print a copy for Yuan's perusal, they would be able to
receive the subsidies.[14] It was said that all Shanghai newspapers,
before they reached Yuan's eyes, had to be screened first by his
personal staff and his eldest son. If they contained objectionable
materials, another copy without such passages would be printed
and presented to Yuan.[15] Under these circumstances, we have,
perhaps, the most farcical case in the history of journalism—the
case of the false *Shih pao*. If an old and influential mandarin had
not been visiting Yuan and happened to notice that his host's copy
of the Shanghai paper was different from his own copy at home,
Yuan would never have known the truth.[16]

Yuan's imperial rule lasted only eighty-three days in 1916,
but the newspapers suffered heavy casualities. The number of
papers in Peking, for instance, dropped from one hundred to
twenty during his reign.[17]

New Ideology and Literature

The fall of Yuan Shih-k'ai would have been inevitable even if
he had lived longer. Before he died in 1916, a new China was being
born and forces much more formidable than anyone could have
conceived were threatening to break the dikes. The event that first
aroused the clamor for changes was Japan's presentation of the
Twenty-one Demands in 1915, accession to which would obviously
soon destroy China's semblance of sovereignty. Feeling they could
no longer stand aside, Chinese intellectuals rose in angry rebellion.
Since most of them expressed their ideas in periodicals, which

required less money to run and were not so closely watched as newspapers, periodical essays now became the principal means for the spread of revolutionary views.

The first trumpet call sounded in 1915 when Ch'en Tu-hsiu launched a magazine in Shanghai called *Hsin ch'ing-nien* (*La Jeunesse*). As Ch'en searched for the roots of China's trouble in her cultural tradition, current developments made him wonder whether the nation's age-old institutions were fit for survival in the modern world. To save China, he averred, traditional ideas had to be reexamined. He would rather "discard all traditional ideals, create new political, economical and moral ideals, and build up a new spirit suitable to the new society."[18]

The real avalanche, though, did not start until after Yuan's death, when the weakness and instability of the central government caused a relaxation in official control and thus enabled new ideologies to develop and grow. Peking University, under its new president, Ts'ai Yuan-p'ei, became a hotbed of new thought. Ch'en Tu-hsiu, now Dean of Humanities, became the students' idol, and Hu Shih, a young professor who returned from Columbia University in 1917, also propounded modern ideas that swayed youthful minds. The Literary Revolution, in which the above scholars played leading roles, was to change China's intellectual climate forever. The May Fourth Movement of 1919, when Peking University students demonstrated in the streets against the decision reached at the Paris Conference in regard to the Shantung question, marked the beginning of the great influence of youth on Chinese politics. As fermenting minds began to seek expression in periodical literature, many magazines were published in those days by groups of professors or various departments of Peking University, all using the colloquial style. Students also started magazines of their own, one of the most effective being *Hsin ch'ao* (*The Renaissance*). In 1919 more than four hundred magazines appeared on the market.[19] Also, many progressive newspapers began to publish literary supplements. Alongside resurgent nationalism, communism began to rise. The proposal of the Russian Deputy Commissar for Foreign Affairs, Leo M. Karakhan, to discuss the cancellation of the unequal treaties and to give up special rights and privileges in China was ignored by the Peking government, but it deeply impressed Chinese intellectuals.[20] Radical groups began to study Marxism and Soviet Russia in earnest, and leftist periodicals began to flourish.

The warlords, many of whom were poorly educated, of course could not understand these new theories. Their natural reaction was alarm, and efforts were made to suppress all writings containing new ideas. In March 1919, therefore, the Minister of Education wrote to Dr. Ts'ai to complain about the "radical" student publication *Hsin ch'ao*. In his reply, Ts'ai upheld freedom of publication as well as academic freedom. He pointed out that, in order to expose young people to all points of view, his students were also publishing a magazine advocating traditional Chinese culture.[21]

On April 9, 1919, the governor of Kiangsu sent a directive to his Secretary of Education and all magistrates and school principals in the province, maintaining that traditional Chinese culture was the foundation of the country. All new teachings, it said, could only confuse and harm the young who "crave for strange and uncanny theories." Therefore, they should be prohibited from buying or reading any publications which harbored "absurd opinions."[22]

In May 1919, students in Peking published a daily entitled *Wu ch'i* (The seventh of May) to remind readers of the "National Humiliation Day," the day when, four years earlier, Yuan Shih-k'ai had accepted Japan's Twenty-one Demands. The police asked Peking University to suppress the publication, charging that it had violated Articles 3 and 11 of the Publication Law. Several hundred policemen were dispatched to close the printing shop, arrest the printer and peddlers selling the paper, and confiscate all available copies. Four student representatives went to the police station to protest and were arrested too. *Chiu-kuo chou-k'an*, a weekly publication of the students, was also suppressed because of its stand on the Shantung question.[23]

On May 21, 1919, in order to maintain "friendly relations between China and Japan," the Peking government banned all publications that attacked the Japanese or advocated the boycott of Japanese goods. *I-shih pao*, the most militantly anti-Japanese paper, was suspended and its editor arrested.[24] The next day, editors of nine other papers were summoned to the police station for questioning. On May 23, as a result of Japanese protests, censors were sent to *Ch'en pao* and *Kuo-min kung pao* to censor their page proofs, because they had encouraged the student movement and got into an argument with *Shun-t'ien shih pao,* a Chinese-language paper owned by the Japanese.[25] The government also suppressed the anarchist *Chin-hua tsa-chih* (Progressive magazine) and the socialist *Min-sheng ts'ung-k'an* (People's livelihood miscellany), *Kung-jen pao-chien* (A treasury for the workers), *T'ai-p'ing* (Peace) and *Min sheng* (The voice of the people), because of their alleged devotion to such "absurd theories as social revolution, anarchism, strikes and Communism." On May 31, a pamphlet entitled *Chün-jen hsü-chih* (What a soldier needs to know) was discovered in the market and promptly confiscated because of its radicalism. On June 11, Ch'en Tu-hsiu was arrested on suspicion of being the mastermind of a handbill entitled "A Declaration of the Citizens of Peking."[26]

The censoring of publications was generally done by the police at the post office. The simplest method was to seize periodicals sent for mail. Several issues of *Hsien-tai p'ing-lun* (*Contemporary Review*), edited by Hu Shih and his Peking University friends, for instance, were detained.[27] At least one issue of *Ku-chün chou-pao* (The lonely soldier weekly) met the same fate.[28] Lu Hsün wrote about magazines that never reached the hands of intended readers.[29] The postal ban on *La Jeunesse* in 1920 led to T'ao Meng-ho's suggestion to discontinue its publication when the periodical had become politically radical and there was a disagreement among the editors about its future.[30]

Sometimes, entire passages or articles would be deleted by the censors. In vol. 5, no. 110 of *Contemporary Review,* all of pages 104 and 105 and part of pages 103 and 106 were blank. According to the table of contents, the space was intended for an article discussing the finances of the Canton government in the South. The editor indignantly announced in the following issue that this article had been deleted for "some reasons," hence the blank pages. In order to observe the publication schedule, they would henceforth simply leave the spaces blank should the same situation arise again.[31]

The police were prompt in closing down publications which the authorities did not like. *Mei-chou p'ing-lun* (Weekly review), founded by Ch'en Tu-hsiu and Kao I-han, was edited by Hu Shih after Ch'en's arrest in June 1919. Two months later, it was closed down by order of the Minister of the Judiciary, Chu Shen, because it had published an article, "The Independence of the Judiciary and the Independence of Education," by Jo Yü, who asserted that the judges should not allow themselves to become the running dogs of the warlords.[32]

Many publishers complained during these days that the government would invoke a law when it served its purpose and ignore it when it proved inconvenient.[33] At any rate, clever publishers could always make deals with the authorities, who might also change their minds after satisfactory explanations were offered.[34] *Contemporary Review* had trouble with the police for a while, but the issue which had been detained was finally released and mailed to subscribers later, as the editors announced in a subsequent issue.[35]

In 1924, *Chih-sheng chou-k'an* reprinted an article from *Hsin-wen pao* in Shanghai critical of a powerful man. Wu Chih-hui, the editor of the weekly, was accused of having "insulted the government." Since Wu lived in the foreign settlement in Shanghai, orders were sent to various military commanders as well as to a magistrate in the Mixed Court in Shanghai to obtain the cooperation of the Shanghai Municipal Police in obtaining his arrest. The orders were later rescinded upon the intercession of many influential persons.[36]

The zealous but naïve authorities created many farcical cases. In the 1920s, when young people were rebelling against parental authority and struggling for freedom in love and marriage, authorities in Peking decided to suppress all books on love. A book on stage techniques for amateur players by Ch'en Ta-pei was banned because the title began with the Chinese transliteration of the word "amateur" "*ai mei ti*" (*ai* meaning love). The Chinese translation of Edward

Carpenter's *Love's Coming of Age* was also banned because the same offensive word appeared in its title.[37]

In July 1919, Marxism was quite popular in Japan, and many books advocating it also arrived on the Chinese market. The government in Peking had somehow heard of the danger of Marxism and thus ordered the police to seize all books propagating such ideas. Different translators had given Marx different Chinese names, however, and, as a result, books allegedly written by Ma-erh-ko-ssu were confiscated, while those by Ma-k'o-ssu remained safely on the market.[38]

At about the same time, the Peking government learned that many "radical" magazines were being published in Shanghai and instructed the local authorities to suppress them. The Chinese police forces in Shanghai replied that they could not find any publications admittedly written by "radicals."[39]

When *Mei-chou p'ing-lun* was suppressed in August 1919, the eager censors in Peking also seized *Hsing-chi p'ing-lun* because its title ended in the same characters, *p'ing-lun* (critical review), and because both *mei-chou* and *hsing-chi* mean "weekly." In 1924, authorities in Wuhan once arrested some socialists and then confiscated all publications that bore the term "society" because both socialist and society in Chinese bear the same characters, *she-hui.* Fortunately, such efforts were soon abandoned.[40]

As a matter of fact, because of the warlords' stupidity, no one could tell for sure which publications would be suppressed and which would not; there seemed to be no set pattern. An examination of the publications of this period shows that many really radical books were permitted to circulate. *Kai-tsao* (*La Rekonstruo*), a scholarly magazine edited by Liang Ch'i-ch'ao and Chang Chün-mai, was once suppressed in Peking because a picture of the statue of a "naked" woman was shown on its front cover. And yet, at the same time, pornographic literature filled the market. Liu Shih-fu's *Min-sheng,* which advocated anarchism, was also easily available.[41] Books such as *Chang Tsung-hsiang* and *Ts'ao Ju-lin,* denouncing these two high officials as traitors, could run into several editions in a short time.[42] On the other hand, *Tzu-chi ti yuan-ti* (My own garden), a collection of essays on literary criticism by Lu Hsün's famed brother, Chou Tso-jen, was banned. *Hu Shih wen-ts'un* (Hu Shih's collected works) and *Tu-hsiu wen-ts'un* (Ch'en Tu-hsiu's collected works) were also banned by the Peking police. In a letter written to the Prime Minister, dated July 3, 1924, Hu Shih complained that copies of these books confiscated by the police had not yet been returned to him, though the Prime Minister had denied outlawing these works. He asked the Prime Minister to put the following questions to the Ministry of the Interior: Why were they banned? Why was no reason for outlawing them ever made public? Why were the retailers' copies confiscated? Which agencies of the government carried out these orders? Naturally, Hu never received a satisfactory answer.[43]

Corrupt Journalists and the Warlords

While the favorite media of the rebellious intellectuals were the periodicals, few newspapers challenged established interests openly and violently in the era of the warlords.[44] Not many of them, therefore, got into trouble for ideological reasons. The stupidity, inefficiency, and transiency of the warlord regimes in fact allowed the press more freedom than ever before. A number of arrests were made and newspapers suspended in Peking, but such cases usually happened only when the warlords and their minions felt personally insulted.[45] Most of the journalists managed to get along by refraining from political comments or criticizing only a government in a different part of the country.[46] People were free to set up newspapers, as long as they had the permission of the owner of the premises. No government approval was necessary. Special postal rates for newspapers could easily be obtained, and imported newsprint could be bought without restrictions. News agencies were not centralized; newspapers competed freely. In one sense, this was the most free period for the Chinese press in twentieth-century China.[47]

On the other hand, the widespread, rampant corruptions affected journalists as well as people in other walks of life. As Yuan Shih-k'ai had forced journalists to choose between money and bullets, Tuan Ch'i-jui added a new bait: official titles. Cooperating newspapermen could become consultants, councillors, or special secretaries and draw several hundred yuan a month without having to set foot in an office. Gratuities and gifts were accepted voluntarily or involuntarily, and some writers resorted even to extortion or blackmail.[48] Any rascal could set up a newspaper, which did not necessarily have its own premises. Sometimes, several papers could use the same articles and dispatches, which they cut from larger papers, but assume different titles with perhaps different "editorials," and thus enjoy the patronage of different sponsors. The same type forms could be used for several such papers; the printer needed only to substitute a different title and perhaps a short "editorial" praising another sponsor for a different paper. Since such papers were not actually meant for the public, they were nicknamed "phantom papers." A magazine writer reported in 1923 that there were then over one hundred such phantom papers in Peking, though fewer than twenty papers could be found on the market. Only about five or six of the legitimate papers had a circulation of 2,000 or more.[49] The actual number of the phantom papers in China is impossible to ascertain because of their ephemeral nature.

Even the larger papers could not always preserve their integrity. When Ts'ao K'un and Wu P'ei-fu were in power, all the papers in Peking and Tientsin, except those few that were protected by foreign powers, praised them unashamedly and reported their military failures as victories. When Feng Yü-hsiang came into power, all erstwhile followers of Ts'ao and Wu turned around to praise Feng.[50] Newspapermen changed sides as quickly as warlords succeeded one another as masters of Peking.

In April 1926, Chang Tsung-ch'ang and Chang Hsueh-liang marched into Peking with their soldiers. A few journalists hitherto hostile to them were shot. Lin Yutang described them as innocent victims:

That was the time when to do propaganda for the Kuomintang at the old capital was to make oneself the "instrument of communists" and to be "red." With his intense hatred of the communists, and on the plea that such revolutionary papers received "roubles" from Russian sources, Chang Tsungch'ang, the last of China's colourful warlords, shot two editors without trial as a warning to others. They were Shao P'iao-p'ing editor of *Chingpao* and Lin Poshui editor of *Shehhuei Jihpao*. These two editors were arrested at midnight and shot at about one o'clock in the morning.[51]

The death of the two editors did succeed in scaring newspapermen. Before the execution of Shao P'iao-p'ing, they had shown no fear of imprisonment. Kung Te-pai in his memoirs wrote proudly that he had been arrested eight times in his career and the circulation of his paper had soared because of the ensuing publicity. Once, in spite of an advance warning, he had deliberately let himself be arrested because, he wrote, "at that time, no journalists had been shot. To be arrested a few days would only make the paper better known."[52] The execution of these journalists was a profound shock to the press, but their deaths had nothing to do with ideological reasons, as Lin Yutang appears to have suggested. Contemporary records reveal an entirely different picture.

Shao P'iao-p'ing was the founder and editor-in-chief of *Ching pao,* one of the best papers in Peking, whose literary supplement contributed much to the new literature of the time. Although talented, Shao was unfortunately not a man of principle. An opium addict, he led a dissipated life and had to elicit money from the most stingy warlords. In March 1914, for instance, *Ching pao* changed its attitude completely within twenty-four hours toward Wellington Koo, then the Minister of Foreign Affairs, after Koo agreed to a huge payoff.[53] Chang Tso-lin, father of Chang Hsuehliang, had also made large payments to Shao. In 1925, however, one of Chang Tso-lin's chief commanders, Kuo Sung-ling, rebelled against Chang, gave Shao even more money, and made him write against Chang. When Chang Tsung-ch'ang and Chang Hsueh-liang came to Peking in triumph, Shao escaped to the Legation Quarters. A friend of his lured him out of his hiding place on April 24, when he was wondering whether he should return home to settle a fierce quarrel between his wife and one of his two concubines, and he was arrested in the streets. When thirteen representatives of the Peking press pleaded his cause with Chang Hsueh-liang, the latter simply replied that Shao had advocated Red theories and done great harm to the young, and that even death was insufficient punishment for his crimes. He was executed on April 26 because of alleged complicity "with the enemy," but no evidence was ever given.[54] Chang Tsung-ch'ang did not suspend the paper, because he thought that, as long as he left it intact, he had not destroyed freedom of the press.[55] After Shao's death, Shao's family closed the paper voluntarily.

The execution did not arouse much indignation or sympathy. Of those who cared to write about the case, no one seemed convinced that Shao had been a Red agent.[56] One writer raised a feeble protest: even if Shao had advocated communism, should he be condemned and executed without a trial?[57] Hu Cheng-chih, himself a famous journalist and a friend of Shao's, insisted that the latter had printed some "absurd writings" in *Ching pao* only to please the young and to promote the paper. He praised Shao's talent, wealth, and ability to get along with high officials, but added:

> He was not upright in conduct, but was vain, without much culture or learning . . . He lived beyond his means, which brought about his death.[58]

Kung Te-pai was even more outspoken: Shao's real crime was blackmailing and the spreading of rumors. If no one had yielded to his demands for money, he would have died long ago.[59] But his execution ironically made him a martyr for the cause of freedom of the press.

Three months later, Lin Pai-shui, founder and editor-in-chief of *She-hui jih-pao,* a daily in Peking, was also executed. Lin had made a great contribution to Chinese journalism in his younger days by setting up several revolutionary newspapers in the vernacular, such as *Chung-kuo pai-hua pao*. But like Shao, he had led a debauched life, and attacked all those who had refused to pay him off. He had demanded money from Chang Tsung-ch'ang, and when the latter did not comply, Lin attributed his refusal to the influence of Prime Minister P'an Fu, Chang's favorite, and abused P'an in his paper. Consequently, on August 5, 1926, Chang ordered the Commander of the Gendarmes, also an enemy of Lin's, to have him arrested and executed immediately.[60] Though Lin had always prided himself on being a man of the world, his good friend Hu Cheng-chih described him as ignorant of the ways of the world, not very original in thought, vile of tongue, and too free with money.[61]

In fact, brutal as the warlords were, they were not always unfair. In 1926, Ch'eng She-wo, a dedicated and honest journalist who had been arrested more than ten times by various warlords, was arrested by Chang Tsung-ch'ang. He was accused of having received 100,000 yuan from the KMT in Canton to carry on propaganda for the Reds. But an influential old man interceded on his behalf, and, when Chang found out that Ch'eng was really impecunious, he released him immediately. He had been in prison only four days.[62]

Indeed, the warlords' brutality was often the result, as well as the cause, of the newspapermen's unscrupulous practices during these years. In 1923, a magazine writer felt so disgusted that he wrote:

> Had there not been the parasitical journalists to spread rumor, incite contention and serve as tools for them, the warlords, bureaucrats and politicians could not have done so much harm.[63]

Censorship was thus only a part of the complex relationship between the press and the warlords. A subservient press not only connived at, but even abetted, corruption.

All the above cases happened in Peking. In the provinces, local warlords were often even more capricious, their actions more unpredictable. They would have heartily approved of Article 11 of the Publication Law, which would enable them to condemn any publications that might offend them. But warlords often preferred to govern by their fancies and whims, rather than laws, and most areas were probably without any organized censorship or elaborate laws and regulations. Censorship cases often occurred in a haphazard manner. A few examples will suffice.

In 1913, *Kuei-sui jih-pao* in Kweisui reported that Outer Mongolians were going to invade Suiyuan. The military leader of Suiyuan regarded the report as rumor, and ordered the paper suppressed and the editor, Chou Sung-yao, arrested. But, when the report proved to be true, the imprisoned editor instead became an honored guest and was consulted on how to stop the invasion.[64] Soon afterwards, Wang Ting-ch'i took over the paper. After its discontinuation in 1914, Wang founded the *Sui-yuan jih-pao,* but it offended the officials by exposing their corruption, and Wang was finally executed.[65]

In July 1925, the editor of the newly-established *Kuo-min pao* in Tsingtao, which was believed to be affiliated with the KMT, was arrested, severely beaten by the military, and executed the next day. No public announcement was made, but it was reported in other newspapers that he had incurred the displeasure of Chang Tsung-ch'ang for "certain inflammable utterances in his paper," and for urging the workers in the Japanese mills to go on strike.[66]

Also in July 1925, two bookstores in Nanking were closed down by the warlord Sun Ch'uan-fang, and their manager arrested, for selling progressive magazines such as *Chung-kuo ch'ing-nien* (Chinese youth) and *Su-sheng* (The voice of Kiangsu). The *Hangchow Daily Herald* and the *Hangchow News,* both newspapers in Hangchow, were suspended for offending Sun Ch'uan-fang.[67]

In Hunan, where progressive publications enjoyed a popularity second only to their reception in Peking and Shanghai, the provincial government had its own newspaper regulations, in addition to those promulgated by the Peking government. The control of the press was so rigid that no report on foreign or domestic affairs could safely be printed unless it had already appeared in a paper in large cities. For items that were censored, editors would at first leave a note, "deleted by censors," in the blank space left by the deletions, but this practice was soon forbidden.[68] Outlawing newspapers and magazines and arresting editors and writers were familiar sports to those in power, although there was still no elaborate system of secret agents. In August 1919, *Hsiang-chiang p'ing-lun* (Hunan review), edited by Mao Tse-tung, was seized by the troops of Chang Ching-yao, the highhanded military governor of Hunan, when the fifth issue was in the printing press. The printer received a serious warning not to print this magazine any more, and Mao became the editor of *Hsin Hu-nan* (New Hunan), a weekly, from the seventh issue. It was suppressed after the tenth issue came out in October,[69] thus ending Mao's short-lived career as an editor.

Mao was lucky in escaping unscathed; other newspaper editors suffered more. About the time *Hsin Hu-nan* was suppressed, T'an Tu-kung, manager of a newly-established paper, was executed because of the paper's attack on Chang Ching-yao. During this period in Hunan, as an editor for *Ta-kung pao* in Changsha told us, "it was a common practice to raid or close down newspapers. Many newspapermen were arrested, banished, imprisoned, or even executed."[70]

Foreign missionaries and governments played a part in persecuting Chinese journalists, too. When such cases occurred, however, the provincial governments always seemed to support the papers. In 1914, *Hu-nan t'ung-su chiao-yü pao* published a colloquial-style version of an article on American mistreatment of the Filipinos, which, the editor maintained, had appeared originally in *Tung-fang tsa-chih* (*Eastern Miscellany*). An American missionary complained to the American consul in Hankow about the article, and the latter to the government of Hunan, but they received no satisfactory answer. Such a small incident soon became blown out of proportion. Washington instructed its Minister to China to protest to the Peking government. The local government, though, remained as stubborn as before. Finally the paper was suspended for a week, and ordered to print pro-American stories for twenty-one days. In May 1915, *Hu-nan kung pao* attacked the Twenty-one Demands, and proposed a boycott of Japanese merchandise. The Japanese Minister protested to the Peking government, demanding that the paper be closed and an apology be published. The local government, however, would not give in.[71]

The press fared no better in South China. To be sure, writers in the South could attack northern warlords and imperialists freely, but they could not antagonize southern warlords.[72] Even in Canton, where "revolutionary" regimes followed one after another for a decade after 1917, the government's control of news was rigid, and many reporters were bribed. As one journalist reported from his personal experience:

> Reporters' being shot or imprisoned was not accidental . . .
> Papers often had to print what the government required them
> to print . . . The quality of reporters was low . . . Some used
> the papers for extortion.[73]

Revolutionary enthusiasm soon brought intolerance in its wake. The clamor in North China that the alliance between the KMT and the Communists meant "selling out to Russia"[74] increased the KMT's bitterness toward "reactionary" journalists. A speech delivered by Pai Yü at Whampoa Military Academy in 1925 clearly exhibited their attitude:

> We have to use very harsh, compulsory measures to advocate
> [our beliefs] in the teeth of those who are against the
> [revolutionary] movement. I also advocate that we create
> immediately China's "reign of terror," and use extraordinary
> measures to suppress ractionaries. When our Northern
> Expedition begins, we shall have to massacre the reactionary
> running dogs of the imperialists on a large scale . . . I believe
> that a revolution cannot be successful without a reign of
> terror, or be worthy without massacres.[75]

It is obvious that, under these circumstances, there was no possibility of having a free press.

Arguments for Freedom of the Press

Amid all these suppressions, whether for ideological or personal reasons, the demand for freedom of publication grew louder than ever before in China. Freedom of speech and of the press was discussed publicly and enthusiastically. In 1920, liberals such as Hu Shih and Chiang Monlin, together with radicals such as Li Ta-chao, issued the "Manifesto for the Struggle for Freedom," demanding certain basic freedoms, including those of speech and publication.

Much of the discussion of this period was conducted from a theoretical point of view. Western ideas of freedom of speech and condemnation of government intervention were very popular in academic circles.[76] Western thought found able exponents and began to influence the nation profoundly. To refute an old man who suggested that the best way to eradicate the new ideas flooding into China was to suppress all newspapers except for the organ of the government, Kao I-han declared that what China needed was not unity in thought but diversity, that it was from such diversification that truth would emerge.[77]

Applying his views to a real issue, Kao criticized the Police Regulations for legalizing official interference with freedom of speech, assembly, and publication. He pointed out that such regulations were designed to perpetuate injustice and corruption, and cited examples from European history to show that such laws really belonged in the eighteenth century, not the twentieth.[78]

One of the most vehement writers was, of course, Ch'en Tu-hsiu, who pointed out that, according to the Constitution of China, people should enjoy such freedom "unless restricted by the law." The qualifying clause left a loophole that the government had been exploiting. "The law is made to preserve the civilization of the present," he said. Freedom of speech and publication, which is a major premise of law and civilization, is needed to create the civilization of the future. There must be absolute freedom of speech, unrestrained by any law, in order to discover the weakness of the present system and the shortcomings of the current laws. If there is no freedom of speech, or if the press has no freedom to violate the law, only the established institutions will be preserved; nothing better will be created.[79]

This advocacy of absolute freedom regardless of the law was, perhaps, the most bold and radical plea ever made in China. Other writers were more moderate. They only hoped that the government would either repeal restrictive laws, such as the Police Regulations, the Martial Law, the Publication Law, and the Regulations Governing the Press, or make no attempt to go beyond them. The legality of the Regulations Governing the Press was challenged, as these regulations, harsher than the Publication Law, were enacted and enforced by the police, who had no legal authority to make any law. In fact, even the legality of the Publication Law was questioned because it was promulgated by Yuan Shih-k'ai without the approval of the Parliament. Demands were also made for the limitation of police power, and the cessation of the practice of using military men as commissioners of police, who had played an important part in censorship.[80]

The critics also realized that current high government officials such as Chang Shih-chao and I Yin-ch'u, who had once clamored for freedom of the press, now wished to suppress freedom of expression,[81] that revolutionaries wanted freedom for only their own party and not the others,[82] and that many journalists were corrupt.[83] To have real freedom of publication, they reasoned, one must eliminate not only the feudalistic warlords, but also the black sheep in the fold.[84]

The attitude of the revolutionaries may be illustrated by an article in *Hsiang-tao* (*Guide Weekly*). It called "democracy" and "freedom of speech" pretexts used by every party to protect its own organs from enemies. Therefore, papers in China should be divided into two categories according to their attitudes toward the revolution, and treated in different ways. The article then gave a list of papers supposedly working for the warlords, the Japanese, and the British "imperialists." "If democracy and freedom of speech are for these papers," it asked, "what is the value of democracy and freedom of speech?"[85] Clearly, the self-righteous left could become as intolerant as the reactionary right.

Foreign Authorities in Shanghai

A discussion of censorship in China would be incomplete without mentioning the part that foreigners played in the settlements. When China was torn by civil wars and the Chinese press oppressed by warlords and their henchmen, peace and prosperity continued to exist in the foreign settlements in the treaty ports, especially Shanghai, and a certain degree of freedom for the press was tolerated there.[86] During the days of Yuan Shih-k'ai, the press in Shanghai alone dared criticize his ways. Chinese revolutionaries, adventurers, and writers thus flocked to Shanghai to engage in writing and publishing, especially after 1925, and that city became the center of their activities.

The illusion of British impartiality resulting from the *Su pao* case was soon destroyed by harsh reality. The Shanghai Municipal Council, in protecting the Chinese press from the Chinese government, was really trying to assert and increase its own power. As early as 1903, when the *Su pao* case was still in the court, the Municipal Council made its first attempt to regulate the Chinese press by legislative measures, but objections raised by the diplomatic corps blocked this initiative.[87] Nevertheless, three categories of materials were generally banned: attacks on certain Chinese political or military figures whom the foreign authorities wished to please;[88] attacks on foreign powers; and, of course, ideologically subversive writings.

In 1913 and 1915, asserting that the outspoken opposition to Yuan's monarchical scheme and the anti-Japanese feelings in the Chinese press endangered normal life in the settlement, the Shanghai Municipal Council drafted another municipal law for controlling the press. In March 1916, the Council proposed a resolution asking for certain amendments in the municipal bylaws and regulations to license printed matter. The proposed provision to be included under Bylaw XXXIV would give the Council the

right to refuse, withdraw, or suspend licenses at its own discretion.
As Kotenov wrote:

> Frankly speaking, the Council in its attempt to solve the
> complicated problem of the regulating of the native press in
> the Settlement resorted finally to the same "administrative
> discretion," which characterized the notorious Chinese
> legislation of the 3rd year of the Republic. The only exception
> was that the exercise of this "discretion" did not this time
> rest in the hands of ignorant and corrupt Chinese officials, but
> in the hands of the representatives of the Shanghai foreign
> community.

The proposed measures were severely criticized by the ratepayers
(voters). Then the Council modified its proposal and submitted the
new bill in 1917 and 1918. It was still rejected by the Consular
Body, which objected, among other things, to the licensing of the
foreign press, as the "Consuls wished to see licensed only the
Chinese press."[89]

At this time, the anti-Japanese movement was growing in
China. The Chinese newspapers in Shanghai took up the campaign,
first by refusing to accept any Japanese advertisements and later by
printing reports concerning the boycott of Japanese goods, a most
widely discussed subject in those days. Several newspapers openly
supported the boycott.[90]

The French consul-general, who was empowered to "keep
peace and order" in the French Concession, on June 20, 1919
issued an ordinance in regard to Chinese newspapers published in
the Concession, enjoining that: (1) no newspapers or magazines
might be established in the French Concession without the permission of the French consul-general; (2) each paper should submit
one copy to the police in the French Concession and the French
consulate-general before it appeared on the market; (3) the publisher, writer, and printer of any printed matter which violated
public peace and order would be prosecuted in the French Mixed
Court; (4) the police could suspend any publication which had not
had official approval.[91] Thus the French Concession in Shanghai

joined the British Concessions in Hankow and Tientsin in drawing up its own regulations for governing the press.

On May 17, 1919, the editor of the KMT organ *Min-kuo jih-pao* (*Republican Daily News*), Yeh Ch'u-ts'ang, was charged before the Mixed Court with inciting readers to murder General Chang Ching-yao. The article, "Quickly Do away with Chang Ching-yao, the Military Governor of Hunan," was described by the prosecution as set in unusually large type in a prominent place in the newspaper, and published every day from April 16 to May 17. Yeh was warned to use proper discretion. In July, he was again arrested for publishing on July 4 an article entitled "Essential Ways for the Salvation of the Nation," and on July 18 "A Wicked Official Denounced by the People of Chekiang Residing in Kwangtung." Yeh argued that the July 4 article, which denounced the Peking government as an agent of Japan, was an announcement by members of the Chinese Parliament residing in Shanghai. The July 18 article was a circular telegram from the Chekiang Association in Kwangtung, calling the military governor of Chekiang "a robber and murderer." The paper was suspended for two days, and Yeh was released on bail after he promised not to publish such articles again.[92]

In July 1919, the additional bylaw with the licensing regulations submitted by the Council was passed at a special meeting of the ratepayers because of the Japanese block vote, but it was later vetoed by the Consular Body.[93]

Antiforeign feelings kept rising. As Shanghai's Captain-Superintendent of Police reported in 1921:

The spirit of unrest, or of self-expression, noticeable during recent years continued during 1921. Various movements were in evidence; among them being . . . meeting in connexion with China's cause at the Washington Conference, Chinese representation on the Municipal Council, activities of socialist extremists and strikes . . . Signs are that a movement akin to Bolshevism is slowly but steadily gaining ground in Shanghai and other places.

The Captain-Superintendent was quite pleased that

other activities of this nature under observation of the police during the year led to the successful prosecution of four publishers and disseminators of communist literature and the seizure and confiscation of large quantities of handbills and pamphlets.[94]

This report clearly shows that the British officials in Shanghai, like the Chinese warlords, attributed the resurgence of Chinese nationalism, abetted by so many obvious insults to Chinese pride, to Communist agitation. The more arrogant the attitude of the British, treating China only as a potential market for their goods and the Chinese people as inferior colonial subjects, the more irresistible the siren voice of communism would become. So said Chang Hu in 1925:

> The British are afraid of Bolshevism on the one hand, but oppress the poor on the other hand. The more they keep on oppressing the weak, the more credit they will get for a leftist China than the Ministry of Propaganda in Moscow. The poor and weak nations in the world have now awakened and are fighting for their freedom. They need not wait for the Communist Party to wake them up.[95]

In their fear of communism, the foreign authorities in the settlement forgot all about freedom of speech and of the press. Their police vigorously suppressed all publications that they considered Bolshevistic[96] or immoral; newspapermen were often visited by the representatives of the Municipal Council and were ordered to delete undesirable items.[97] Editors and managers of publishing firms or bookstores were often brought before the Mixed Court, which had gained complete independence from Chinese jurisdiction since 1911.[98] Neither the police nor the court appeared to be always fair and incorruptible. Chang Ching-lu, later a well-known publisher, was once employed by a newspaper as a "social secretary" to appear in court on behalf of the paper whenever it was prosecuted. In 1923-1924, while managing a publishing firm, he was prosecuted and fined seven times in six months, and appeared before the Mixed Court on the average of once a week. Sometimes the police would bring charges for the purpose of extorting money from the publishers.[99]

To be sure, the Communists were quite active.[100] The Shanghai Book Company, established on November 1, 1923, was ostensibly a retail agent for some publishers. Its real purpose, however, was to print and secretly distribute Communist publications at night. As its manager reported years later, they had very little business in the retail department, but the clandestine circulation of their Communist publications was not wide either. Even their best seller, the *Guide Weekly,* sold only a little over 1,000 copies of each issue.[101]

Although the Municipal Council's attempt to pass a law for licensing printed matter failed again in 1919, the Council was undaunted, and submitted the same proposal to the ratepayers every year between 1920 and 1925. Not only was this initiative greeted with a lack of enthusiasm by the ratepayers, but it stirred up strong opposition throughout the entire Chinese community. In 1924, twenty-six Chinese organizations representing practically all the Chinese mercantile and professional groups in Shanghai issued a joint protest against the proposal. In April 1925, the Chinese opposition, headed by the Chinese Chamber of Commerce, flatly declared the new attempt of the Council as *ultra vires* and an encroachment upon China's sovereign rights.[102] The special meeting of ratepayers could not convene because it lacked a quorum, and the proposal did not even have a chance to be presented.

Failing to pass its own laws, the Municipal Council resorted to the Chinese Publication Law of 1914, although the latter had been ignored in China since the death of Yuan Shih-k'ai. The first case in which this law was invoked occurred on January 23, 1925, when Shao Li-tzu, vice-president of Shanghai University, was charged as a menace to the peace and order of the settlement because a large stock of books and pamphlets in Chinese and English "related to Communist teachings" was discovered on the premises of the institution. Article 11 of the Publication Law was invoked. Counsel for the accused argued that Communist doctrines had not been declared illegal in China and that these books and pamphlets formed a part of the university library. He also questioned the legality of the Publication Law because it had never been presented before the Chinese Parliament. The court held that the law had not been officially repealed and thus was still in force. Shao, a bona fide resident of the settlement for more than twenty years, was allowed to remain in the settlement after posting a personal bond of 1,000 yuan. The books and pamphlets were confiscated.[103]

On February 25, 1925, the editors of *Min-kuo jih-pao, Shanghai shang pao,* and *Chung-hua hsin pao,* all Chinese newspapers published in the International Settlement, were charged under Articles 3 and 11 of the Publication Law. Shao Li-tzu, editor of *Min-kuo jih-pao,* was again charged as an "undesirable" and the paper suspected as affiliated with Shanghai University. The article in question appealed to the workers in the Japanese mills in Shanghai to rise up and oppose the "Japanese capitalists," who "treated the Chinese as slaves or cows and horses." The establishment of Japanese mills in China was, this appeal asserted, "an encroachment upon China's sovereign rights." The court found the article antiforeign, and the accused were fined.[104]

In February and March 1925, fifty-eight persons, including workers of the Nagai Wata Kaisha Company mill, were brought before the Mixed Court on various occasions to answer for the first strike in the Japanese mill on February 26. Fifty-two of the accused were fined, although the court did not follow the suggestions of the prosecution to connect the strike with "Communist propaganda" carried on in some native newspapers. Several papers were fined, however, for having printed the manifesto of the labor union.[105]

Having learned bitter lessons, most Shanghai papers remained silent when a second strike at the Japanese mill was called and a Chinese foreman was killed by the Japanese. Chinese students, nevertheless, held a peaceful demonstration on May 30, during which twelve Chinese students were killed by the police under the command of a British officer. Many more were wounded and/or arrested on the grounds that their "Communist activities and antiforeign propaganda were a menace to peace and order in the

Settlement." Charges were preferred against forty-nine persons, forty-seven of whom were students, under Articles 164 and 165 of the Chinese Criminal Code and Article 11 of the Publication Law. The prosecution again brought in Bolshevism. The defense contended that the movement was motivated by patriotism, although communism was not outlawed in China. Evidence from the accused and several foreign witnesses also bore out this statement. None of the students admitted the influence of communism. All the defendants were released on bail.[106]

On June 12, 1925, seven persons participating in the June 1 demonstration were charged under, among other things, Article 11 of the Publication Law for distributing "inflammatory pamphlets." The defense pointed out that the Publication Law concerned the author, publisher, and printer, but not the coolies sent out to distribute the publications. The case was then dismissed.[107]

After the May Thirtieth Incident, British authorities increased their efforts to hunt for Red writers. On June 2, the diplomatic corps instructed the foreign press in China to exploit to the fullest the possible relationship between Chinese students and Soviet Russia in order to turn public opinion against the student movement. Within a week, foreign-language papers were labeling the Chinese masses as Bolshevistic and antiforeign, and lavishly employing such words as "mob," "demagogue," "anarchy," "uprising." The Municipal Council announced in the *North China Daily News* that strict censorship would be imposed if the Chinese papers should publish "inaccurate" information. On June 30, the Council published the first of the three issues of *Ch'eng-yen* (Sincere words) in Chinese to present the British side of the story, which the Chinese attacked as mere distortions. In August, it published *Chiu-kuo wu pao,* which the Chinese called reactionary, absurd, and imperialistic. When *Shun pao* and *Hsin-wen pao,* the two largest Chinese papers in Shanghai, printed *Ch'eng-yen* on July 11 as an advertisement, the Chinese community was furious. The Students Union withdrew its advertisements from the two papers, and interfered with their sale outside of the Settlement. The two papers finally yielded to the students' demands.[108] Instead of winning the loyalty of the Chinese population, the Settlement authorities were to have more difficulties with them.

On July 10, a police detective-sergeant saw a copy of the *Union,* a weekly published by the Students Union, in the window of the Intelligence Press. He purchased a copy for three coppers, and found it seditious. As a result, the Intelligence Press was searched, and about twenty titles were seized, including one book by Tagore on character, which had nothing to do with Bolshevism, and another publication entitled *Hsing-shih* (The awakening lion), which was actually anti-Bolshevik. The accountant and the submanager of the Press were arrested. The Mixed Court decided that the confiscated works were dangerous readings liable to incite the Chinese to violence. The accused were released on bail, on condition that they would cooperate with the police in suppressing inflammatory literature.[109]

On September 17, the manager and the printer of the *Shanghai pao* were charged in the Mixed Court with publishing seditious reports involving Tuan Ch'i-jui and the Peking government. The police raided the printing shop and seized all unsold copies. The accused complained of discrimination, since the *North China Daily News* and the *China Press,* both English-language newspapers in Shanghai, had published with impunity the same reports, worded in much stronger language. The police's reply implied that what might be legal in the English press would still be illegal in Chinese papers. The defendants were fined on October 3 and required to post bonds, and the printer was also cautioned on a second charge of issuing an "inflammatory" booklet. This booklet attacked the "barbarous and brutal" massacres of the Chinese by the British in Shanghai, Shameen, Hankow, Nanking, and Chinkiang, saying:

> Rumours that we are Bolshevik and anti-foreign are being circulated so that they may shirk their responsibility [in China]. . . Their battleships are patrolling our rivers and blockading our seaports, which is a great insult to a weak race. How can we tolerate such things any longer?

It called for a declaration of war on the British. "Even when almost every one of our countrymen anticipates defeat, let me say that we will win the war . . . The proud are invariably defeated."[110]

The most famous case consequent upon the May Thirtieth affair was the trial of Wang Yun-wu because of a special issue of the *Eastern Miscellany* covering the incident. The *Eastern Miscellany* was a conservative magazine, but the police considered the articles in this particular issue "highly inflammatory." Wang Yun-wu, chief editor of the Commercial Press, which published the magazine, was charged before the Mixed Court on September 17, although he was not a resident of the International Settlement, nor did he transact business there. Later the manager of the Press's sales department in the Settlement was also prosecuted. The defense counsel showed that the cartoons were similar to those in the foreign publications, and that the photographs of dead students, bloody clothing, and so forth, were the same as those in the local newspapers. Wang, obviously hoping to remain in the good books of the authorities, offered a feeble defense. The police had really no case against the defendants; they wished only to suppress the facts. On October 24, the accused parties were required to post a security.[111]

Naturally the KMT organ *Min-kuo jih-pao,* the arch-offender, could not help getting involved. On September 25, 1925, Yeh Ch'u-ts'ang was again charged under Articles 3 and 11 of the Publication Law for publishing a report on September 7 of a riot on Honan Road, in which several workers were injured or killed by the municipal police. It also stated that the Students Union in Shanghai had sent a protest to the Peking government. The prosecution contended that the report exaggerated the inhumanity of the British. It also cited an old Chinese law forbidding students and criminals to engage in politics, although Chinese students had been most active in politics for years. Yeh was required to print an apology for the "obnoxious article" in his paper, and was fined for failing to print his name therein[112]—an apparent pretext, since very few papers in China ever printed the names, addresses, ages, and native towns of their editors, publishers, and printers in accordance with the Publication Law.

Sometimes, even reading a pamphlet in the street could get

the reader into trouble. On December 6 of the same year, a man was charged with almost all the crimes the police could think of because he was found reading a pamphlet in the street and having more issues of the same in his sleeves. The accused insisted that he had just picked up the pamphlet and was trying to find out what it was about when arrested. Nevertheless, he was expelled as an undesirable element and handed over to the Chinese authorities for trial.[113]

The unscrupulous use of the Publication Law irritated the Chinese to no end. Many protests had reached Peking. On April 3, 1925, the Shanghai Publishers Association, the Joint Association of Book and Newspaper Publishers, the Daily News Association, and the Book Dealers Association jointly petitioned the Peking government again to repeal the law.[114] After the *Eastern Miscellany* case, even more people complained. Under public pressure, the Chinese government rescinded the law on January 29, 1926.

To be fair, it should be pointed out that, in all these censorship cases in the Settlement during this period, the accused were usually only fined or required to deposit a security; no one lost his life. The Chinese nevertheless seethed with fury. The reason for their anger was well summarized in an editorial in the *Contemporary Review.* Commenting on the raid on Shanghai University in 1925 and the subsequent confiscation of allegedly Communist books, the editor wrote:

> The concept of freedom of speech and publication came from the West. Why should the white men alone have [such] freedom, but not the Chinese? . . . Furthermore, all the weeklies and monthlies that talk about "-isms" often print just literal translations of works by the white men. Why do you [white men] call such writings anti-foreign, once they are translated into Chinese?[115]

Following the May Thirtieth Incident, spontaneous strikes against foreign interests—especially the British and Japanese—came one after another all over the country, involving people in all walks of life. The "very damaging weapon" they had, as the *Times* called it, was the boycott of British and Japanese goods in China. Western policy played right into the hands of the Communists. Michael Borodin, Soviet adviser to the KMT government in Canton, said happily: "We did not make May 30. It was made for us."[116] Public interest in the social sciences had greatly increased, as was borne out by library circulation figures. The years of 1925-1927 were the heyday of progressive books and periodicals.[117]

In the face of strong antiforeign sentiments, the Consular Body announced on June 19, 1926 that the Printed Matter Bylaws proposal would not be placed before the ratepayers' special meeting that year. After that, no more was heard about the suggested bylaws. On January 1, 1927, the Mixed Court, which had been partially responsible for the disorder on May 30, 1925, was handed over to the Chinese authorities. In less than three months, Chiang Kai-shek's National Revolutionary Army marched into Shanghai, and China was soon under the control of the KMT government in Nanking.

In conclusion, it would seem that China's national fortune reached its nadir during this period, especially in the decade following 1916. Intellectually, however, it was the most brilliant and important period in modern Chinese history. The May Fourth Movement and the subsequent Literary Renaissance openly challenged and weakened the authority of the Confucian tradition. Western democratic thought, communism, and the Three People's Principles all became generally known and discussed in periodicals—which had become the forum of the liberals—if not in newspapers. Cruel as the warlords could be, they usually suppressed publications only when their personal interests or reputations were endangered. Having no systematic ideology of their own, they could not recognize, and therefore often did not persecute, dissent. Besides, some of them also shared the fervor of nationalism, which led to many severe conflicts between the foreign authorities and the Chinese population in the International Settlement in Shanghai.

Equally anxious to uphold their interests and prestige, the foreign authorities also punished the offenders and made them pay with their purses. This seemingly most chaotic period, ironically, was also one of relative freedom of thought and great significance in China's intellectual history.

Chapter IV

THE KUOMINTANG REGIME BEFORE THE WAR,
1927-1937 (1)

On June 9, 1926, KMT troops, led by Chiang Kai-shek and backed by a united front with the Communists, pushed northward from Canton. Under the banner of anti-imperialism and anti-warlordism, a none-too-strong army won the full support of the people and made miraculous progress. On January 1, 1927, the KMT government in Canton, comprising many Communists, moved to Wuhan. Chiang Kai-shek, however, established on April 18 another KMT government in Nanking, composed mostly of conservative elements. The rift between the KMT and the CCP soon became irrevocable. The KMT expelled the Communists from their ranks and started a bloody purge. The two KMT governments merged in September. With the death of Chang Tso-lin in June 1928, the Peking warlord government ceased to exist. On October 10, 1928, the government in Nanking became the only national government of China, and the KMT the only official party in power. Although powerful, semi-independent militarists still occupied some provinces, nearly all of them, though not always under Chiang's thumb, claimed to be KMT members.

The government's most urgent problem was now the suppression of the "Communist bandits," who had their base in parts of the provinces of Kiangsi and Fukien. On the military front, the government's efforts to combat communism were obviously successful. In October 1934, Chinese Communists, under the leadership of Mao Tse-tung, Chu Teh, and Chou En-lai, began the fabled Long March. When they reached northern Shensi one year later, only a small group of diehards were left in their ranks. But on another front— the so-called "propaganda front"—the government's success was not so obvious.

79

Leftist and Communist Literature

The Communist conquest of China started with ideological persuasion. Realizing the importance of influencing the young and the politically aware, the CCP in 1925-1927 flooded the market in Shanghai with its literature. Although the Red tide was slightly checked during the great purge of 1927, from 1928 on, Marxist works and books on Soviet literature and literary theories kept appearing in the market. In 1929, books in the social sciences, most of them Marxist, were in their heyday.[1] On June 22, 1930, the League of Chinese Social Scientists came into existence.

At this time, the persecution of Communists was in full swing, with many students and alleged Communist agents being imprisoned or executed. Adopting a subtler approach, the Communists turned to literature, especially to the novel. They believed that they could win over more innocent young converts simply by realistically exposing existing poverty and social injustice. On March 2, 1930, the League of Left-Wing Writers held its first meeting in Shanghai. The roster of its fifty-odd charter members included some of the best-known writers in modern China, such as Lu Hsün, Mao Tun, Yü Ta-fu, Ch'ien Hsin-ts'un, Ting Ling, and T'ien Han. The government vigorously suppressed leftist magazines, such as *Meng-ya* (New growth), *T'o-huang che* (The pioneer), *Wen-hsueh chou-pao* (Literature weekly), *Pei-tou* (The dipper), *Wen-hsueh* (Literature), *Tso-chia* (The writers), and *Chung-liu* (Currents).[2] The post office was again busy confiscating objectionable publications. Publishers or booksellers of leftist writings were threatened by hoodlums and warned not to make such works available any more.[3] Others were closed down by government orders and their owners or editors arrested.[4] As Lu Hsün wrote in 1931, even book covers with characters printed in red ink would arouse suspicion. Translations of such Russian novelists as A. Serafimovich, V. Ivanov, N. Ognev, A. Chekhov, and L. Andreev, were banned.[5]

Direct and indirect pressures were constantly applied to writers on the "black list." Seven members of the League of Left-Wing Writers were arrested on January 17, 1931, and secretly executed in Shanghai on February 7.[6] On May 14, 1933, Ting Ling was kidnaped in a street in Shanghai. The authorities denied any knowledge of her whereabouts, but she emerged unharmed some time later from a prison in Nanking. P'an Tzu-nien was kidnaped in Shanghai on the same day;[7] Ying Hsiu-jen plunged to his death from a building in an attempt to shake off suspected abductors;[8] Hung Ling-fei was arrested in 1933 in Peiping, and was shot;[9] T'ien Han, a famous dramatist, was arrested with thirty-three other writers and intellectuals in Shanghai in 1935, but released after recanting;[10] Kuo Mo-jo fled to Japan and did not return to China until after the beginning of the Sino-Japanese War in 1937.

In order to elude the watchful eyes of the police, most of the famous leftist authors had to resort to the use of pen names or pseudonyms. Shen Yen-ping, for instance, had to publish to support his family, but none of his writings could appear in print in his own name. He thus used "Mao Tun" (spear and shield, a phrase meaning "paradoxical") as a pen name when he submitted a short story to a literary magazine late in 1927. The editor, a friend of his, replaced the first character with a homonym to make the name look more like a real one and thus avoid suspicion.[11] This new form has come down as Shen Yen-ping's nom de plume. For the same reason, Ch'ien Hsing-ts'un also had to take a pseudonym, A Ying, which has become better known today than his real name.[12] Lu Hsün, one of the greatest writers in modern China and the recognized leader of this group, published some of Ch'ü Ch'iu-pai's essays as his own,[13] because Ch'ü was a known Communist and not even his nonpolitical writings could be published.

Lu Hsün himself was said to be under the constant surveillance of secret agents, and went into hiding three times before he died in 1936.[14] Because of his political leanings, he often had trouble finding a periodical for his articles. As he wrote in the preface to his *Erh-hsin chi*:

In 1930, the number of [leftist] magazines was decreasing. Some of them could not be published on time, probably because of increasing pressure. *Yü-ssu* and *Pen-liu* were often confiscated by the post office or banned by local authorities, and finally could not continue any longer. At that time, *Meng-ya* became the only magazine I could contribute to, but it too was suppressed after the fifth issue . . . In that year, all I wrote was but the ten short essays included in this collection.[15]

In 1933, many of his articles intended for a literary supplement of *Shun pao* in Shanghai never went into print because of the references to current events. As it became increasingly difficult for him to publish his writings under his well-known pen name, he had to use other aliases—according to his wife, at least eighty different ones. Sometimes, to keep the editor from recognizing his handwriting, he would have his manuscript copied by someone else.[16]

The government's intense effort to suppress Communist literature, which was usually coordinated with its military campaigns against the Communist army, simply drove the Communist press underground.[17] Editorial offices might be located anywhere and were always on the move. Publications might be printed at night, either at a secret spot with the help of sympathetic typesetters and pressmen, or at a legitimate press without the knowledge of other staff members or the management. Sometimes the month and the day were printed but not the year. To avoid arousing the suspicion of the police, magazines changed titles readily. For instance, only one issue of *Ch'ien-shao* (*The Outpost*), "the organ of the Left-Wing Writers League of China," came out, and its title was immediately changed into a conventional one—*Wen hsueh tao pao* (Literary post).[18] Periodicals that did not change titles might use covers showing false titles and/or fictitious publishers or writers, with the real titles printed on the inside front cover or the first page. *Hung-ch'i* (Red flag), the CCP organ, appeared sometimes under titles ranging from "The Goddess of Happiness," or "The Love History of Miss Hung Ni," to "The Statistics of Finance" or "The Publishing World." Other magazines, such as *Hung-ch'i chou-pao* (Red flag weekly), *Lieh-ning ch'ing-nien* (Leninist youth), and *Pu-erh-sai-wei-k'o* (Bolshevik), also used false titles.[19]

The same deceptive practices were used for books. Ch'ü

Ch'iu-pai's *She-hui k'o-hsueh kai-lun* (A general survey of social sciences) was changed to *She-hui k'o-hsueh yen-chiu ch'u-pu* (An introduction to social science studies), written by Pu-lang-te-erh and translated by Yang Hsia-ch'ing. *Min-chung ko-ming yü Min-chung cheng-ch'üan* (People's revolution and people's Regime), a collection of essays from *Hung-ch'i chou-pao,* was labeled as *Sun Wen chu-i chih li-lun yü shih-chi* (The theory and practice of Dr. Sun Yat-sen's doctrine). *Kung-ch'an chu-i ABC* (Communism ABC) appeared under the title of *Tzu-pen chu-i chih p'o-chieh* (The anatomy of capitalism). Books published by the Northern People's Press would often give the Northern Country Books Company or the New Life Book Company as publishers. Most of these books were printed at night in stores that sold only government-approved books and stationery during the daytime.[20]

To outwit the postal ban, the Communists often resorted to their own distribution system. In an issue of *Hung-ch'i,* the editor told interested readers to contact its responsible officers if they wanted to subscribe. No names or addresses were given, but obviously those who were interested knew where and how to seek the representatives. Readers were also requested not to destroy their copies after reading them, but to pass them on to other comrades.[21] Often publishers took advantage of booksellers sympathetic to their cause to promote the sale of such magazines.[22]

Another method of eluding the censors was to avoid all obviously Communist terms, such as "class struggle," in one's writings. Ai Ssu-ch'i's *Che-hsueh chiang-hua* (Discourses on philosophy), for instance, tried to explain dialectical materialism to readers without using Marxist terminology. In one article, the author described how he had to avoid all explicit references and incriminating examples.[23] Many other devious ways were employed to disguise Communist teachings. I have found a copy of *Yang-chou shih-jih chi,* reprinted in Shanghai in 1936. No one would have suspected any Communist ideas in this seventeenth-century eye-witness's account of the Manchu invaders' massacres in Yangchow, if he had not read the preface.[24]

Methods of Control

Communist activities made the government nervous and suspicious, and induced minor functionaries to watch all newspapers and news agencies very closely to prevent the printing of news that might be prejudicial to the government. Various news censorship regulations were promulgated by the central as well as local governments.[25] On September 21, 1933, the KMT Central Executive Committee passed the Revised Measures on News Censorship in Important Metropolises, which stated the general principles for censorship. Two weeks later, it passed the Revised Standards for News Censorship, which specified that "newspapers in publishing news shall use the dispatches of the Central News Agency as their guidelines."[26] Censors were stationed at relevant telegraph offices. To play safe, they often interpreted the rules and regulations in the broadest possible sense.[27] Often they could not make up their minds. Thus news items already published in one local paper might not be allowed to travel to a different city;[28] a report might pass through the censors' hands at one office, but not another;[29] what was tolerated by the central government might be banned by a local government;[30] reports of no great consequence were unnecessarily deleted; simple narratives of actual happenings, such as the movements and activities of high government officials, would often be suppressed, leaving the editors completely baffled.[31]

On October 14, 1934, for instance, Yü Hsueh-chung, chairman of the Hopei provincial government, left Peiping for Hankow. A news agency in Peiping reported Yü's trip, but the next day it was ordered to deny the report. Yü's activities were reported in Chinese newspapers elsewhere but not in Tientsin and Peiping, even though they appeared in foreign language newspapers in these two cities. After Yü's return to Peiping, *Ta-kung pao* (*L'Impartial*) used this case to illustrate the absurdity of news censorship in an editorial entitled "Where Did Chairman Yü Come from?" The paper received a stern warning from the Censorship Commission.[32]

On the afternoon of October 24 of the same year, Chiang Kai-shek arrived in Peiping. When the evening papers in Peiping submitted their page proofs for censorship, the report on his arrival was banned.

At midnight the censors lifted the ban, but instructed all papers to consult the Central News Agency for information on Chiang's movements. On October 27, a Central News Agency dispatch about the Mongolian Political Council's expressed readiness to welcome Chiang to inner Mongolia was deleted. At noon on November 3, Chiang left Peiping for Chahar and Suiyuan. Two hours later, Reuter's News Agency dispatched the news in English and displayed the report on a bulletin board in a hotel in Peiping where foreign correspondents stayed. Yet, on the next day, Chinese newspapers in Peiping were only allowed to say that Chiang had gone to visit the Ming Tombs.

When Madame Chiang accompanied her husband to Peiping and gave a press conference to foreign correspondents on November 2, Chinese reporters were excluded. Her interview contained no confidential information, but she denied that China would adopt Fascism, and that a Blue Shirt Organization existed in China. Although her interview was published in English-language papers in Peiping the next day, a Chinese translation, designed for publication by Chinese newspapers on November 4, was suppressed by the censors.[33]

Examples such as the above are too numerous to be cited here. So much news was suppressed that the people hardly knew what was actually going on in their own country.[34] Good reporters had to use various ruses to phrase telegrams in such a way that their reports might appear acceptable to the censors and yet also comprehensible to editors or readers. One method was to send out several telegrams to report an important news items with varying degrees of obscurity in the language, so that, in case the clearer messages were detained, at least the more obscure ones could get through. Some reporters used the long-distance telephone to report to their home offices, but this service was then available only along the Nanking-Shanghai-Hangchow Railroad.[35]

What was worse, officials could sometimes compel a newspaper to say what they wanted it to say, and then claim that the paper was expressing its own views. A newspaper would be severely punished if it should refuse to publish, or should reveal the real source of, such writings. The public might catch up with the truth several weeks or months later, or they might never do so. *Ta-kung pao* once questioned the wisdom of such propaganda practices in peace time, and voiced the fear that people would lose confidence in newspapers and put their trust in rumors.[36]

Books and magazines were also prevented from publishing material unpalatable to the government. In addition to the Publication Law of 1930 and the Regulations concerning its application in 1931, the Regulations for Punishing Counterrevolutionaries were promulgated in 1929, and the Emergency Law Governing Treason and Sedition in 1931, prescribing capital punishment or life imprisonment for those engaging in seditious propaganda by writings, pictures, or word of mouth, with intent to subvert the Republic.[37]

At first, the Publication Law of 1930 does not seem to have been very effectively carried out. The Ministry of the Interior admitted that few publications were submitted for registration before February 1932. But the situation soon changed. While only 375 titles were registered in March-December 1932, 855 titles were registered in 1933, 5,225 in 1934, and 1,693 in January–June 1935. By June 1935, 4,500 newspapers and magazines had been registered, among which about 400 had ceased publication either by government orders or of their own volition.[38]

To facilitate prepublication censorship of books and magazines, the Censorship Commission for Books and Periodicals was established in Shanghai in 1934. The Rules for Censoring Books and Periodicals were phrased in such ambiguous language that a censor could interpret them in many different ways to suit his own whims. Rule no. 5, for instance, insisted on "correct thought" without giving an exact definition for the word "correct."[39] The complaints of Chinese writers in Shanghai during those days recall the objections raised by Milton in his *Areopagitica:* "That he who is made judge to sit upon the birth or death of books," instead of being "above the common measure, both studious, learned and judicious," was often "either ignorant, imperious, and remiss, or basely pecuniary." Middle school graduates who had no love for literature often meddled with the manuscripts of good writers, but their tampering was not openly known until after the disappearance of the Censorship Commission in 1935. Unacknowledged deletions or corrections by clumsy censors often marred the originals.[40] Sometimes half a sentence would be deleted, leaving the other half meaningless; or censors might insert revisions in bad Chinese or at variance with the author's meaning.[41] Lin Yutang remembered how, in a passage discussing love, the clause "as preached by Tolstoy" was deleted from an article for his magazine. The article was concerned principally with the Chinese New Year, but Tolstoy, being a Russian, was according to the censor's logic a Bolshevik.[42] Speaking of the extensiveness of such deletions, Lu Hsün reported that, of a 6,000-character article on the downfall of the Ming dynasty he wrote for the January 1935 issue of *Wen-hsueh,* three-fourths was deleted, and a description of female factory workers' life in tenement houses was cut out completely. Of the essays intended for the *Erh-hsin chi,* the majority were withheld by censors, obliging the publisher to print merely the remnants in a volume entitled *Shih-ling chi* (A collection of remnants).[43] Disgusted with such practices, Lu Hsün would often compare the published version with his original manuscript and mark the deletions made by censors or editors. From such original manuscripts, an edition of his complete works was published in 1938 in Shanghai, when the city was again under foreign control. With this unexpurgated edition, readers had an unusual opportunity to study the censors' operations.[44] None of the censored passages or essays tried to preach Communist doctrines or, to a layman's eye, in any way violated the Publication Law. But they were usually satirical and could thus be interpreted as critical of the government.

Some censors even took advantage of their position. Chang Ching-lu, a publisher, reported that he was not allowed to bring out Kuo Mo-jo's *Wo-ti yu-nien* (My childhood), which was labeled as "reactionary," after he had refused to accept a censor's book on the latter's terms. Soon afterwards, a sequel to *Wo-ti yu-nien* appeared in the market with the imprint of a different publisher, who had accepted the censor's terms and published the latter's pornographic novel.[45]

In spite of all these preventive measures, offensive writings continued to appear in print. As in the previous periods, the customs and post offices were often ordered to stop their circulation. From August 16 to October 16, 1934, postal delivery was denied to *I-shih pao* in Tientsin because of its editorial of August 10 criticizing the military areas in North China. *Ch'en pao* in Peiping lost its postal privileges from September 17 to November 3 in the same year. The same punishment was imposed on *Shih-shih hsin pao* (*China Times*) in Shanghai, also on September 17.[46] Because of its critical attitude towards the government and its publication of news items which other newspapers dared not print, *Ta-kung pao* in Tientsin was not allowed to circulate south of the Yangtze River. From December 4, 1936, it also lost its postal privileges. Hu Shih deemed the ban a testimony to the paper's integrity and a cause for congratulation.[47] *Sheng-huo* (*Life Weekly*), edited and published by Tsou T'ao-fen in Shanghai, was denied the use of the mails in 1932.

Even when a publication was accepted for mailing, it might still be detained or confiscated by the authorities. In January 1934, *Tu-li p'ing-lun* (Independent review), a magazine edited by Hu Shih and published in Peiping, was notified by the Peiping Post Office that 121 packages of the magazine mailed to Kiangsu had been detained by the censors at the Gendarmerie Headquarters in Nanking. Upon investigation, the editors found the issue in question to be no. 81. Less than three months later, 139 packages of its issue no. 91 were detained by the postal and telegraphic censors in Nanking, and again no reasons were given.[48] The publishers, however, were not always informed officially. A magazine might reach readers in one town but not those in another. A publisher often had no way of knowing until many subscribers complained. *Tu-shu tsa-chih,* a magazine in Shanghai devoted to the study of all schools of social thought, often mysteriously disappeared, and its editors repeatedly had to assure subscribers that the magazine had been published and mailed on time and that they could not be held responsible if any issue should fail to reach a reader.[49]

Publications might be allowed to circulate in one place but not in another. *Ching pao* of Peiping was banned in Shanghai in 1929 because it allegedly printed "anti-Nanking" news.[50] In April of the same year, twenty-eight Shanghai tabloids, generally known as "mosquito" papers, were banned by the Garrison Headquarters in Nanking because they "libeled the central government."[51]

For worse offenders, the government would simply suspend their publications temporarily or permanently. On March 7, 1932, *Cheng-i pao* in Hankow was suspended for three days because of an editorial criticizing the central government.[52] In June 1934, *Hua-pei jih-pao* (*North China Press*), the KMT's own paper in Peiping, was suspended because of its report on May 31 about the railroad service between North China and so-called "Manchoukuo." Its director and editor-in-chief were ordered to return to Nanking, and it was restored on July 1 under new management.[53] In September 1934, Hua T'e News Agency in Nanking was suspended because of a news story about three generals demanding certain concessions from the central government.[54]

On April 3, 1935, *Jen-yen*, a weekly in Shanghai, was suspended for a month, with no reason given.[55] In December 1933, *Life Weekly* was closed by the government after it had been rumored for fourteen months that a suspension order was imminent. Tsou T'ao-fen's two other weeklies in Shanghai met the same fate: *Ta-chung sheng-huo* (*Public Life*) in February 1936; *Sheng-huo hsing-chi k'an* (Life Sunday edition) ten months later.[56] Also in December 1936, *Tu-li p'ing-lun* was closed down by government order because of its comment on the situation in the Hopei-Chahar area, although three months later, after Hu Shih's protest, it was allowed to resume publication.[57]

More than once Chiang Kai-shek himself was directly involved in the suspension of newspapers. In December 1935, *Ch'en pao* in Shanghai printed a report on the manipulation of the stock market in Shanghai by a Japanese company. The paper was suspended on the grounds that it was attempting to create confusion in financial circles and to disrupt the government's program of nationalizing all silver coins. Chiang wanted the reporter arrested, but changed his mind after his most trusted aides spent several hours convincing him that he was not a Communist.[58] In July 1937, the Central Publicity Department suspended Kung Te-pai's *Chiu-kuo jih-pao* in Nanking for three days because of an editorial criticizing Madame H. H. Kung, wife of the Minister of Finance and sister of Madame Chiang, for her manipulation of the stock market in Shanghai. After the paper resumed publication, it carried another editorial on the same subject, and this time it was suspended for one month. Somebody asked Chiang to intercede, and he did. On August 7, an official of the Central Publicity Department told Kung Te-pai on the telephone that he could resume publication immediately, although the ban was not officially lifted. The paper reappeared on August 15.[59]

Among the numerous cases of postal ban or suspension, those cited above are but a few of the better-known examples. Many of the suppressed publications were simply labeled "reactionary," the meaning of which was never clearly explained. In 1929, the Ministry of Education repeatedly ordered schools to prohibit students from reading "reactionary publications."[60] On May 26, 1929, *T'ung-hai hsin pao* in Nantung, Kiangsu, which was often critical of the KMT authorities, was closed down by government order because it was "reactionary."[61] In March 1931, several bookstores in Shanghai were sealed off because they sold "reactionary" books.[62] After the Mukden Incident in 1931, an article in *Tu-shu tsa-chih* that criticized the government's failure to resist Japanese invasion was labeled "reactionary." As its editor pointed out in a later issue, the whole country was then unhappy with the situation and could therefore be called "reactionary," and if everybody was already "reactionary," how much more harm could a "reactionary" article do?[63] Even in areas not entirely under Nanking's control, authorities learned to apply this favorite epithet to books and magazines they disliked and banned those publications accordingly.[64]

To make sure that suppressed publications would not be available to the public, the government inspected bookstores and compiled lists of prohibited books and magazines in an attempt to control distribution. Eight such lists for this period, a total of 1,803 titles, are included in Chang Ching-lu's collection of source materials for the history of Chinese publishing.[65] The following are the three main lists, each with its date and number of titles:

1931	228 titles
February 19, 1934	149 titles in the humanities
August 1936	662 titles in the social sciences

The five supplementary lists, which have inclusive dates, are:

1929-1931	92 titles
1929-1931	211 titles
1929-1936	307 titles in the humanities
January-March 1936	24 titles
November 1936-June 1937	130 titles

There was some overlapping among these lists. The Communist magazines *Hung-ch'i* and *Pu-erh-sai-wei-k'o,* for instance, were listed more than once under their aliases. Though these lists were not exhaustive,[66] they nevertheless give some idea of the nature and extent of prohibited publications.

Whereas the majority of the blacklisted publications were Marxist, a considerable number of them were written by members of other minor political parties or KMT members involved in intra-party power struggles.[67] The reasons given for the outlawing of these works included "libeling this Party and criticizing national leaders," "advocating reactionary [ideas]," "criticizing the present government and inciting [readers] to contention," "absurd ideas," and "radical statements." A history of the Revolution of 1911 was banned in June 1930 because of "inaccurate records satirizing Dr. Sun Yat-sen." A book on the different forms of government was banned in 1932 because it was "in favor of despotic monarchism, expressing preposterous ideas." A book on the primary sources of contemporary history was banned in June 1934 because it "mocked the responsible committeemen of the [KMT] Central Headquarters." A collection of speeches made by important Party and government officials was banned in January 1935 on the ground that it "libeled the leaders of this Party." Five books and two magazines on "Latinxua" (Latinization of the Chinese language) were banned in February 1937, and three more such magazines one month later, probably because of official disfavor of this scheme of writing Chinese with an alphabetic script.[68] Most interesting of all was the inclusion of eight farmer's almanacs in 1930 because the use of the lunar calendar was "contrary to government policy."[69] None of the prohibited publications was obscene or indecent.

The most famous list was the one issued on February 19, 1934, in which 149 books in the humanities were outlawed for "advocating class struggle."[70] While some titles had been banned for years, many of them, as the twenty-five affected publishers pointed out, had been duly approved by and registered with government agencies in accordance with the Publication Law. They were mostly novels, poems, and plays written or translated by leftist writers, including some of the best produced in modern China.[71] Kuo Mo-jo's famous book on ancient Chinese society was included, along with his other works. Some were reference books: a dictionary of Chinese and foreign writers, a world history, a dictionary of literature for students. Foreign writers who made the list included Maxim Gorky, A. V. Lunacharsky, K. A. Fedin, A. Fadeev, A. Serafimovich, Upton Sinclair, Theodore Dreiser, Maurice Maeterlinck, Romain Rolland, and Bertrand Russell. The government felt that the subtle approach of the leftist "proletarian school" writers made it difficult for the censors to pick out the objectionable passages that advocated class struggle and subversion.[72] A list of leftist writers was thus compiled and all their writings outlawed. Instructed by KMT Central Headquarters, the Party officials in Shanghai visited booksellers and publishers on February 19 and ordered them to submit all copies and stereotypes of such books to the Party headquarters to be burned. The ban aroused protests from all quarters.[73] To protect their financial interests, the publishers petitioned the local KMT headquarters, requesting the government to reexamine the books in question and impose prepublication censorship. They promised never again to publish any works, except purely academic ones, by those authors whom the government regarded as "reactionary." One month later, on March 20, the Central Publicity Department issued the following order disposing of the 149 titles in question. Thirty works which had already been banned must be burned; 30 works which "advocate proletarian literature and class struggle, or libel the Party or government authorities" must be banned from the market; 30 works which "introduce proletarian literary theories, are translations of Soviet Russian writers, or contain incorrect thought" must be outlawed during the period of "bandit suppression"; 22 works which contain some "improper" sentences or phrases might be released again after the objectionable passages were deleted; 37 works featuring love stories or written "before the Revolution" and containing no objectionable passages would be allowed to circulate temporarily in the market.[74] The negotiations resulted also in the establishment of the Censorship Commission for Books and Periodicals in Shanghai (see Chapter I).

As in the previous periods, the government sometimes vented its ire on the authors' or editors' persons, not just on their writings. On November 4, 1930, Lo Lung-chi was arrested in Shanghai for six hours because of his alleged criticism in *Hsin-yueh* (New moon) that the KMT disregarded the people's civil rights. The local KMT headquarters accused him of being "reactionary and insulting to Dr. Sun Yat-sen" and suspected him of being a Communist. In 1931, another article of his in *Hsin-yueh* (3.8:1–26), criticizing the Provisional Constitution of the Political Tutelage Period (1931), brought more trouble to the magazine. "Ever since the publication of the *Hsin-yueh* monthly," a KMT directive asserted, "it has often published writings hostile to the Party. Recently, in its eighth issue, it even calumniated the Constitution and vilified this Party." It was thus "semireactionary." The said issue was banned in Peiping and Tientsin. More than a thousand copies of the issue were confiscated and an employee and a visitor arrested when the magazine's Peiping office was raided in July 1931.[75]

On July 24, 1934, Ch'eng She-wo, publisher and editor of *Minsheng pao* in Nanking, was arrested. Ch'eng had been arrested many times before by the warlords; this time his "crime" lay in exposing in May the embezzlement by P'eng Hsueh-p'ei, a favorite of Premier Wang Ching-wei, in the construction of the new Executive Yuan building. By order of the Executive Yuan on May 24, *Minsheng pao* was suspended for three days. P'eng brought a libel suit against Ch'eng on June 5, but could not win the suit at the court of law. In July, Min Tsu News Agency in Nanking released a news story about Chiang Kai-shek's offer to mediate a dispute between Wang and Yü Yu-jen, President of the Control Yuan, in regard to the impeachment of the Minister of Railways. Although this news had been passed by the censors and printed in many papers, Ch'eng was singled out to be arrested by the Garrison Commander in Nanking at Wang's order, along with three members of the Min Tsu News Agency. He was detained in the Garrison Headquarters for more than one month, and his paper was permanently suspended. Finally, on September 2, he was released after promising never to publish another paper in Nanking.[76]

Even factual reporting could sometimes bring woes to the journalists. In the summer of 1931, for instance, one of the "mosquito" papers in Hankow reported that certain high provincial government officials had placed high stakes in a mah-jongg game in a hotel. The local satrap at once ordered the arrest of the editor, who had fled. An order was then issued requiring each newspaper or news agency to submit a bond of at least 2,000 yuan. As a result, about forty newspapers, mostly "mosquito" papers, and seventy news agencies were forced to close down, leaving only two Party papers, four private papers, and three news agencies in the province.[77]

Although the Publication Law provided no role for the military, military officers, like the warlords before them, often took the law into their own hands.[78] In 1930, the T'uan Wu News Agency in Chungking complained of unclean food in a local restaurant. An army supplies officer, who was a part-owner of the restaurant, arrested the news agency's director and editor and detained them for several days. Again, when *K'uai pao,* a newspaper in the same city, criticized a women's association, a brigade commander, whose favorite concubine was on the association's board of directors, suspended the paper, arrested its editor-in-chief, and threatened to shoot him unless he apologized by bowing three times to the concubine. The editor had, of course, no other choice but to comply.[79] Szechwan, where Chungking is located, was then the domain of a semi-independent satrap; but military officers in other provinces behaved no better. In 1934, *Tung-nan jih-pao*, a newspaper in Hangchow, somehow offended an officer of the local garrison. On the night of October 4, the officer arrested the head reporter for questioning, and did not release him until the reporter's superior interceded.[80]

In Canton, under semi-independent General Ch'en Chi-t'ang, journalists fared even worse. Tan Pei-yuan was imprisoned from 1933 to August 1936, when Yü Han-mou, commander-in-chief of the Kwangtung Army, ordered his release. A few days later, Hsia Tzu-pan, editor of the International News Agency, told the world that he had been secretly arrested by Ch'en in April 1935 and jailed until about one week before Ch'en's downfall in 1936. His relatives and friends had pleaded for him in vain, because the Canton police had denied any knowledge of him.[81]

Since local governments and the KMT headquarters did not always work hand in glove, curious tragicomedies often took place. On April 30, 1929, for instance, the police of Hangchow, by order of the chairman of the Chekiang provincial government, suspended *Min-kuo jih-pao*, a local Party paper, arrested its editor, Hu Chien-chung, and sent him to Nanking for punishment. Meanwhile, the Party's Provincial Executive Committee passed a resolution to impeach the provincial government officials and pleaded for Hu. Hu was released in Nanking by the Central Publicity Department, where he was given a new position. *Min-kuo jih-pao* resumed publication under new management.[82]

Editors who were sentenced to imprisonment could sometimes consider themselves fortunate. The most luckless met death, especially in the interior areas. In January 1931, the Yü-chung News Agency of Chungking issued a news story depicting the extravagant funeral ceremonies for the father of a certain General Fan, who was then the garrison commander of the Szechwan-Hupei Border Area. Wasting no time on the proper legal proceedings, the general simply sent a group of soldiers to arrest the editor, Liu Shu-tan. Although he had only joined the agency three days before, the unlucky editor was immediately beheaded, while the agency's manager and a clerk were jailed.[83]

On July 26, 1932, Liu Yü-sheng of *Chiang-sheng jih-pao* in Chinkiang was arrested by the provincial government of Kiangsu for alleged Communist sympathies, and detained for several months without a trial. The case, which took place right under the nose of Nanking, naturally aroused public indignation. The Control Yuan investigated the case and, on January 22, 1933, recommended that General Ku Chu-t'ung, chairman of the provincial government, be impeached and punished, but Liu had been shot the day before. Repeated recommendations from the Control Yuan to impeach Ku brought no result at all. On January 25, he reported that Liu had been a Communist, and gave as evidence the literary supplement sections of his paper. According to the Control Yuan, most of the short stories and articles contained therein "depicted only the social conditions and life in China." In a reply to the Executive Yuan on January 31, Ku asserted that Liu "intended to incite class struggle and Red terrorism." Among the passages quoted from his writings as evidence of his crime was the sentence, "Red currents have swept over the whole country"[84]—which, even though we have no data on Liu's political leanings or background, seems to be very slim evidence for killing a journalist.

Many more tragedies may have taken place in the interior without our knowledge, for any writer or editor could have been shot simply as a "Communist" and reported as such. Since, in areas close to the national capital, open arrests or executions could be embarrassing (as the above example shows), assassins were perhaps sometimes employed.[85] On June 16, 1933, Yang Hsing-fo, executive secretary of the Academia Sinica and the League for Civil Rights, was assassinated in Shanghai. The League had been organized only five months before by Madame Sun Yat-sen, elder sister of Madame Chiang Kai-shek, to offer aid to political prisoners and support the freedom of the press. At the time of Yang's death, the League had been active in attempting to obtain the release of an allegedly kidnaped Communist woman writer, Ting Ling. It was said that Yang had to be killed because the League had gathered enough evidence to prove that Ting had been kidnaped by KMT agents.[86] His death put an end to all the activities of the organization.

In 1934, *Shun pao* of Shanghai, the oldest and largest newspaper in China, incurred the government's anger because of its strong anti-Japanese attitude. On November 13, Shih Liang-ts'ai, its owner and editor-in-chief, was mysteriously assassinated on the Shanghai-Hangchow Highway. Rumors circulating during those days asserted that the government was involved in the plot. Such rumors naturally cannot be proved, but the paper was reorganized after Shih's death, and, although it remained in his family, it changed its editorial policy to fit the government line.[87]

Again, as in the earlier periods, instead of coercion, the government would often resort to temptation. The quality of the journalists was on the whole much higher in this period than in the previous years; but still many of them, particularly in the interior areas, remained corruptible. One writer bitterly complained in an English-language journal in 1932:

> The doling out of various subsidies to newspaper correspondents and editors, both Chinese and foreign . . . seems to have become the only function of the various publicity organs in the government.[88]

Money was not the only bait, however. In a 1934 magazine, we find the following observation:

> In the past year or so, some newspapers and magazines had made stimulating [i.e., critical] comments on the authorities and current events. But such periodical publications either soon changed their attitude, or were banned secretly.[89]

One means of inducing the more prominent writers or editors to "change their attitude" was evidently to offer them official positions.[90] Ch'ien Hsing-ts'un was once offered an editorship in the

Shanghai Bureau of Education on condition that he would change his stand. (He declined.) T'ien Han was arrested in 1935 for being a Communist, but, after his release, he became an official for cultural activities in the KMT government. Early in 1936, two high-ranking officials were sent to Shanghai to win over Tsou T'ao-fen. Declining an invitation to confer with Chiang Kai-shek in Nanking, Tsou later learned that Chiang had probably intended to give him a government position there.[91]

Some publishers had to change their policies in order to stay in business. In 1931, the Hsien Tai Book Company, the publisher of some suppressed leftist magazines, was sealed up, but it was later reopened when the principal shareholder agreed to the conditions set by the local KMT Headquarters: to reorganize the company, employ KMT officials on its editorial staff, and switch to publishing magazines for the "nationalistic school of literature," which the KMT was sponsoring to counteract the "proletarian literature."[92]

To make sure that people read the right kind of publication, the KMT financed *Chung-yang jih-pao* (the Central daily news) and many other Party newspapers in various cities and towns. In spite of their low subscription rates, these well-financed Party papers failed to attract a large reading public. The reasons for their unpopularity were well explained by *Min-kuo jih-pao,* the Party paper in Nanning, Kwangsi: all news issued by government or Party organizations had to be approved first by their responsible officers, who could invent all kinds of excuses for withholding reports that they disliked. Crimes and other sensational stories were not permitted to appear in print, nor were unfavorable financial news such as depression, failure of commercial concerns, and the like. As a result, the local news section of such a paper became an official gazette, recording only the resolutions of meetings and the promulgation of laws and regulations. Sometimes it did not even carry an editorial, since any slight error might mean trouble.[93]

In order to make sure that reporters would not go astray, government offices often employed press liaison officers, and high-ranking officials sometimes gave press conferences in which mimeographed information sheets would be passed out to reporters and news agencies.[94] For important national and international news, the Central News Agency had the monopoly. Established in 1925 in Canton by the KMT and moved to Nanking with the government in 1927, it enjoyed many special privileges; it alone had its own radio and other news-gathering facilities in various towns and cities all over the country, and was the only Chinese news agency that could afford to send correspondents abroad. Commercial news agencies, such as Kuo Wen and Fu Tan, had to withdraw from the competition voluntarily. Official releases and Party propaganda became almost the only sources of information available to the common people.[95]

The government's frequent interference with the press probably gave students, workers, and certain influential groups the impression that they could do the same. On May 30, 1929, the premises of *Min-kuo jih-pao* in Shanghai were damaged by several hundred students and factory workers because the paper had refused to suspend publication on that day to commemorate the May Thirtieth Incident. *Shun pao* was also slightly damaged.[96] On March 9, 1930, the printing plant of *China Times,* another large newspaper in Shanghai, was damaged by a mob of over thirty people because it had not reported a strike in a certain factory. The paper claimed that the omission was made by order of the local KMT headquarters and complained that it had been made a scapegoat.[97] In April of the same year, several scores of students, workers, and children destroyed the printing equipment of *Ch'en-kuang pao* and *Kuo-chi hsieh pao* in Harbin because they had refused, two days earlier, to print a "manifesto" advocating strikes among students and factory workers.[98] On June 19, 1934, militant Mohammedans in Tientsin damaged three bookstores and injured several clerks in the stores because they had on sale a popular novel entitled *Nien Keng-yao p'ing-hsi,* which described the Ch'ing dynasty general's conquest of Chinese Turkestan, and which the Moham-medans claimed was an insult to their people.[99]

The Moslems were also responsible for the interesting "Piggy" case in 1932. In "Why the Mohammedans Do Not Eat Pork," published in the July 16 issue of *Nan-hua wen-i* (South China literary magazine), a little-known semimonthly in Shanghai, Lou Tzu-k'uang quoted a story which insulted the Moslems. The folktale, supposedly circulating in Kansu, had appeared in a collection published by the Pei Hsin Book Company in Shanghai a few months earlier without any incident.[100] But the article did not give the necessary reference or include the original recorder's comment that the tale could have been invented by a few narrow-minded Han Chinese. It appeared also to suggest that anti-Moslem feelings were justifiable, and contained a provocative sentence in its concluding section. Consequently it aroused widespread indignation among the Moslems, and their protest soon brought *Nan-hua wen-i* to its knees. According to a letter written by the Shanghai Islamic Association dated October 3, the magazine had yielded to the four demands of the Moslems, including an apology from the editor and the destruction of all unsold copies.[101] The irate Moslems were still not satisfied, and, late in October, a delegation of prominent Mohammedans from North China went to Nanking to lodge a strong protest with the government.

The case is of particular interest to us because it shows that direct government intervention, however just it may be, is not always wise. Had the case been argued at court as it should have been, it might have occasioned interesting discussions of academic freedom and responsibility, and led to a sounder verdict. As it was, it soon became an emotional issue. Even Hu Shih, who criticized Lou first but later made a qualified apology to him, did not read his article carefully. Chiang Shao-yuan, a folklorist who defended Lou's article as an academic essay, did not read the original version or know the recorder's comment.[102] Other people did not bother to read the article or examine the supposedly "folk" origin of the tale.[103] They just sympathized with the Moslems, and supported the demand for religious freedom.

On November 7, the KMT Central Executive Committee ordered the Pei Hsin Book Company and *Nan-hua wen-i* closed and the authors punished. The Executive Yuan was instructed to enforce the decision immediately. The Central Publicity Department was further instructed to examine all textbooks and publications in order to eliminate remarks that might appear to violate the principle of religious freedom. Accordingly, the Executive Yuan issued orders, on November 8 and November 13 respectively, stressing religious freedom and prohibiting any publications which might offend the Moslems.[104] Both the Pei Hsin Book Company and *Nan-hua wen-i* apologized to the Mohammedans and closed their businesses. None of the editors or writers seemed to be punished, although Lou Tzu-k'uang, fearing vengeance by an unruly mob, became frightened and went into hiding.[105] Thus ended one of the rare cases in China that involved religious freedom.

Because of the need to rally the Moslems, no one in China blamed the government then for taking drastic action to preserve national unity.[106] Hu Shih was the only one who raised the important question of legality. Could a government that claimed to rule by law order the closure of a private commercial concern without due process of law?[107] As a matter of fact, this is one of the crucial questions which one may ask in regard to many other censorship cases during this period.

Chapter V

THE KUOMINTANG REGIME BEFORE THE WAR,
1927-1937 (2)

In 1928, the Municipality of Greater Shanghai, which covered all of Shanghai outside the foreign settlements, was established by the Chinese government and placed directly under the control of the Executive Yuan. Whereas the Shanghai Municipal Council with its Municipal Police still existed in the International Settlement and the French authorities in the French Concession and the foreign residents enjoyed the same extraterritorial privileges as before, the Mixed Court was returned to China in 1927 and became the Shanghai Provisional Court under the control of the Kiangsu provincial government. In 1930, in an agreement between China and some of the foreign powers, China was authorized to establish a district court and a branch high court in Shanghai with jurisdiction over all criminal and civil cases involving only the Chinese. Chinese laws were applicable in these courts, which were a part of China's judicial system, and all appeals had to be made to the Supreme Court of China.[1] Chinese-language newspapers in Shanghai were censored by the News Censorship Bureau, established jointly in the International Settlement in March 1933 by the local KMT headquarters, the Shanghai municipal government, and the Shanghai Garrison Headquarters.[2] Arrests of Chinese residents or raids on Chinese properties in the Settlement would be made by the foreign Municipal Police and handed over to the Chinese authorities. In July 1935, for instance, the Shanghai Municipal Police began a campaign against unregistered "mosquito" newspapers and confiscated copies of more than forty such dailies or semiweeklies, most of which carried no names or addresses of their publishers. The list, it was understood, was furnished by the Chinese authorities.[3] Ch'en Tu-hsiu was arrested in October 1932 by the Shanghai Municipal Police in the International Settlement, and Tsou T'ao-fen by the French police in the French Concession in November 1936. Both were tried in the

Chinese courts.[4] Foreign settlements, though still under foreign control, were no longer a haven for rebellious Chinese writers.

Suppression of Anti-Japanese Literature

Although the Western authorities in the foreign settlements in Shanghai lost some of their grip on the Chinese press, Japanese interference with Chinese publications everywhere grew steadily in the few years before the outbreak of the Sino-Japanese War. On September 18, 1931, the Japanese army attacked Mukden under flimsy pretexts, and then extended its sway over all of northeastern China, the richest and most fertile part of the country. As soon as it occupied that vast territory, it established "Manchoukuo" and lost no time in revising textbooks and outlawing Chinese patriotic writings. Strict censorship of newspapers and magazines was imposed by the Japanese army and the Japanese Embassy in cooperation with the puppet government officials.[5]

On January 28, 1932, Japanese Marines attacked Shanghai. One week before the invasion, on January 21, *Min-kuo jih-pao* in Shanghai reported a fire at a Chinese factory which had been started by Japanese hoodlums on the previous day. On January 22, a Japanese Navy lieutenant went to the paper with a protest demanding an apology, the dismissal of the reporters involved, and a guarantee not to print similar reports in the future. On January 23, members of the Japanese Residents Association tried to destroy the paper's premises. Meanwhile, Japanese warships closed in on the city. In order to appease the Japanese, the Shanghai Municipal Council advised the paper on January 26 to cease publication, and sent armed foreign policemen to seal up the paper's premises. The Municipal Council agreed on March 29 to reopen the premises, but insisted that the paper had to apply for a special permit before it could resume publication. *Min-kuo jih-pao,* which had had a long history of conflicts with the foreign authorities, thus came to an end.[6]

The Japanese invasion of Shanghai met with fierce resistance from the Chinese Nineteenth Route Army. Although a cease-fire agreement reached in May stipulated the suppression of all anti-

Japanese activities, the Chinese people's hatred for the Japanese remained intense. Japan's ambition to conquer China became more and more clear as the days went by. Numerous incidents were created to wring concessions from the Chinese government. On April 10, 1933, Generalissimo Chiang Kai-shek made his position clear: "Before all the [Communist] bandits are destroyed, we must not talk about resisting the Japanese. Whoever disobeys this order will be given the severest punishment."[7] Whatever were the reasons behind this policy, it was difficult for the people to accept emotionally. Since the Communists were clamoring for resistance to Japan, the government seemed to feel that anyone who advocated war with Japan must be either Communist or Communist-inspired. Patriotic student demonstrations were often dispersed by armed police and soldiers. Campuses were raided, and the possession of any prohibited publications was sufficient reason for the owner's arrest.[8]

In order not to offend the Japanese, the government in its proclamations and notices avoided using the term "Japan." In all publications, seemingly anti-Japanese expressions, including reports on the movement of Japanese troops in North China, were outlawed. The symbols "x x" were used to represent the two characters for Japan, should that nation be referred to in any unfavorable light. All negotiations with Japan were kept secret.[9] The credibility gap between the government and the people soon became extremely wide, and the government had to take drastic measures to forestall popular dissatisfaction. In July 1934, for instance, press censors in Shanghai and other cities, following instructions received from Nanking and personal orders from Chiang Kai-shek, sent circular letters to the editors of all newspapers warning them against reporting or commenting on public indignation at the revised, pro-Japanese tariff policy which had become effective on July 1. Chiang declared that the government could no longer tolerate the "unreasonable" attitude of the public and would ban all newspapers indiscreet enough to support the stand of "ignorant merchants." Rigid censorship was imposed on cables to prevent them from reporting the Chinese people's indignation to foreign readers.[10]

While Westerners were amazed at the speed with which Japan was asserting primacy in China, Chiang managed with considerable skill and astuteness to avoid an open breach with Japan by authorizing sweeping concessions to Japanese demands. Despite the fact that Chinese writers and journalists were very careful not to give the Japanese a pretext to make further demands, the *New Life Weekly* case still took place.

Hsin-sheng chou-k'an (*New Life Weekly*) began publication in Shanghai in January 1934, soon after the suspension of *Life Weekly*. Its editor and publisher, Tu Chung-yuan, was an industrialist and an admirer of Tsou T'ao-fen. On May 4, 1935, it carried in its vol. 2, no. 15, an article entitled "Random Talk on the Emperors," written by I Shui (pseudonym of Ai Han-sung, who edited *Life Weekly* during its last days when Tsou, being an officer of the League for Civil Rights, had to go abroad for his personal safety). The article, which described the decline of monarchies all over the world, began by discussing the powers emperors had once enjoyed and the tragedy of some of the least fortunate emperors in China. Then it said:

Today, most emperors have only the name but not the substance; i.e., they are emperors in name but not emperors in power. As far as we know, the emperor of Japan is a biologist. He is the emperor by hereditary rights. He actually does not have the real power, though everything is done in his name. When it is time to receive foreign visitors, the emperor is needed; when it is time to review the troops, the emperor is needed; when it is time for any important ceremonies, the emperor is needed. Otherwise the emperor is ignored by the people. *The Japanese War Office and capitalistic class are the real rulers of Japan.* As it has been mentioned above, the present Emperor of Japan is interested in studying biology. If he were not an emperor and thus had to be bothered with many irrelevant duties, his achievement in biology would be greater than it is now. It is said that he has made many discoveries in biology. [His being an emperor] is a great loss to scholarship. And yet, contemporary Japan would not give up her antique—the "emperor." Of course, an emperor is useful in governing Japan now in order to alleviate the conflicts between different classes and to sanctify the crimes of certain people. The functions of the emperors of Italy and the British Empire are the same . . . The British regard their emperor as a figurehead . . . unlike the Japanese who regarded their emperor as sacred. Yet, in fact, all these emperors are but puppets of the real rulers of today. We had better call all the emperors of the present time puppet emperors.

It ended with calling Henry P'u Yi, Emperor K'ang Teh of the so-called "Manchoukuo," "a puppet of the puppets."[11]

This relevant passage has been extensively quoted so that readers may judge for themselves whether the article is "a great insult to the Emperor of Japan," as the Japanese claimed. A short article of no value, it attracted little attention at first. But in June, it suddenly aroused the belated wrath of the Japanese community in Shanghai. The central government in Nanking as well as the Shanghai municipal government was confronted with Japanese demands for apologies and other kinds of remedial action. To give point to those demands, a Japanese cruiser deferred its scheduled departure from Shanghai.

On June 10, the National Government issued a mandate calling for the promotion of friendly relations with all neighboring countries. The mayor of Shanghai, General Wu Te-chen, promptly apologized to the Japanese and ordered a ban on the magazine, the punishment of the persons responsible, and the destruction of all remaining copies of the issue; he also guaranteed that similar incidents would not recur. Still the Japanese were not satisfied. Since the article had been passed by the censors, the Japanese claimed that the responsibility for the offense rested with the KMT Central Headquarters. The Central Publicity Department immediately dismissed all seven local censors, and issued an exceedingly long statement reiterating the government's determination to suppress and punish publishers of articles designed to jeopardize Chinese relations with friendly nations. Meanwhile, arrangements were made to bring Tu Chung-yuan to trial.

Tu was summoned before the Second Branch Kiangsu High Court on July 1 for preliminary inquiries. He claimed that he did not know I Shui's real name and address and that the article had been published without his knowledge when he was on a business trip to Kiangsi. On July 9, the court was convened. Tu was formally charged with committing an offense under Articles 310 and 116 of the New Criminal Code, and Article 325 of the Old Criminal Code, for insulting the head of a friendly state. The conviction was made easy by the defense, who made no attempt to justify the article. The trial resulted in the sentencing of the defendant to fourteen months of imprisonment—two months short of the maximum penalty prescribed. All copies of vol. 2, no. 15 of the magazine, in which the article appeared, were to be confiscated. Furthermore, the judge deemed the sentence final and declared that no appeal would be allowed. As the *North China Herald* observed, "it is difficult to imagine any government acting with greater promptitude and determination than has the Chinese government in this affair."[12]

Although Yeh Ch'u-ts'ang, chairman of the Central Publicity Department, declared on July 10 that the incident was now considered closed, the Chinese people could not forget the case so easily. Early in August, a number of copies of the August issue of an American magazine entitled *Vanity Fair,* which contained a caricature of the Emperor of Japan, appeared in Shanghai but were promptly banned. A Japanese Foreign Office spokesman admitted that the cartoon was "worse than the recent article in the *New Life Weekly.* Nevertheless, the Japanese ambassador in Washington merely requested United States Secretary of State Cordell Hull to take whatever action possible to remedy the situation without lodging a formal protest, and appeared well satisfied when Secretary Hull expressed regret that such a "misunderstanding" should have occurred. The Japanese could only ban the issue in Japan and her possessions, as well as in China.[13]

Although the contrast between the two cases was all too obvious and painful to the Chinese, most of them appreciated the difficult position the government was in and refrained from criticizing it. No feature article was written about Tu's prison life. While some people felt that more care had to be exercised to prevent further humiliation, others only dared protest the judge's decision from a legal point of view when Mrs. Tu's appeal on behalf of her husband was rejected by a higher court. The president of the Supreme Court finally stepped in and ordered a rehearing of Tu's appeal. But before anything was done, Tu completed his prison term and was released on September 8, 1936.[14]

After the *New Life Weekly* case, the campaign to suppress anti-Japanese literature grew even more intense. On July 14, 1935, a book peddler, who had been arrested at a street corner by a Japanese officer of the Shanghai Municipal Police, was brought before the First Special District Court in Shanghai for displaying eight booklets advocating the boycott of Japanese products. The judge sentenced the accused to two months' imprisonment or a two-year suspended sentence, and ordered the confiscation of the books. On the day before, the same court had given another peddler a three-month sentence and ordered the confiscation of many allegedly anti-Japanese books. The general manager of the Wen Hua Bookstore, where the peddler had obtained his copies, was punished eight days later because of the possession of 2,840 volumes allegedly advocating ideas contrary to the mandate of the central government. On August 5, seventy copies of *Chin-hsiu shan-ho* (The beautiful scenery of China) were seized at a neighboring bookstore. Three bookstore managers were brought to trial on December 1, and one peddler and another bookstore manager on December 9, all for selling anti-Japanese books in Shanghai.[15]

Such incidents multiplied, as many people were found guilty of this "crime."[16] The Chinese authorities also took steps to make sure that various political agencies, educational institutions, and their teaching staffs be made fully aware of the situation and exercise restraint. Agitations to boycott Japanese goods, as well as anti-Japanese speeches and organizations, were all proscribed. Various orders and proclamations were issued to suppress patriotic activities and writings. On December 20, 1935, martial law was proclaimed for the Nanking-Shanghai area, and, on February 20, 1936, the

Emergency Regulations for Keeping Peace and Order were promulgated. Despite these measures, Japan still found fault with the Chinese government. In August 1935, because of Japanese objections, one sheet in a new primary Chinese reader prepared by the Shanghai Municipal Government for adult education was destroyed, since it contained a reference to the Mukden Incident which was not to Japan's liking.[17] In December 1935, the Central News Agency released the following dispatch in English:

> The Ping Min (Common People) News Agency in Tientsin was subjected to an unexpected search yesterday morning conducted by nationals of a certain "foreign country," who were accompanied by special police of the Bureau of Public Safety.
>
> Upon the expiration of the search, Tai Ting-chao, director of the news agency, was carried away. No reason was given for the raid and the "arrest" of the director. The Ping Min News Agency was established in Tientsin in 1929.[18]

This news item is interesting not only because it presented an unusual case, but also because it shows how the Chinese press avoided using the word "Japan." In September 1936, Chang Chi-luan, editor-in-chief of *Ta-kung pao,* was prosecuted in Shanghai for "disturbing peace and order" because of an article in his paper on August 16 entitled "A Play Which Cannot Be Performed," which contained some satirical references to "Manchoukuo" and was therefore regarded as "increasing tension among readers."[19] The year 1936 saw many magazines suppressed for being anti-Japanese—fourteen of them in December alone.[20]

The ban on anti-Japanese literature actually whipped up patriotic feelings among the Chinese, who found it increasingly difficult to tolerate the government's humiliating efforts to preserve peace. Various patriotic organizations sprang up. On April 3, 1937, seven prominent leaders of the National Salvation Association, who had been arrested in Shanghai, were put on trial. They were accused of communicating with the Communists, instigating unrest among workers and students, disturbing peace and order, and intending to overthrow the government. All the evidence submitted was taken from their writings, including *Chiu-wang ching-pao* (Bulletin of the National Salvation Association), which advocated releasing all political prisoners and putting an end to the civil war in order to resist foreign aggression. Also presented in evidence was a copy of *Tou-cheng* (The struggle), a Communist periodical, seized in the home of Tsou T'ao-fen, one of the defendants.[21] The Shanghai Seven were of course convicted and imprisoned, but were released soon after the outbreak of the Sino-Japanese War.

The Foreign Press in China

Compared with their Chinese counterparts, foreign correspondents and publishers had much more freedom because of their extraterritorial privileges. News stories which were forbidden in the native press might be found in newspapers owned and operated by foreigners. The Japanese, especially, made full use of this privilege. Chinese writers under severe censorship alluded repeatedly to the freedom enjoyed by the foreign press and to the many prejudiced or deliberately distorted stories in foreign-language papers in China. This double standard, they pointed out, caused Chinese readers to distrust their native press and to fall prey to foreign rumor-mongers.[22]

The Chinese government, to be sure, was as anxious as the Chinese journalists to regulate the foreign press, and it tried hard to do so. In 1932, the Regulations Concerning the Registration of Newspapers stipulated that all foreign newspapers published in China must be registered with the Ministry of the Interior as well as the KMT Central Publicity Department or face a postal ban. The British, American, and French Ministers in Peiping promptly lodged a protest with the Chinese Ministry of Foreign Affairs, maintaining that there was no provision in the Chinese Publication Law requiring foreign newspapers to register with the Party organ. The Chinese government quickly backed down. Another attempt in 1934 met again with staunch opposition from the foreigners, who maintained that the foreign press should refuse to be muzzled when its views differed from those of the KMT on petty political questions.[23]

The most important weapon of the Chinese authorities to curb the influence of the foreign press was to deny it the use of the mail, so that it could not circulate beyond the settlements. On August 3, 1927, for instance, the Chinese Post Office refused to deliver the *North China Daily News* in Shanghai. No official explanation was given for the refusal, but the paper believed that the postal authorities acted under the instructions of a local general, who considered himself affronted by the paper. The ban lasted for two months. In 1928, a postal ban was placed on *Shun-tien shih pao,* a Japanese-owned Chinese-language newspaper in Peiping. Early in 1929, a similar ban was imposed for several weeks on the *North China Star,* an American-owned paper in Tientsin, because of an objectionable article written by C. D. Bess of the United Press.[24]

On April 18, 1929, the Standing Committee of the KMT Central Executive Committee decided that George E. Sokolsky, an American contributor to the *North China Daily News,* should be asked to leave China, that a postal ban should be imposed on the paper and also on its Sunday edition, the *North China Herald,* and that the customs authorities should be ordered to prevent their circulation through bulk shipments from Shanghai by steamers. The *North China Daily News* had often disparaged the Chinese national character, but this time it had aroused the government's ire by an attack on the Shanghai Provisional Court and an exposé, in a series of articles by Sokolsky, of power struggles within the KMT. The paper protested vehemently against the ban, but this did not change the decision of the Chinese government.[25]

On December 23, 1932, the government canceled the postal privileges of the *Far Eastern Review,* an English-language monthly, on the grounds that its editor and publisher, George Bronson Rea, had become an adviser to the puppet "Manchoukuo" government and had been actively engaged in malicious propaganda against China in Geneva and elsewhere.[26] In 1934, the *Oriental Affairs,* edited and published by H. G. W. Woodhead in Shanghai, lost its postal rights because it had also been engaged in propaganda for "Manchoukuo." The postal ban raised a storm out of all proportion to the importance of the incident, or of the journal in question. In an article entitled "Banned from the Mails for Seeking the Truth," included in its July issue, Woodhead complained that his paper and postage stamps had been "filched" without an explanation by the Chinese government. He also sent two circulars to the foreign press. In response, British newspapers in Shanghai suggested in editorials that the spirit, if not the letter, of "sacred" treaties had been disregarded, and that the liberty of the press was at stake. The question of the postal ban on the journal went even to the British House of Commons and was commented on by such magazines in London as *Truth* and *Newspaper World*. The latter said:

> The latest form of censorship of the press comes from China, and the periodical does not even know that it has been banned until complaints of non-delivery begin to come in from subscribers.

As the *People's Tribune,* a Chinese-owned English-language monthly in Shanghai which came to the government's defense, pointed out:

> This way of dealing with "objectionable" periodicals is not Chinese at all and . . . the method is practised by the British, among other authorities, when it suits them to put it into operation.

The *People's Tribune* should know, as it had been a victim of a postal ban imposed at Singapore, a British Crown Colony, in exactly the same manner as that which had caused Woodhead to raise such a storm.[27]

Beginning on May 25, 1931, all telegraphic and radio messages to and from China had to pass through the hands of censors at the Chinese government telegraphic and radio offices. In 1934, complaints against the censoring of cables from foreign correspondents in China abounded in papers all over the world. One of the complaints was that, whenever there was a reference to "Manchoukuo," the censors either inserted quotation marks or qualified the term with "the so-called," and/or "puppet state," and also that to "Emperor

K'ang-Teh" they would always add the words "puppet ruler," thereby increasing the cost of the cable. Such protests ignored the fact that the three northeastern provinces were an integral part of China. More legitimate was the complaint that press messages were blue-penciled so erratically that nobody really knew what principles, if any, the censors had followed. The indignant sender of a mutilated message could not know what had happened to it until he saw it printed. The censors refused to meet newspapermen or to inform them under whose orders they operated, and they would not divulge what kind of news was permissible. Besides, there was no consistency at all. Shanghai was then the clearinghouse of most foreign news agencies operating in China, and in some cases one agency might be permitted to receive a telegram from Nanking or Peiping while another was denied the same.[28]

The efforts of the Chinese government were often futile as well as ridiculous, however, because the Japanese had a cable of their own from Shanghai to Nagasaki, and Chinese censors were not allowed in their office. As a result, Japanese correspondents alone could cable any version of any event in China. Reports distinctly untrue or harmful to China were often relayed from Tokyo, while impartial correspondents of other nationalities could not tell the truth.[29]

Telegraphic privileges were occasionally withdrawn from foreign-registered papers, as the *China Press* discovered in September 1934. This paper was then owned by the Chinese, though the company was still incorporated under the laws of the State of Delaware. It provoked official ire by publishing a Washington dispatch about an allegation made at a hearing of the United States Senate that China had spent the American wheat loan on the purchase of armaments.[30]

Another method sometimes used was to protest to the authorities of the offender's country and demand his deportation, as happened with George E. Sokolsky, Charles Dailey of *The Chicago Tribune,* and Hallett Abend of *The New York Times* in 1929. Mr. Dailey had incurred the Chinese government's displeasure through a speech delivered at Manila, in which he described China as in chaos. Mr. Abend's dispatches, according to Chinese officials, failed to reflect the truth and were pro-Japanese.[31] This method of suppression was seldom effective, except perhaps in the case of Harold R. Isaacs, an American editor of the *China Forum,* and this was because his presumably leftist leanings made him *persona non grata* to the American as well as the Chinese authorities. In 1932, the Shanghai Municipal Government lodged a protest with the American consul-general asking for the suppression of the weekly on the grounds that Isaacs had published articles and comments insulting to the Chinese government and the KMT and that he openly supported the Chinese Soviet government. H. G. W. Woodhead wrote for the *Shanghai Evening Post and Mercury* (July 26, 1932) condemning this leftist periodical and claiming that Isaacs "would have been suppressed immediately had the editor been under Chinese jurisdiction." Since the Chinese government had no jurisdiction over Isaacs, the police arrested in August the Chinese proprietor of a printing house which had printed two issues of this weekly in July, even though the printer argued that he had discontinued his contract when he discovered the "reactionary nature" of the journal.[32]

Foreign journalists often actively participated in Chinese politics. W. H. Donald, an Australian and the first editor of the *Far Eastern Review,* became at first an adviser to Chang Hsueh-liang and then entered the service of Generalissimo Chiang. Like their Chinese counterparts, foreign correspondents and editors did not hesitate to receive subsidies from the Chinese government. However, as one correspondent pointed out in *People's Tribune:*

> The acceptance of a subsidy did not necessarily turn the particular paper into a mouthpiece of the government, or for the pecuniary consideration, make it at least attempt to interpret its policy fairly and in accordance with the facts.[33]

Arguments about Freedom of the Press

Meanwhile, among Chinese writers the clamor for freedom of speech and the press was as loud as it had ever been in China. What made these years unique, however, was the nature of the arguments for thought control advanced by official or semiofficial agencies. The KMT had always insisted that "nothing incompatible with the Three People's Principles" could be tolerated; but now, when it applied this canon to communism and ruled it seditious, many people became confused. Dr. Sun Yat-sen, for instance, had said about his Principle of People's Livelihood on August 3, 1924:

> The Principle of People's Livelihood is the same as socialism and may also be called communism, and [its final goal] is universal brotherhood.

He then explained:

> Communism is the ideal goal of People's Livelihood, and that the doctrine of Livelihood is the practical application of communism; such is the difference between the doctrine of Marx and the doctrine of the Kuomintang. In the last analysis, there is no real difference in principle between the two; they differ only in method.[34]

Chiang Kai-shek, in defending Sun's policy, wrote in 1925:

> If the two "-isms" [i.e., Three People's Principles and communism] were fundamentally incompatible, wise as was Dr. Sun and loyal to the Party as was the First Kuomintang National Congress, how could they rashly make such a decision [i.e., the KMT-Communist coalition in 1924] and leave our party in danger? . . . Dr. Sun's Three People's Principles may not exactly be communism, but both are revolutionary. Dr. Sun felt deeply that [the Three People's Principles] must include communism in order to be the true Three People's Principles, and the [KMT] must include the Communist Party in order to be the true Kuomintang.[35]

He also wrote then that he dared to answer for the Communist elements in the KMT:

I would die for the people's revolution. I would die for the Three People's Principles, which would also mean dying for communism.[36]

Later on, young readers simply could not understand why Communist writings should be outlawed while Sun's teachings were worshipped as infallible and sacred,[37] and why they were not allowed to discover for themselves the differences and similarities between the two.

Liberal thinkers, who worshiped Western ideas of freedom and democracy, questioned the government's policy of banning all publications "incompatible with the Three People's Principles." Could Sun's theories be further improved? Did the government authorities interpret them correctly? In April 1929, Hu Shih, in his article "Human Rights and the Constitution," published in *Hsin Yueh*, criticized the government and the KMT organizations for violating the people's rights. "All books, magazines, or newspapers are banned if only labeled 'reactionary,'" he said. Two months later, he published another piece in the same journal, this one entitled "It Is Difficult to Know, But It Is Not Easy to Practice Either." Both articles were regarded as "insulting to Dr. Sun." On October 21, the KMT Central Executive Committee instructed the Ministry of Education to warn Hu and to order all teachers in China to devote at least an average of half an hour each day to the study of Sun's doctrines.[38]

Liang Shih-ch'iu wrote three articles for *Hsin-yueh* criticizing the KMT's efforts to "regiment thought," which he did not believe could succeed. He quoted Sun's own words to show that the latter had become a revolutionary partly because of his resentment at the restrictions imposed by the Manchu government on people's freedom of speech and the press.[39] Lo Lung-chi also wrote several articles to expound his ideas on freedom, in which he too quoted Sun's denunciation of the Manchu government's suppression of the press and drew examples from history to show the futility of suppressing these freedoms. He concluded that truly good theories could stand the test of criticism and discussion.[40]

After a police raid on the magazine's Peiping office in 1931, *Hsin-yueh,* the mouthpiece of liberal thinkers, soon became a purely literary magazine. Although few writers ventured to question openly Sun's doctrines, numerous protests and petitions were made to the government demanding freedom of the press.[41] The complaints seem to have been directed at the manifold arbitrary and discretionary powers claimed by the government that enabled ignorant government officials to counter criticism with force instead of with argument or explanation of their cause, and to take administrative action regardless of the Publication Law, which, although galling to most writers, had at least allowed the accused a chance to defend himself in court.[42] As matters stood, however, few censorship cases ever went to the court. Postal bans, persecution of authors and editors, raids, suspensions, and the like, were usually carried out in secrecy and seldom announced officially.

Many attempts were made to call the government's attention to the importance of drawing a line between subversive writings and subversive activities. Reading a book, it was maintained, did not necessarily mean believing in the ideas expressed in it, and the outlawing of all books on Marxism or Soviet Russia was therefore unnecessary. Besides, literature exposing social injustice and poverty was not necessarily Communist. As Hu Shih pointed out, according to the government's interpretation of subversive views, both Mencius and Tu Fu (A.D. 712-770), some of whose lines depicted the unequal distribution of wealth and the miseries of the poor, should be regarded as Communists and banned.[43] Long before Karl Marx was born, such descriptions, indeed, abounded in classical Chinese literature, including *Shih-ching* (The odes).

All critics, however, conceded that the situation in China was not ripe for allowing as much freedom as existed in the United States or the United Kingdom. None of them suggested the immediate adoption in China of the ideas espoused by Thomas Erskine and Lord Chancellor Camden in England and Thomas Jefferson in the United States; namely, that a government should not restrict people's right to speak and to print, even to save itself from destruction, because freedom of the press is one of the natural rights of man.[44]

Even the most radical protagonists took the same position as Sir William Blackstone and Chief Justice Lord Mansfield in eighteenth-century England. While the press should be free from previous restraints such as licensing, they agreed, it would be punishable by law should it abuse its freedom.[45] In other words, they all believed that some forms of restraint were necessary and that the government had a legitimate right to define the limitations. The only problems they could not agree on were what should be allowed in print, who were to be the arbitrators, and what were to be the safeguards against abuses by the authors and oppression by the government. The petition submitted to the KMT by over twenty leading newspapers and news agencies in December 1934, for instance, did not ask for the abolition of censorship, but for the following: (1) that censors be required to adhere to the press regulations issued by the KMT; (2) that no newspaper or newspaperman be punished except by law; (3) that all journals suspended for reasons other than having advocated violent revolution be allowed to resume publication; and (4) that all imprisoned newspapermen be brought to trial. Still, to what would appear very reasonable requests by Western standards the government turned a deaf ear. Those high officials who, in their earlier revolutionary days, had also clamored for a free press became now as obstinate as the downgraded Manchus and warlords. Ironically, writers now looked back nostalgically to the last years of the Ch'ing dynasty as the "golden age" of the "free press."[46]

While clearly authoritarian and autocratic, the KMT government still wished to appear democratic. It agreed with its critics that people should have a free press and repeatedly assured the people of their constitutional rights. In fact, there was scarcely any important KMT congress that did not offer a reassurance to this effect. On December 27, 1929, Chiang Kai-shek sent a circular telegram to all newspapers promising to take heed of all constructive criticisms based on facts.[47] On January 22, 1934, the plenary session of the KMT Central Executive Committee adopted a proposal sanctioning the extension of civil rights, freedom of speech and the press, and freedom of organization and assembly.[48] On November 16, 1935, the Fifth KMT National Congress passed a resolution instructing the KMT Central Executive Committee to adopt better measures in regard to press censorship. As a result, in December of that year, the National Government issued identical instructions to its subordinate organs, ordering them to protect the freedom of the press. The directives specifically mentioned the protection of newspapers that expressed constructive and legitimate opinions on current affairs.[49]

Nevertheless, with regard to the application of the above principles, the government seems to have come much closer to the kings and queens of Tudor and Stuart England, arguing that restraint had to be imposed in the face of harsh realities. Chiang Kai-shek alone knew what was best for the country, and the people must trust him completely.[50] Any critic who disregarded his difficult position and attacked his policies had to be Communist-inspired, or at least "reactionary." On January 18, 1931, for instance, the *China Times* in Shanghai printed a brief comment on the way the Ministry of Foreign Affairs had handled the return of the Belgian Concession in Tientsin and the planning of the legation quarters in Nanking. Chiang reviled the paper vehemently the next day:

A newspaper . . . should not indulge in emotional attacks on foreign affairs, the government, or individuals . . . If a person forgets his position as a citizen and gets off the right track, the government will have to stop him. To disobey the Three People's Principles is reactionary.[51]

As compared with the previous regimes, the KMT was not just repressive; it had legions of spokesmen to defend its repressive policies. The argument once used by the Peking Police—"if there is no government, how can there be a country?"—was now repeated and fully rationalized. On March 25, 1932, for instance, Premier Wang Ching-wei said: "If there is no KMT, there can not possibly be the Republic of China."[52] It was indeed a pity, one government supporter wrote, that people could not understand the nature and mission of this great party:

> Kuomintang is a revolutionary party . . . therefore . . . China can have only one Kuomintang, not any other political parties . . . Under the rule of this party, only those opinions which support the national revolution or sympathize with the Kuomintang are worthy of [our] support and protection. All other public opinions, whether of the opposition parties or of the counter-revolutionaries, are not only unworthy of [our] support and toleration, but must be suppressed.[53]

Another writer believed that people could find more freedom in China than in any other country except perhaps the United States and the United Kingdom:

> Press censorship, restrictions imposed on publications, suppression of books or magazines . . . do not deprive [one's] freedom. They only limit [one's] freedom because no one can have unlimited freedom . . . The present Chinese government is truly a responsible government . . . It would certainly be wrong for an incompetent government to refuse to be criticized or opposed by its people. Fortunately, the present [Chinese] government is not such an [incompetent] government.[54]

During the warlord era, some people had joked about an old pedant's suggestion that only one paper should be allowed in the country so that absurd ideas could not spread. Strangely, this idea seemed to gain ground in this period. While criticizing the severe censorship policy in Japan, one writer categorically supported the KMT government's efforts to control news for the sake of "national security." He believed that the Central News Agency, under the Central Publicity Department, should be made into the strongest, and perhaps the only, news agency in the nation. The Central Publicity Department should make the central government's views on any important domestic measures or diplomatic events known to all newspapers so that they could editorialize accordingly. Better still, the central government should write the editorials and distribute them to all newspapers. Of course, such editorials could also be written collectively by the editors-in-chief of large papers and then distributed to all the others. The Central Publicity Department should operate a school of journalism to train loyal newspapermen. For the time being, all journalists should be screened and controlled by the government, which should also control the supplies and equipment needed by the press and prescribe the number of pages each newspaper could publish. Eventually all the newspapers should be nationalized.[55] As we shall see in the following chapters, many of these ideas would actually be put into practice during and after the war.

Effects of Control

Advocates of thought control did not seem to realize that there was no foolproof method of achieving their ends. The intensive efforts to suppress Communist writings did not eliminate them,[56] but merely made Communist propaganda retreat to subterranean channels, where it could not be very easily attacked by its opponents. Moreover, censorship led also to some not very desirable trends.

As compared with the limited number of books published each year,[57] magazine publishing seemed to be more vigorous.[58] Magazines did not require much capital and thus also enjoyed more flexibility than books and newspapers. A magazine which was outlawed could easily appear under another title. On February 1, 1933, the first issue of *Tzu-yu yen-lun* (Free speech), a semimonthly, appeared on the market. The editors announed that in the previous year they had published *Chu-chang yü p'i-p'ing* (Opinions and criticisms), which had been banned secretly by the government after its fourth issue because of an article entitled "What Will the Kuomintang Do?", and that henceforth the journal would appear under the new title.[59] Although such a candid declaration was rather unusual in China, it was a well-known fact that when a magazine was banned a new one would soon appear, edited and published by the same people. The more radical the magazine was, the sooner it changed its title. This is one of the reasons why, during this period, there were so many magazines; most of them had but a short life.[60]

Outwitted by their elusive enemy, the baffled censors often viewed with suspicion all serious studies in the social sciences or works concerned with current affairs. According to Chang Ching-lu, seventeen social science books published in 1928 by his Lien Ho Book Company in Shanghai—about 50 per cent of its total annual output—were not allowed to circulate.[61] During this period, many publishers hesitated to publish books in the social sciences. Chinese historiography was advancing very rapidly during these years, but few worthy studies of contemporary history were published, probably because of the chilling fear of unwittingly offending important government officials or being suspected of having a leftist slant. As a result, the Confucian classics, which the KMT had once considered obsolescent, became again respectable and profitable. Reprints of other old books, also "safe" business, kept many publishing companies in the black, with the years 1934-1935 marking the climax of the reprinting business. Not only Chinese classics, but also popular chivalric fiction and ancient obscene literature reappeared on the market, some bringing in huge profits. Elementary science books also sold well. The number of popular, do-it-yourself books in science, technology, history, geography, and military science increased markedly, especially in 1936.[62]

When people dared not speak out directly, some writers, such as Chou Tso-jen, took a negative attitude by giving up serious writing, living in seclusion, and devoting their time to such hobbies as "talking about ghosts," "painting snakes," or collecting antiques. Others expressed their cynicism in short essays written in a witty, humorous, or cynical style, which became a contemporary vogue, especially for periodical literature.[63]

As the large papers, uncertain of the censors' intentions, published only dull reports supplied by official news agencies and refrained from discussing all controversial subjects in their editorials, the people began to turn to "mosquito" papers for information and enjoyment. Printed in small printing shops with primitive hand-operated machines, these papers could change their titles and dismantle their plants with much less difficulty than their more respectable compeers; hence they enjoyed a little more freedom. While some of these smaller papers presumably supplanted the larger ones and played a useful role in China, some others, avid for profit, indulged in sensationalism. A few newspapers and magazines in Shanghai almost specialized in atrocious murder and sex cases. Violence and sex often monopolized the front page, accompanied by lurid photographs and banner headlines. When there was no murder case, these papers would concentrate on other crimes or devote page after page to the private lives of movie actresses, dancing hostesses, and the like. Quack doctors and shady medicines were advertised in large type. Control of such a degenerate yellow press was often suggested by citizens, but rarely exercised by the authorities.[64]

Other "mosquito" papers were organs of blackmailers from whose dirty tricks the innocent victims would very rarely receive government protection. Still other papers, especially some in small towns in the interior, were the tools of ambitious and irresponsible politicians, and would publish any false report or misleading editorial in order to have subsidies.[65]

The worst effect of censorship, however, was that, in banning all Communist publications and denouncing all anti-Japanese activities as Communist-inspired, the government deprived the people of any reliable ways of learning the motives that prompted the Chinese Communists to promote anti-Japanese sentiments. Beside being motivated by true patriotism, the CCP was also concerned with the possible Japanese threat to the Soviet Union.[66] *Hung-ch'i chou-pao,* for instance, printed a directive dated April 15, 1932, and signed by Mao Tse-tung and others, which showed an equally uncompromising attitude toward the KMT government. It instructed the Red Army first of all to eliminate KMT armies in areas close to those under Japanese occupation.[67] Although the directive reflected the justifiable hatred of a small group cornered mercilessly by their own countrymen, still, if the common people had been free to read these documents, many of them might have had second thoughts about the Communist position. Unfortunately, through its stupid censorship policy, the KMT allowed the Communists alone to exploit Chinese nationalism. Many young people regarded the Communists as the only true patriots and suspected the government, which prohibited them from criticizing Japan, of harboring treacherous intentions. Instead of serving the government, the KMT's censorship policy actually helped destroy it.

Finally, an entirely fair evaluation of this period, one must admit, is difficult because the background of some of the most important historical events has not yet been completely understood. Nevertheless, a comparison of this period with previous ones reveals some interesting differences. First, whereas writers were more often persecuted in the earlier years because of their attacks on individuals, in this period the principal cause for censorship was ideological and was aimed chiefly at the Chinese Communists and their fellow-travelers. Second, although the methods for the control of the press became subtler and seemingly less barbaric (except in areas still controlled by regional militarists), they were apparently more effective. It appears that a well-defined ideology upheld by a more stable government actually proved more inimical to freedom of the press than did the warlords' whims. Third, the Chinese government had recovered some of its sovereign rights and could sometimes deal directly with foreign correspondents in China. Foreign authorities in the settlements now played only a minor role in regard to the Chinese press, although Japanese pressure began to mount.

Some readers may disagree with my assessment of this period, the most prolific in modern Chinese history. Because of the nation's increasing stability and prosperity, notably in the coastal provinces, the volume of publications grew apace. Scholarly output advanced rapidly with the progress of higher education, and literary works, especially prose fiction, flourished. The pressure from the government for conformity, though, obviously had a dampening effect on the development of thought. Almost all the major writers of this period had launched their creative careers before 1927. Whether their indirect approach in this period or the bolder, more powerful voice of their predecessors (or that of their own earlier days) has produced better literature is outside the scope of this study. The sentimentality of some novels and the sardonic decadence of some others make me miss the unrelenting critique and profound insight of, for instance, Lu Hsün's *Ah Q cheng chuan* (Story of Ah Q, 1921) and other clarion calls for thorough reexaminations of the Chinese tradition and character which the May Fourth Movement had inspired. The painful soul-searching started by that movement could have led to the elucidation of many complex issues, the improvement of the nation's mental health, and ultimately the revitalization of an ancient civilization. Suppressed and abandoned during this period, the quest for the solution to thorny problems was bound to resurface, even in disturbing guises. In the recent Cultural Revolution, for example, a number of the same issues were brought up again, but in a very different atmosphere. At any rate, all speculation about what China could have become if the not yet completely corrupt KMT government had truly united and brought peace to the entire country is but academic guesswork. Chiang's government had scarcely been settled in Nanking for one decade when the Japanese invasion of China turned from threat into reality. The ensuing war, bringing unprecedented suffering and grief to the Chinese people, was soon to destroy the fragile stability which the KMT had managed to establish in China.

Chapter VI

THE WAR OF RESISTANCE, 1937-1945

On July 7, 1937, Chinese and Japanese troops clashed near the Marco Polo Bridge, and a large-scale war soon flared up. The Chinese people were elated by the government's determination to resist Japanese invasion, in spite of the obvious disparity in the military strength of the two nations. To combine their efforts, the KMT and the CCP formed in September a united front for the second time in Chinese history.[1] This temporary reunion resolved, if only in name, most of the problems which political disagreements between the two parties had produced within the country. Many literary magazines and traveling, amateur dramatic groups sprang up, aimed at arousing the people's patriotism.[2] Hankow became the temporary political as well as publishing center. It appeared that there might be more freedom in wartime China than ever before.[3]

Any person who harbored such hopes was soon disillusioned, however. After Hankow fell into Japanese hands on October 25, 1938, the deterioration in the KMT-CCP alliance became apparent. Patriotism gradually yielded to partisan interests, and mutual distrust developed into outright hostility. The New Fourth Army Incident in January 1941, in which many Communist soldiers were besieged and butchered by government troops, brought the conflict into the open. As the relationship between the two parties worsened, control of the press became much more stringent. According to "rumors," the central government, which had moved to Chungking after the war broke out, compiled a blacklist of eight hundred leftist writers, many of whom soon fled to Hong Kong for temporary refuge. The mayor of Chungking burned thousands of books in the wartime capital.[4] In restaurants, theaters, and other public places, a warning "Do not talk about current affairs" was prominently displayed. The iron fist of the government showed itself now without a velvet glove.

With the possible exception of the years 1937 and 1938, control of the press was effectively enforced throughout the time of the war in Free China.[5] The Publication Law of 1937 specified that regulating publications was the responsibility of the Ministry of the Interior together with the local governments, although other regulations delegated much power to the Ministry of Information. In fact, however, many other government agencies, including the military, the Youth Corps (organized by the KMT in 1938), and the secret agents, could all handle censorship cases as they pleased.

The war brought several important changes to China, among them the development of the inland areas. The cultural centers, which had been situated along the eastern seaboard, shifted now to the interior. The publishing center in Free China, after the fall of Hankow, moved to Chungking, with Kweilin and Kunming as secondary centers.

Persecution and Decadence in Japanese-occupied Areas

In areas occupied by the Japanese, the control of the Chinese press was very stringent. All anti-Japanese expressions were, of course, strictly forbidden, and the idea of the "Greater East Asia Co-prosperity Sphere," a brainchild of Ishihara Kanji, was vigorously promoted. Many newspapers went out of existence.[6] The situation in the International Settlement in Shanghai, which remained a publishing center, was, however, quite complex.

After the Chinese army withdrew from Shanghai in November 1937, the Chinese News Censorship Bureau disappeared, the Shanghai bureau of the Central News Agency was closed by the order of the Shanghai Municipal Council, and many papers temporarily ceased publication. The foreign settlements maintained their neutrality, and Chinese papers once again sought European protection. Many papers, including four KMT-operated ones, resumed publication under foreign registration and refused to be censored by the Japanese-organized News Censorship Bureau.[7] There were also papers published by Chinese collaborators with the Japanese. To camouflage their pro-Japanese leanings, they occasionally printed documents dispatched from Chungking. For a couple of years, most of the Chinese papers in the International Settlement were not seriously molested.

The picture changed in 1939. Patriotic newspapermen at first received anonymous letters threatening their lives. Then, the Japanese consul-general in Shanghai protested to American and British consuls as well as to the Municipal Council against the alleged anti-Japanese publications. Soon, on April 22, newspapers registered under British ownership received a memorandum from the British consulate-general, prohibiting the printing of any writings that might encourage anti-Japanese sentiments or terroristic activities, including the texts of and comments on all documents and declarations issued by the KMT or similar groups, references to Chinese collaborators as "Chinese traitors," Chinese soldiers as "the brave fighters," and the Japanese as "the enemy," "the devil," or "X X."

The papers protested. On April 24, they published verbatim the Outline for Propaganda in War Zones, issued by the Political Department of the National Military Council in Chungking. *Mei-jih i pao* (*News Digest*), for unknown reasons, was the only paper ordered by the police to refrain from publishing the third installment of the document. On May 6, the Settlement's Captain-Superintendent of Police warned all newspapers not to publish, without the prior permission of the police, any speeches or documents on the war situation or reports on political activities tending to incite violence. Violators might lose their license. Chinese newspapers nevertheless stubbornly refused to obey the order. On May 9, the Japanese presented the Municipal Council with a blacklist, and demanded the suppression of a number of papers and the arrest of some newspapermen. Many newspapermen also received anonymous letters threatening that their entire families would be murdered if they refused to do things in the Japanese way. The Municipal Council did not comply with the Japanese request, but in August it began to censor all Chinese newspapers in the Settlement. Two foreign censors and two Chinese censors took turns visiting the papers, toning down all words and terms that might provoke the Japanese. News emanating from Chungking or reports encouraging Chinese patriotism were generally suppressed, and, as a result, blanks often appeared in the papers. However, the papers could argue with the censors if they felt they were too severe or unreasonable.[8]

In view of the tremendous pressure exerted by the Japanese, penalties imposed upon Chinese newspapers by the authorities of the International Settlement during 1937–1941 were light and reasonable. In May 1939, *Hua-mei ch'en pao* printed an article in its literary supplement that advocated the extermination of all Chinese traitors. Its license was revoked on the ground that it had "disturbed peace and order in the Settlement." Yet on the following day, the license was returned to the paper, which immediately resumed publication. On May 19 of the same year, *Wen-hui pao, Mei-jih i pao, Ta-mei jih-pao,* and *Chung-mei jih-pao* were suspended for half a month because they had published the full text of a speech by Chiang Kai-shek without police permission. On September 18, 1940, *Chung-mei jih-pao* was suspended for three weeks because it exposed the activities of pro-Japanese Chinese elements in educational circles in the Shanghai area. On January 30, 1941, the same paper was once again suspended for two weeks because it ridiculed the so-called "peace movement" advanced by the Chinese collaborators. On June 25, 1941, *Hua-mei wan-pao* was suspended for one month because it printed an article praising the heroic deeds of the guerrillas in the Chungtiao mountain range in southeastern Shansi.[9]

The reasonableness of the sentences in the above cases, as contrasted with the highhanded methods for suppression which the Settlement authorities had adopted in the 1920s, clearly suggests the secret sympathy of the Americans and Europeans in Shanghai with China's struggle to maintain independence. Gone was the bitterness between the Chinese population and the Anglo-Saxons. Their alliance to fight against common enemies was close at hand.

On January 24, 1941, the Japanese-sponsored puppet "National Government," headed by Wang Ching-wei in Nanking, promulgated its own Publication Law. Except for a few slight modifications, it was almost identical, article by article, to the KMT government's

Publication Law of 1937. In the Wang government's law, the local
authorities referred to were the police, and all books were required
to be registered with the Ministry of the Police, which, together
with the Ministry of Information, performed the same duties as
those assigned to the Ministry of the Interior under the KMT government. Among the five articles devoted to restrictions on the contents
of the publications, only Article 21(A) was changed from "Calculated
to undermine the Kuomintang or violate the Three People's Principles" to "Calculated to undermine the Three People's Principles
or violate the national policy." An additional Article, 21(D), was
added to ban all materials which had been "forbidden to be printed
by the order of the Ministry of Information."[10] Needless to say, the
materials forbidden under this law were anti-Japanese and anti-
Wang writings.

The methods used by the Japanese and Wang's government in
press control were also largely the same as those of the KMT.
Newspapers were allowed to print only dispatches released by the
Japanese Domei News Agency or the Chung-yang tien-hsin she,
Wang's counterpart of the Central News Agency.[11] In 1939, the
puppet government operated a school to train newspapermen.
Fifty graduates were sent out to work in the provinces of Kiangsu
and Chekiang, where they established their own papers and tried
to buy opposition papers. In the spring of 1939, when *Wen-hui pao*
and *Mei-jih i pao* in Shanghai were suspended, Wang bought them
at high prices. The staff, however, refused to cooperate and
announced their intention to resign; so the papers had to cease
publication. Two other Shanghai newspapers, *Tao pao* and *Kuo-
chi jih-pao,* met with the same fate.[12]

When money failed, force followed. The year 1940 brought
much suffering to Chinese newspapermen in Shanghai. In May,
most Chinese-language papers again received anonymous letters
warning them not to publish materials antagonistic to Wang and his
peace movement; otherwise some recalcitrants might be "executed."
On July 1, Wang's government issued a list of eighty-three "most
wanted men"; forty-three of the names on the blacklist were newspapermen, who hurriedly went into hiding. From August 1939 to

December 1941, thirteen journalists were kidnaped, six were
assassinated, three were wounded by gunmen, and four staff
members of different newspapers died when bombs were thrown
into their premises. Some newspapers received threatening letters
at least twenty times, and their premises were bombed a total of
seven times. Newspaper delivery boys were often robbed by
hoodlums if the papers they carried contained any anti-Japanese
articles. Careless readers who used such papers as wrappers could
lose their lives outside the Settlement. Foreign newspapermen
unsympathetic to Wang's regime were also threatened with bombs
and bayonets. On July 14, 1941, the mayor of Shanghai was
ordered to arrange the deportation of seven Western journalists:
J. B. Powell, C. V. Starr, Randall Gould, Carroll Alcott, Hal P.
Mills, Norwood F. Allman, and J. A. E. Sanders-Bates. Some of
them later left of their own accord.[13]

Finally, on December 8, 1941, Japanese Marines took over
the International Settlement in Shanghai, and Chinese publications
were plunged into total darkness. All anti-Japanese and anti-Wang
papers disappeared. *Shun pao* and *Hsin-wen pao* alone were later
allowed to reappear, but only under the supervision of the Japanese
Navy. All manuscripts had to be censored before going to the press.[14]
Many Chinese writers were arrested and tortured. Lu Hsün's widow
was arrested by the Japanese gendarmerie in Shanghai on December
15, 1941. She was released two and a half months later, and most
of the papers seized in her home were returned to her, but Lu Hsün's
diary for the year of 1922 had mysteriously vanished.[15] Since
books had often brought disasters, not only to their writers but
also to their owners, many Chinese secretly destroyed books during
these years.[16] The lists of banned books announced by Wang's
government were very long. All volumes advocating the KMT
programs, the war of resistance, Chinese patriotism, and the like,
were prohibited.[17] In order to undermine the people's morale,
most newspapers were ordered to print only cheap trash in their
literary supplements, and for a few years Chinese collaborators
produced much inferior literature in order to earn subsidies from
the Japanese. An unprecedented crop of so-called "women writers,"

including Eileen Chang, often with their photographs preceding their trivial writings, began to appear.[18] The market was flooded with pornographic and decadent works, and the Chinese publishing world reached its lowest ebb under Japanese control.

Prepublication Censorship and Other Means of Control in Free China

On the other side of the battle front, life was quite different. The great exodus of refugees to interior China began late in 1937, when it was apparent that the war was going to last a long time. Most of the people who deserted their homes and gave up their worldly belongings to fight for their fatherland were ready to make any sacrifice. Strict news censorship by the government was thus accepted without demur, and, in fact, many regarded it as indispensable. They felt that during the war there could be freedom only for the nation, and not for individuals. Even liberals such as Chang Chi-luan, editor-in-chief of *Ta-kung pao,* felt it necessary to let the Central News Agency handle military news exclusively, and hoped that the agency would be greatly expanded to meet the need.[19] Most of the Chinese papers, however, could not afford to move to the interior, a few government papers and several large privately-owned papers, such as *Ta-kung pao, China Times,* and *Hsin-min pao,* being the fortunate exceptions.

The war dragged on, and more and more people became disillusioned with the leadership supplied by the KMT. As demands for freedom of speech grew louder,[20] government censorship also increased in severity. During wartime, the government claimed, personal freedom for every citizen had to be curtailed. P'an Kung-chan, chairman of the Central Censorship Commission, wrote in 1944 that China had learned her "censorship system, whether in the past or at the present, from foreign countries." He pointed out that censorship was much stricter in the Soviet Union than in China, and that it was also practiced in the United Kingdom. There was no reason why the Chinese alone should complain.[21] All military, political, diplomatic, or economic news reports had to be issued and approved first by the responsible government offices, and then turned over to the Central News Agency, which would supply all the news stories that a newspaper needed, including headlines. With other articles and reports of a less serious nature the censors also did a thorough job. Any writing considered disadvantageous to the government or to the war effort was censored. As a result, the weaknesses in the government, the corruption of high officials, social injustices, and the like, were seldom exposed.

Reporters and editors of the Central News Agency had their woes, too. Correspondents who went to the front with the army often found the reports they had sent back mutilated beyond recognition. Even when their long reports were passed by the censors, there was often no space to print them because newspapers were generally reduced to four, six, or eight pages as a wartime economy measure. City reporters would go to government offices only to be told that the news stories they looked for had already been relayed to their news agency. Editors and reporters became scarcely more than copyists. Victories were always exaggerated and defeats minimized. Instead of reporting facts, the Central News Agency became almost a propaganda agency.[22]

Consequently, almost all newspapers became virtually official gazettes, dull and monotonous. High officials, lacking a sense of humor, tended to regard all human interest stories about themselves, not to mention satires or cartoons, as insults. It was probably the similarity and monotony of many papers that prompted Lin Sen, chairman of the National Government, to suggest that they should all be combined into one so as to avoid repetition and waste.[23] There was even a suggestion that the government nationalize or requisition all newspapers during wartime. Others proposed that all newspapers publish one and the same edition and that all deficits be borne by the government.[24]

To produce loyal journalists, the KMT's Central Political Institute set up a department of journalism. Various cliques in the government, the Party, the Youth Corps, the army, and local governments, all ran their own papers without any overall plan for coordination.[25]

Since no publication could be printed without government

approval, suspension of papers, imprisonment of editors, and the like, were much rarer than before.[26] In areas where control was not so complete, however, such cases apparently still took place. In 1944, for instance, the chairman of Hunan provincial government, an army commander, ordered the local authorities to ban some newspapers which were critical of his administration on the grounds that such writings wasted ink and paper and stirred up unrest. On April 11 of that year, *Ta-kang pao* in Hengyang was suspended for three days for the same offense. The writer of the offending article had to flee to another town, where he was arrested.[27]

One of the most notorious cases was that of *K'ai-ming jih-pao,* also in Hengyang. This paper, published since August 1939, was raided after midnight on January 16, 1941 by dozens of plain-clothesmen who took with them documents, ledgers, and eleven staff members, including the editor-in-chief. These raiders had no warrant; they refused to give their names or reveal which government office they were working for. They did order the paper, however, to continue publication. On February 27, the paper sent a circular to all journalists in China, asking for their assistance in obtaining the release of the eleven arrested men, who had not yet been brought to trial or told of their alleged misdeeds. Meanwhile the whole affair had been kept secret, it complained, at the insistence of an unspecified agency which had made the arrests. On the same day, *K'ai-ming jih-pao* also printed a long account of the case and tried to refute the "rumors" that the paper or the arrested, who were KMT members, had any connection with "another political party." The tragedy that had befallen it, the paper charged, was motivated entirely by "personal grudge." On March 27, in an editorial, it reasserted its loyalty to the KMT and the Three People's Principles, but appealed to the government to have more respect for human rights. As far as I can ascertain, in June, five months later, ten of the arrested newspapermen were still in prison.[28]

While almost all newspapers strove to conform, the *Hsin-hua jih-pao* (the *New China Daily*) was perhaps the only paper in Free China that dared to differ.[29] The establishment of the *New China*

Daily in KMT-held areas was one of the terms required by the Communists for their coalition with the KMT in 1937. Its original plan to begin publication in November 1937 in Nanking fell through because of interference by KMT officials, so that its first issue did not come out until January 11, 1938, in Hankow. On October 25, when Hankow fell, that edition ceased publication and the Chungking edition began. The paper was under the direct supervision of Chou En-lai, then the head of the Communist delegation in Chungking, until its removal to Yenan in March 1947.

The purpose of the CCP organ was of course to advance the cause of the CCP by publishing important Communist documents, advocating Communist theories and practices, and reviling the KMT government. Almost everything it did contradicted the Publication Law and other regulations for press control. The KMT government, while respecting the paper's legal status, secretly hated it. Thus, the changing relations between the two parties were clearly reflected in the changes of the government's attitude towards the paper. Since closing it would endanger the coalition, the government adopted a policy of permitting its printing but blocking its distribution. After June 1939, when the Measures for the Restriction of the Activities of Other Political Parties were passed by the KMT Fifth National Congress, the government began to apply more and more pressure to the *New China Daily*. Its methods, the paper charged, included the following: (1) strict censorship to prevent the paper from becoming an effective tool for propaganda; (2) severe punishment for other newspapers that dared to follow its example; (3) warnings to all businessmen not to advertise in its pages; (4) employment of secret agents to make sure that no peddler hawked the paper in the streets; (5) implied or explicit threats to would-be readers; (6) confiscation or detention of the paper at the post offices; (7) closing of the paper's branch offices to restrict its circulation.

On the other hand, the paper also resorted to all kinds of wiles, legal and illegal, to stay in print and get its copies into readers' hands. Undoubtedly, it was the loudest claimant for freedom of speech and of the press. While in Hankow, of all papers, it alone refused censorship. In Chungking, it became subject to censorship, and the censors watched it closely. Immediately after the New Fourth Army Incident, it complained bitterly of their interference, and asserted that, on January 8, 1941, eleven out of the fifteen items submitted for censorship were detained. The paper then compiled a long list of words and passages which the censors had deleted in the first four months of 1941; among them were news about Communist guerrilla activities and the Communist Eighth Route Army,[30] the advocacy of freedom and equality for all minority races, and the use of the term "united." An editorial designed for the January 9, 1941 issue, commenting on President Roosevelt's message to the United States Congress in regard to China, was so radically revised that even the censors suggested the paper might as well omit the item altogether.

The *New China Daily* remained still the only paper which dared to indicate the deletions by using such symbols as "✕ ✕ ✕," "□ □ □," and "○ ○ ○," or printed the characters for "deleted," or just left blank spaces—practices that were then strictly prohibited. It was also the only paper that dared ignore the government's warnings or temporary suspension orders. Although its editors realized that the government dared not close down the paper, they still tried not to provoke the authorities unnecessarily. The censors' instructions on minor matters were usually followed, but documents and announcements on important issues were always published, in spite of possible retaliation. In 1939, for instance, considerable friction existed between the two parties, and the government promulgated various laws and regulations to restrict the Communists' activities. On September 16, 1939, Mao Tse-tung made the Communist position clear to the correspondents of the Central News Agency and two Chungking newspapers. The *New China Daily* published Mao's interview on September 19 without having submitted it to the censors, and its staff printed and distributed the issue several hours earlier than usual. When the government discovered the contents of that issue and started to seize the copies in circulation, many readers had already read Mao's words.

A more dramatic event took place in 1941, after the New

Fourth Army Incident. On January 17, the KMT announced the disbandment of the New Fourth Army, alleging that it had rebelled against the government. The account of the incident in the *New China Daily* was censored. To fill up the large blank space, Chou En-lai's "Elegy" in his handwriting was to be printed instead. The paper realized the seriousness of the political situation at the time, and made necessary arrangements to meet every eventuality. Of the two hundred-odd members of its staff, only eighty remained in Chungking ready to die with the paper; all the other members were evacuated to Yenan and other Communist-held areas. The censors came to the editorial office with soldiers and policemen. While the editor-in-chief was entertaining the censors in the living room and other staff members were dealing with the soldiers and the police, editors and printers were busy working on two different editions of the issue. The edition shown to the censors contained a version which could be accepted by them. Meanwhile, the edition with Chou's elegy was given to the paper's own delivery boys to be distributed. Police and soldiers discovered the trick and started arresting the delivery boys. But their attempt to stop its distribution was foiled when Chou En-lai himself hawked the paper in the street, and his example was immediately followed by his Communist comrades.

The Communists did not have a news agency of their own at that time, and their chief source of information was the Communist delegation in Chungking. With the help of the Communist underground organizations, the editors obtained publications from Communist-held guerrilla areas behind the Japanese lines. Many of the articles printed in the paper's "local correspondence" column were actually written in Chungking, though based on such local publications. Their "foreign correspondence" column was written in the same manner, based on Communist publications in other countries.

The *New China Daily* also encountered peculiar problems in distribution. Since it could not depend on the post offices, which could confiscate its copies, nor, for local distribution, on newspaper wholesalers, who dared not handle it, it had to establish its own distribution network. In a few cities and towns, such as Chengtu and Kunming, it had branch offices. In Chungking, it recruited more than one hundred poor boys aged eleven to sixteen, housed them, fed them, and trained them to deliver the paper. These boys traveled by foot or by bus to places miles away. They were often harassed by secret agents, police, or soldiers, and very often were beaten and arrested on such pretexts as "disturbing peace and order in the street," "violating traffic regulations," "violating the New Life Movement for not walking on the left side of the street," or "spitting in the street." They might be detained for a few hours before their release, but their papers were invariably confiscated. These little rascals soon developed into shrewd and resourceful agents. They devised various stratagems to outwit their opponents and seemed to enjoy such cat-and-mouse games. Many of them later joined the CCP.

The paper, of course, did also use the mails. Since many copies might not reach their destinations, its staff members often used envelopes with the printed addresses of government agencies or schools, and dropped them into different mailboxes. Sometimes they mailed the paper in the wrappers used by the *Central Daily News* or *Sao-tang pao* (*The Broom*), a daily published by the Army. Immediately after the New Fourth Army Incident in 1941, because of government interference, the paper was for a while reduced in size to one small sheet and, for a few months, its circulation dropped from 50,000 to 200 copies.

Since no other printer dared to print the paper, it had its own printing equipment, with another set of equipment hidden in a secret place to make sure that the paper could continue publication even if the equipment should be damaged by hoodlums. Paper was rationed during the war, and the *New China Daily* could never get enough of it from the government. It did, however, have its clandestine sources of supply and owned a secret, small paper mill in a little town in Szechwan where bamboo was abundant.

Like all the Communist-operated bookstores before the war, the *New China Daily* served also as a center for Communist activities. Under the direction of Communist underground organizations, it

sponsored many study clubs (some of them secret) and helped
organize factory workers, young people, and women. In addition
to two underground papers, *Chieh-fang jih-pao hsuan-k'an* (Selections
from the Liberation daily) and *Hai-wai hu-sheng* (Protests from
abroad), it published also a weekly, *Ch'ün-chung* (The masses),[31]
and many books on communism. Some of these publications, such
as Ch'en Po-ta's *Lun Chung-kuo chih ming-yun* (On the *Destiny of
China*), were distributed secretly. Others such as *Lieh-ning hsuan-chi*
(Selected works of Lenin) were displayed openly in bookstores.

The liberals, who did not have an army to back them up, did
not fare so well, however. As the government clearly wanted only
praise from the people and could not tolerate any criticism, any
person who dared to speak ill of high officials was courting disaster.
The best-known case in point was that of Ma Yin-ch'u, a noted
economist and educator.

Inflation began to plague Free China in 1939 and increased
its pace after May 1940. H. H. Kung and T. V. Soong, Madame
Chiang Kai-shek's brother-in-law and brother, had been in charge of
the nation's finances for years and had made huge fortunes even
before the war. During the war, their rapacity increased. Other
corrupt government officials, army officers, and selfish businessmen
also started to scramble for the loot, and embezzling, payroll-
padding, hoarding, and black market operations were rampant. In a
July 1940 issue of *Shih-shih lei pien,* Ma Yin-ch'u published his
famous proposal to install a "capital levy" immediately after the
war for the nation's reconstruction. He quoted an article by
Guenther Stein which maintained that the depreciation of Chinese
currency in July 1939 was a direct result of manipulation by
Chinese bureaucrats, asked whether millions of people should
continue to die to support a few super-multimillionaires, and
demanded that the government stop printing more paper money
and instead make war profiteers contribute all of their ill-gotten
gains to the war.

Ma was then the Dean of the College of Business Administration
in the University of Chungking and a member of the editorial board
of the magazine where the article appeared. Although he mentioned

no names and his discussion of the various fiscal problems was on the whole theoretical, his criticism was unmistakably directed against Kung, Soong, and their followers. Three months later, in the October issue of the same magazine, he published another article reasserting his opinion that a tax on the profiteers was the only way to solve the nation's financial problems.[32]

These two articles immediately won Ma enthusiastic public support, and he was hailed as a crusader whenever he gave a speech on the subject. Many "rumors" were then circulated to discredit him, with hints about his secret connections with the CCP, his senility, and so on. In spite of his assertions of loyalty to the KMT and the Three People's Principles, he was asked to resign from the university. When his students heard about this, they held a meeting on December 4. Ma came with his entire family and tried to reiterate his ideas, but he did not have a chance to finish. The commander of the gendarmerie jumped onto the platform and denounced Ma for criticizing the authorities. When the students responded with catcalls and the commander threatened to expel the disruptive individuals, the president of the university adjourned the meeting.

That evening, the commander went to Ma's home and told him that Generalissimo Chiang wanted to see him. Ma spent that night in the commander's headquarters, and the following nights too. On December 5, his students began a campaign to rescue him, but to no avail. Accompanied by the commander, he went to his office on December 7 to clean up his desk. Several thousand students of the neighboring National Central University joined his students to demonstrate their support for him on the campus, but, when he tried to talk to them, the commander interrupted again, hauled him into a waiting automobile, and drove away. On December 8, a report appeared in the papers: "Ma Yin-ch'u was ordered to go to the battle front to study the economic conditions there."[33] Soon it was "rumored" that Ma had been removed to Kwangsi and placed under house arrest there. The authorities insisted that he had not lost his freedom, but nobody was able to see him, and he was mysteriously silent. According to Liu Ya-tzu, Ma regained his freedom and returned to Chungking in 1944 when Owen Lattimore, on a visit to Chungking, expressed a desire to see him.[34]

Ma Yin-ch'u was among the luckier critics. Because of his privileged position, he could make his views known to many before he was silenced. Other critics never had a chance, since they could not escape the censors. The Central Commission for the Censorship of Books and Periodicals and many local censorship offices had been set up in 1938 to institute prepublication censorship.[35] In Chungking, Tsou T'ao-fen told us, the Censorship Commission was reasonable at first and worked well with writers and publishers. After the arrival of a new Commission chairman, censors began to make deletions in black ink so that the words covered by ink would not be legible, and they also began to revise manuscripts. Disapproved manuscripts were not returned to the writers, and arguments with censors were no longer possible.[36]

Many words and phrases became taboo, and censors were quick at spotting them. Chiang Kai-shek could not be referred to by his given name. Before the war he had generally been called Generalissimo Chiang, or the Leader, but now the Highest Leader or the Highest Authority seemed to become his title. The phrase t'uan-chieh (united) was frowned upon, and t'ung-i (unified) had to be used in its stead because it was felt that only parties on an equal footing could be united. The KMT, being above all the others, might make the inferior parties work together and unify them under one authority, but it would not condescend to become one with them.[37] Terms used by the Communists were strictly forbidden, not to mention the usual Marxist terminology. "Minority races" must now be replaced by "special races," and "liberation" by "resurgence." Even traditional phrases had to be reworded. The "liberation of women," for instance, was once changed by a censor to "the resurgence of women," a meaningless phrase because Chinese women had never been treated by men as equals. Some writers found it very awkward, at any rate, to apply the term "special races" to the minorities in Europe after World War I.[38]

Censors were never short of reasons for their revisions. Any criticism of the government or description of corruption in high official circles "handicapped war efforts." The writings of Aristotle and Aristophanes did not "answer the needs of the war of resistance." An objective account of Japanese military power "exaggerated the might of our enemy." Any criticism that not enough had been done for the war reflected a "pessimistic and negative attitude." Any writing referring to the Chinese revolution as a part of the world revolution was Communist, because "our nation and our country must come first."[39] When an open letter written by Ts'eng Ch'i, a member of the Political Council representing the Young China Party, was published in the newspapers in July 1940, many important sentences had been deleted. Another leader of that party protested to a high government official and was told frankly that the deletions were deemed necessary because the letter "discussed the problem of a constitutional government for China. The movement for a constitutional government has now finally subsided. How could we let them stir up the dust again [along the same route] and make a comeback?"[40]

Of all types of publications, the left-leaning and liberal magazines suffered the most at the hands of the censors. *Chung-kuo nung-min* (Chinese peasants), in an announcement in 1945, declared that two-thirds of the articles intended for its vol. 5, no. 1 were deleted and thus the said issue could not be published on schedule.[41] *Min-chu chou-k'an* (Democratic weekly), an organ of the Democratic League in Kunming, complained that four articles intended for its first issue were detained by the censors.[42] Another magazine complained that, out of the ten articles submitted for censorship, only two were passed with some deletions and revisions. Five were detained by the censors, two were refused by the censors because "the handwriting is illegible," and one had to be revised first in accordance with the censors' instructions and resubmitted.[43] The extensive deletions of course created difficult problems for editors. If they were clever, they might turn in more articles to the censors than they could actually print, but then they could be stuck with too many articles for one issue if the censors happened to be lenient.[44]

The Rules for Submitting Periodicals for Censorship, promulgated in 1941, permitted no publisher or editor to hint in any way that deletions or omissions had been made by censors. This rule was strictly followed for some time, but was obviously relaxed after two sets of liberalized regulations came out in 1944. After that, some editors occasionally showed in their notes or announcements the titles and contents of the deleted articles. In an "Editor's Postscript," the editor of *Tzu-yu lun-t'an* (Freedom forum) apologized to his readers and to Li Shu-ch'ing, the author of an article which never appeared in print. The editor even quoted some sentences from the suppressed article on the Regulations for the Censorship of Wartime Publications:

> The government spokesmen referred to wartime censorship practices in the United Kingdom and the U.S.A. [as precedents for censorship in China]. But our [government] makes censorship laws and regulations as if they were designed to guard against robbers and thieves. The governments and people in the United Kingdom and the United States handle this matter with mutual confidence and mutual understanding. There is a world of difference between [their system and ours].

And then the editor added casually, "We can only hope what Mr. Li has said above is irrelevant."[45] In an "Important Announcement," the editor of *Min-chu chou-k'an* mentioned the authors and titles of four short comments on current events which had been held up by the censors. He apologized to his readers for failing to observe the journal's publication schedule, explaining that new articles often had to be written to replace those suppressed by the authorities.[46] By means of such apologies the editors could indirectly inform the public of interference by censors. Many other periodicals at this time had the same difficulty with the censors, who often failed to return the articles submitted to them promptly. Magazines rarely came out on time, and often two issues had to be combined into one.

While the suppression of whole articles occurred quite

frequently, the omission of sentences and passages was almost a matter of course. An article in *Min-chu shih-chieh* (*Democratic World*), commenting on the implications of two news items from official sources, consisted of eight paragraphs or a total of less than four hundred and fifty characters. According to the symbols supplied by the editors, forty characters had been deleted at the end of the second paragraph. At the end of the third paragraph, one whole passage was missing. At the end of the fourth paragraph, five lines (about one hundred characters) had been cut off; while at the end of the last paragraph, there was a notation: "The rest has been deleted." If the article had had anything meaningful to say, it must have said it in the censored passages, for what came out in print amounted to only a few general statements and slogans without any significance.[47] In *Min-chu chou-k'an*, many such examples can be found, too. In one article there was a notation: "Three hundred characters have been deleted." In another article of about two thousand characters, nearly six hundred had been censored.[48] The censors were evidently working with great vigor and enthusiasm during these years, for *Chung-hua lun-t'an* (China forum), a semi-monthly published by the Third Party, insisted that its contributors should not be paid until after their pieces had been passed by the censors, as only then could the lengths of their articles be determined.[49]

As in the previous years, standards for censorship varied from place to place. Books passed by censors in Chungking might still be banned in other cities or towns. The authorities claimed that they had to relax their standards more in Chungking because it was one of the centers of world attention. But in other places, especially the small towns or villages where foreigners seldom set foot, much more severe control was in order.[50] An editorial which P'an Kuang-tan wrote for *Tzu-yu lun-t'an*, for instance, was not tolerated in Kunming until it had been passed by censors in Chungking and had appeared first in *Ta-kung pao* on September 24, 1944.[51] But, even in Chungking, different censors seemed to handle books in different ways, and different writers received different treatment. In 1940, Chao Feng translated a Soviet song book entitled *Su-lien yin-yueh* (Soviet music) and submitted it to the censors in Chungking. After the publisher got the manuscript back from the censors, only the scores were left; all the words of the songs had been deleted. In the same year, Ch'en Yuan translated *Su-lien ming ko chi* (Famous Soviet songs). It was passed by the censors in Kweilin after one year's delay, but later on, when the same translator submitted another translated anthology of Soviet songs to censors in Chungking, he never saw or heard of his manuscript again.[52] Chinese writers in Hong Kong sometimes complained of being discriminated against by censors in Free China. Chiang Hsueh-k'ai's translation of John Gunther's *Inside Asia* was published in Hong Kong but banned in Chungking, although the editor had already deleted passages detrimental to H. H. Kung and T. V. Soong. Another translation of the same book, however, was approved. Gunther's *Inside Europe,* translated by Sun Han-ping and Wang Hsin-wu and published in Hong Kong, was also banned in Free China.[53]

To circumvent the censors, clever editors would resort to all kinds of ruses, just as they had done before the war. Sa K'ung-liao, for instance, wrote a book on journalism while he was in prison. In order to pass censorship, his editors did some subtle editing in the first edition, which was published in Kweilin in March 1945 under a pseudonym. In one paragraph, he described the special privileges enjoyed by the Central News Agency, which had forced private competitors out of the business. The last sentence of the paragraph reads: "Moreover, the establishment of many Party papers and news censorship bureaus in large cities is also among the more important measures." This statement, the author admitted later, was meant to be a left-handed compliment. Many other instances of subtle editing could also be found in this work.[54]

During the relatively tolerant period soon after the outbreak of the war, many magazines and books that had hitherto been outlawed appeared again on the market. With the intensification of the conflict between the two major parties after January 1941, the once prohibited books were suppressed again. Thousands of such volumes were burned in Chungking.[55]

In July 1941, the Central Censorship Commission issued a list of 961 banned books and magazines that were outlawed from October 1938, when the Commission was established, to June 1941, when the list was prepared. For the majority of the forbidden items, no other reason was given than "violating the censorship standards." Most of the publications on the list were, of course, pro-Communist books or the productions of Communist or leftist writers; but included also were a selection of Chiang Kai-shek's letters, which was branded as unsatisfactory, and a translation of a biography of Chiang, which "has not been submitted to the Generalissimo for approval, and [it] used unbecoming language in some places."[56]

In 1942, the Rules for Submitting Books for Censorship were promulgated. Books published between July 1937 and September 1940 could not be sold until they had been censored and listed in the "Books Permitted for Circulation." Even before these lists were released, however, the police, the KMT and its Youth Corps officials, and military personnel as well as secret agents had been seizing books at will. Many booksellers complained that searching parties would sometimes carry off whatever they deemed objectionable, without even giving a receipt, although the publications in question might have been legally approved by the Ministry of the Interior and/or the censorship offices. There was a legend that one such "investigator" trucked away so many copies of what he called "banned books" from bookstores in Hengyang that he finally had enough volumes to open a small bookstore of his own.[57]

The hunt for "subversive" books brought woes not only to publishers and bookstore owners, but also to private citizens. Few Chinese dared to carry books when they traveled during these years because the policemen or gendarmerie, who searched their luggage, were often illiterate or semiliterate and suspicious of all books. The mere possession of banned books could mark a person as "subversive," as had always been the case in China; reading them would almost certainly get him into trouble. Some writers asserted that subscribers to the *New China Daily* were regarded as Communists by the police, and that many students were expelled because of reading an issue of that paper or a book published by the Life

Publishing Company, an allegedly leftist firm.[58] Some of these claims, of course, may have been gross exaggerations. Reading too much leftist literature could indeed arouse the suspicions of the secret police, but an occasional browsing in such writings, so far as I know, was not likely to land a person in jail.

In order to counteract subversive writings, the KMT flooded the market with free or inexpensive publications of its own and required all schools and government offices and employees to buy them. In 1941, the Ministry of Information set up its own publishing bureau and printing plants, with many branch offices to reprint and publish books and magazines which advocated its cause. In that year, the Ministry reported, 506,200 volumes were printed by the publishing bureau. Of the 91 titles, 26 had to do with the Three People's Principles, and 35 with current affairs. In addition, the bureau reprinted 10,000 copies of Dr. Sun Yat-sen's works, half of which were given to government and Party organizations, colleges and middle schools, the other half sold at cost. In the fiscal year 1941-1942, the bureau distributed 3,087,000 volumes (including 63 titles compiled and published by the bureau), 70,000 copies of pictorials, and 2,500,000 copies of handbills to soldiers and local organizations. Periodical reading rooms were set up at many localities. Chiang Kai-shek's speeches were reprinted and sent to Japanese-occupied areas under false titles. In addition, the Youth Corps published four magazines at its central headquarters, and a total of 202 magazines at its various local offices. The Party had 15 newspapers, which claimed a combined circulation of a little more than 300,000 copies.

Lack of transportation facilities, one of the greatest problems for private enterprise in wartime China, did not hamper the Ministry of Information. Besides using the mails, it made all public and privately-owned steamships and buses carry its publications free of charge. For distribution, it set up the Chinese Cultural Service, which boasted of 401 branch offices in 1940, and 83 more in 1941. In the province of Szechwan alone, the service had a network of 115 offices.[59]

Publishers who would say whatever the government wanted

them to say were generously rewarded, even though they had
produced nothing of great value. During these years of skyrocketing
inflation, it was government subsidy that enabled them to issue
books or periodicals carrying few or no advertisements.[60] Even
reputable publishers had to come under the government's wings.
Immediately after the fall of Hong Kong in 1941, for instance,
Chiang Kai-shek sent one of his top aides to see Wang Yun-wu,
general manager of the Commercial Press, the largest publisher in
China. Upon learning that the Press was in financial straits because
of its heavy losses in Hong Kong, Chiang promptly ordered the
four national banks to give it a huge loan at low interest without
requiring any security. Since, by law, no one could borrow money
without security, Wang was allowed to be the guarantor for his
own press. The Ministry of Education also named the Commercial
Press as one of the seven approved publishers for printing and
selling textbooks—lucrative business hitherto monopolized by the
KMT-controlled Cheng Chung Book Company. In 1942, the
Commercial Press received the exclusive rights to publish college
textbooks compiled by the National Bureau of Compilation and
Translation in the fields of the humanities, science, medicine, and
business administration.[61] The Commercial Press had undoubtedly
performed very valuable services to learning and education in China.
Nevertheless, one wonders if it could have received such favors had
it not faithfully followed the KMT party line.

Effects of Censorship

For various reasons, Chinese publishers developed a tendency
to avoid political issues and find escape in imaginative literature.
According to the statistics compiled by the Ministry of Information,
of the 1,891 titles published in 1941, literary productions made up
28 per cent; of the 3,879 titles in 1942, 41.7 per cent were literary;
of the 4,408 titles in 1943, 45.8 per cent. The above figures bear
out what P'an Kung-chan said about this period—that, as inflation
made life more and more difficult, light literary readings became
more and more popular. Many of the titles published were reprints
of old-style popular novels. P'an regarded this tendency as a waste

of wartime manpower and material and wanted to see more books expounding the Three People's Principles and the natural sciences.[62]

Much of the literature produced, however, was not of a high caliber. In the early stages of the war, patriotic writers tried to maintain the people's morale. The necessity of following official lines and avoiding one's own interpretation compelled them to adhere to a set pattern and made their outcries sound hollow. Later, as corruption became more rampant and disillusionment with the KMT became more bitter, many Chinese writers turned to historical novels and plays to elude the censors. Instead of referring explicitly to Free China, they would shift the scene to ancient China or to the Japanese-occupied areas, dropping broad hints that the suffering of the people and the tyranny and dissipations of those high officials described in their works matched closely the conditions that readers could find around themselves.[63] Some turned to lashing landlords in the countryside, who had no power over them.[64]

An even better way to keep off the fangs of the censor was to engage in translation or to write about places far away from China. Anyone who is familiar with wartime Chinese publishing cannot have failed to notice the innumerable translations of Western literature. Since the Soviet Union was now also an ally, many works by Russian writers such as Tolstoy, Gorky, Turgenev, and Dostoevsky also appeared in Chinese in quick succession. But the best sellers were perhaps books usually classified as journalistic reporting, such as Ted W. Lawson's *Thirty Seconds over Tokyo.* [65]

Many translated articles appeared in magazines and newspapers too. *Hsin-wen chan-hsien* (News front), for instance, devoted one whole issue, consisting of ten articles, to the freedom of news reporting. Five of these pieces were translations of articles by American writers (including one by the United States Information Service), and two were by Britishers; only three articles were written by Chinese authors, and they quoted foreign writers and discussed news reporting only in foreign countries. They made no reference to freedom of the press in China.[66] The *Democratic World* was supposedly concerned about the problems for the democratic forces in China, but almost all its articles that professed to discuss such problems were translations. *Tsai-sheng* (Rebirth), an organ of the National Socialist Party, used only translated articles from American and British magazines to show the advantages of the constitutional form of government.

The United States Information Service played an important part in supplying the materials for translation. Since China had lost all her coastal provinces and had to depend largely on air transportation in order to stay in touch with foreign countries, and since the few foreign magazines which found their way to the Chinese market were priced too high for the reading public, assistance from the USIS was deeply appreciated. The editors of the *Democratic World* reported the difficulty they had had in finding relevant foreign works and spoke gratefully of the "praiseworthy service rendered by the USIS" in helping them obtain such materials for translation. Sometimes magazines used translations that the USIS prepared and gave them free of charge.[67] As the Chinese government was chary of offending her most important ally, even censors had to think twice before they deleted or revised a translated article. As a result, liberal writers tried to hide behind the protective shields of their foreign, especially American, counterparts. When they wanted to say something about China, they would simply translate foreign articles that conveyed the same ideas. Government-supported magazines alone carried more original articles, since they would have no trouble with the censors.

The reluctance to discuss domestic affairs induced Chinese periodicals as well as newspapers to give disproportionately large amounts of space to foreign news, especially after the outbreak of World War II. Military strategists commented on operations in foreign theaters, but seldom on those at home. Columnists wrote about political and social problems in foreign lands, but not in China.[68] On August 27, 1943, the *Central Daily News,* the KMT organ, criticized this tendency in an editorial entitled "To Correct a Tendency." "Every day in our newspapers," it complained, "international news occupies about three-fourths of the total news coverage. In news commentaries, the percentage of comments on foreign affairs may be even larger." All readers agreed that the criticism was pertinent, but some of them regretted that the editorial did not probe the problem. Why were most writers forced to seek, as one writer phrased it, this "safest way" out? How could the tendency be corrected unless the government would change its censorship policy?[69]

Tsou T'ao-fen and Government Control of the Press

The worst result of the government's attempt to control the press and thereby control people's thought was that it turned good and honest men into its enemies and rebels. Tsou T'ao-fen was a good example of a patriotic liberal persecuted by the government. Finally the very means designed to make people conform to the government's wishes made him request on his deathbed to become a member of the CCP.

Tsou T'ao-fen was the pen name of Tsou En-jun.[70] Born in 1895 of middle-class parents, he started his literary career in 1926 as the editor of *Life Weekly,* a periodical designed at first to impart vocational skills to young people in the lower-middle or working classes. Its short articles depicting in simple language the woes and aspirations of humble people, its friendly advice urging readers to love their country and work for its betterment, its factual reporting, and its fair, patriotic editorials, soon won the hearts of the young. In a few years, its circulation was reported to have soared from 2,800 to more than 150,000, a record in China.

A sincere and sympathetic friend of unhappy youths, Tsou was never affiliated with any political party during his lifetime. In the mid-1920s, Shanghai was a hotbed of radicalism and anti-foreignism, but there is no record that Tsou ever participated in any of the activities. He did not like Soviet Russia or the Chinese Red Army. He denounced the "tyrannic Russian invasion" of China's northeastern provinces, belabored Marxism, and criticized the CCP's "radical measures to implement class struggle," such as "arson, murder, and brutality." He was for Dr. Sun's Principle of the People's Livelihood, but pointed out that those who gave the principle only lip service while secretly feathering their own nests were actually only helping the radicals. Industrial development was to him the best way to solve China's problems.[71]

The Mukden Incident in 1931 awakened him to the imminent and grave crisis facing his country. His primary duty, he now became convinced, was to arouse his countrymen to resist Japan. His campaign to collect funds for Chinese guerrillas in the north-eastern provinces was a smashing success, but seeing the generous support he received from the poor and lowly and the apathy of the rich and powerful made him wonder if there was some truth in Marxism after all. In his first favorable response to socialism—an article entitled "Our Latest Thoughts and Attitude," published in January 1932—he asserted that a system which exploited the masses for the pleasures of the few would have to collapse, and that socialism was bound to prevail some day. Disgusted with the spine-less government and corrupted officials, he wrote six months later that "if China has any way out, it will have to be socialism."[72] Nevertheless, he still remained a staunch nationalist. Urging all Chinese to unite and save the country, he found it very difficult to accept the government's policy of trying to eliminate the Communists first before it would resist Japanese aggression. Like many writers of those days, he doubted whether military action alone could vanquish communism.

The government reacted promptly to his liberal views. As early as December 1931, his readers in Nanking warned him that the KMT Central Headquarters had decided to penalize his weekly because it had displayed sympathy with a dissident group in the KMT. Tsou replied that he had never tried to advance the interests of any party or clique and had nothing to fear.[73] In July 1932, however, the "highest military authorities" and the KMT Central Headquarters confidentially ordered the post office to cancel the weekly's postal privileges. The weekly was printed as usual, and sent in secret or semisecret ways to other towns. Soon it began to be banned in various places. The Shanghai Newspaper Retailers Association was also instructed not to handle it, and the magazine had to employ over a dozen delivery boys to handle its distribution in Shanghai. Generous readers working on railways, buses, and steamships helped to transport it to other places. For areas too far off to reach in any other way, it was mailed in all kinds of old envelopes.[74]

In January 1933, Tsou joined the League for Civil Rights, which was organized by Madame Sun Yat-sen and Ts'ai Yuan-p'ei, former president of Peking University. The activities of the League came to an abrupt halt after the assassination of Yang Hsing-fo in June. The circumstances were such that Tsou, as an officer of the League, had to leave the country in July for his personal safety. Hu Yü-chih and Ai Han-sung took over the editorship of the weekly. In November 1933, when a group of KMT dissidents set up an independent "People's Government" in Fukien, proposed a liberal domestic platform, and called for a common front against the Japanese, Hu Yü-chih wrote an editorial, "Arise, Our People," for a December 1933 issue of the weekly to support these rebels. Although the dissidents had also incurred the dislike of the Communists, who labeled them the "third party," the KMT government nevertheless ordered the closing of the weekly. Its fate aroused much sympathy. As one writer had pointed out in 1932:

> *Life* [*Weekly*] has said what I would like to say deep in my heart, but have not said. It is not affiliated with any political party, has no secret backing, but has only made some fair comments from the viewpoint of the people.
> To be sure, it exhorted the government, and attacked bad and corrupt officials. But its comments were based on facts. It did not fabricate any fact. It did not deliberately incite [the people]. It is a loyal adviser to the government, a spokesman for the public. Even if it occasionally opposed the government [measures], its opposition was loyal opposition.[75]

At this time, according to Communist sources, Tsou had had little contact with them; nor did he have a clear understanding of the policies of the CCP. He was not yet convinced of the necessity for a world revolution, although what he saw in the Soviet Union made him more friendly toward that country.[76]

Tsou returned to China in June 1935. He began publishing

Ta-chung sheng-huo on November 16, with the aim of advocating democracy, freedom, national unity, and, most important of all, resistance to Japan. A postal ban was immediately imposed on the magazine, and there were rumors of Tsou's imminent arrest. Chiang Kai-shek sent two officials to Shanghai to win him over, but to no avail.[77] The magazine was closed down by government order after its sixteenth issue came out on February 19, 1936. On March 7, *Yung-sheng* (Eternal life), edited by Chin Chung-hua but run by the same staff and dedicated to the same principles as *Ta-chung sheng-huo* and thus really a continuation of that journal, appeared in the market. Only seventeen issues were allowed to come out.

In March 1936, Tsou went to Hong Kong to edit and publish *Sheng-huo jih-pao* (Life daily) and *Sheng-huo jih-pao hsing-chi k'an* (Weekly supplement to Life daily). At this time, he began to have contacts with the CCP, and Communist underground workers began to infiltrate the paper's editorial and business departments.[78] On May 11, 1936, the National Salvation Association was established in Shanghai, and Tsou became a member of its executive committee. He wound up the *Sheng-huo jih-pao* on July 31, moved the weekly supplement to Shanghai on August 23, and changed its name from the twelfth issue to *Sheng-huo hsing-chi k'an*. On November 22, he was arrested with six other officers of the National Salvation Association in the so-called "Shanghai Seven" case, which has been discussed in Chapter V. On December 4, *Sheng-huo hsing-chi k'an* received orders from the government to cease publication. Its last issue (no. 28) came out on December 13.

Immediately after the Marco Polo Bridge Incident in July 1937, Tsou and his six companions were released from prison, and Tsou began publishing another magazine, *Ti-k'ang* (Resistance), in Shanghai. When he moved to Hankow in November of that year, he changed the magazine's name, from its no. 28 (November 19), to *K'ang-chan* (War of resistance), which continued to be published every three days. On July 7, 1938, he combined *K'ang-chan* (from its no. 87) and *Ch'üan-min* (from its vol. 2, no. 6) into *Ch'üan-min k'ang-chan* (War of resistance for all the people). In format and editorial policy, this new magazine was modeled on *Life Weekly* in its later stage, though displaying a more definite leaning to the left. Tsou still pleaded for national unity under the leadership of Chiang Kai-shek and urged all newspapers and magazines to advocate the same. While exposing corruption and social injustice, he never wavered in his support for the government's policy to fight Japan to the bitter end.[79] The magazine was moved to Chungking when Hankow was about to fall in October 1938.

In June 1938, Tsou became a member of the Political Council representing the National Salvation Association, the very organization which had caused his imprisonment. The Council was established by the government as a gesture to placate critics. Although it included representatives from all parties, including the CCP, most of its members belonged to the KMT. Tsou continued to work for freedom of speech and publication. Of the nine bills he sponsored, three were bills for such freedom.

Another successful enterprise of his, the Life Publishing Company, was founded in Shanghai in 1932. After the war broke out, the publisher-bookseller developed very rapidly in Free China. In 1939, it boasted of fifty-five branch offices in fourteen provinces, besides its headquarters in Chungking, and thus earned the envy of petty officials. Because of "rumors" that the company was accepting a large monthly subsidy from the CCP, three KMT officials went to the company's main office to audit its books in June 1939, but found no incriminating evidence. Still, censors began to find more and more faults in its publications, and *Ch'üan-min k'ang-chan,* though properly registered and censored, was often banned or confiscated in various localities. Other publications were also detained at post offices or confiscated by soldiers or police without any reason.[80] In March 1939, the government had begun to bear down on its branch offices. In less than four months, eleven of them were closed down, many volumes were confiscated, and some staff members were arrested. To Tsou's repeated inquiries and protests, the Ministry of Information, then headed by Yeh Ch'u-ts'ang and P'an Kung-chan, gave only evasive replies. On July 4, 1939, the Ministry proposed that his company be merged with the Independence

Press and the KMT-controlled Cheng Chung Book Company, and that the new company be placed under a new board of directors and management. Tsou was requested to join the KMT, offered a top executive position in the proposed new company, and promised government subsidies.

Tsou declined the offer, however. He felt that the miraculous progress the Life Publishing Company had made was the result of hard work, selfless efforts, and democratic management, all of which qualities were unknown to the "Party overlords." The Ministry then modified its proposal: the Life Publishing Company might retain its identity under KMT supervisors. Tsou agreed on principle to the Ministry's closer supervision, but would not accept full-time KMT supervisors; nor would he be coerced into joining the KMT. He could not see why a company that had been supporting government policy and contributing to the war effort should be so humiliated. Like other Confucian scholars, he would not sell his soul to save his life work. Besides, he reasoned, what use would a man be to a party if he was so spineless as to yield to force?[81]

Meanwhile, as the negotiations continued, more and more of the company's branch offices were closed. In June 1940, Tsou wrote directly to Chiang Kai-shek, producing evidence that his company had not sold prohibited books or received subsidies from the CCP, as it had been accused of doing. Chiang's orders perhaps halted temporarily the seizure of the company's branch offices. However, by then only six of them were left.

The dismemberment of the Life Publishing Company had been largely the handiwork of the KMT officials. Ch'en Pu-lei, Chiang's confidential executive secretary, who had been a famous journalist in the warlord days in Shanghai, once told Tsou that the trouble probably stemmed from petty jealousy, as some KMT-operated publishing companies were not doing nearly so well as Tsou's.[82] At any rate, even Tsou's worst enemies could not prove him a subversive. In 1938, when the Youth Corps was first organized, Tsou was offered an important position in its national headquarters, which he declined.[83] The Chief of the KMT's Central

Intelligence Bureau, a former schoolmate of Tsou's, admitted privately to the latter that he had had him under close surveillance for seven years, but had no proof that he was a Communist. Nevertheless, the intelligence chief added: "At this time, if [you are] not a KMT member, you must be a member of the CCP. There is no room for neutrality."[84]

As tension between the two major parties mounted after the New Fourth Army Incident, four more branch offices of the company were sealed off between February 8 and February 21, 1941. Now only two of them were left. Tsou's *Ch'üan-min k'ang-chan* was also suspended. On February 23, he resigned from the Political Council and fled to Hong Kong.[85]

On May 17, 1941, he resumed the publication of *Ta-chung sheng-huo* in Hong Kong. Bitter as he was, he remained loyal to the government and urged his readers to support its war efforts. Referring to the groundless suspicion of some KMT officials, he wrote:

> What is most difficult for us to understand is that they seem to regard all good people and good policies as Communist, and claim all bad people and bad policies as theirs. A British journalist, returning recently [to Hong Kong] from our wartime capital, sighed: "In China of today, any man with intelligence could be suspected as Communist." He is a member of the Labor Party.[86]

After Hong Kong fell into Japanese hands in December 1941, *Ta-chung sheng-huo* of course ceased publication. Tsou walked out of Hong Kong with a group of refugees, intending to return to Chungking. As soon as they crossed the Japanese line in Kwangtung, he was told that the central government had issued orders for his arrest.[87] The door to Free China was closed forever to him. Penniless and homeless, he could only go to the Communist guerrilla areas behind the Japanese lines. When he was with the guerrillas in North Kiangsu in 1942, he became seriously ill. The Communist underground workers smuggled him back to Shanghai where he could receive some medical attention. He was wanted by the Japanese, too, and had to move constantly from one hospital to another, from one house to another. The CCP remitted funds to Shanghai, through Communist underground workers, to pay for his living and medical expenses.[88] On July 24, 1944, he died of cancer. In his will, written on his deathbed, he requested that the CCP take him in as a member.[89] His last wish was granted on September 28. Ch'en Po-ta, a Marxist theoretician, summed up Tsou's life as follows:

> A pure, single-hearted patriot, he came closer and closer to the Chinese Communist Party and became a best friend of the Chinese Communist Party. As a result of developments in his thought and struggles, he [finally] offered to become a Communist . . . His love for the Chinese Communist Party stemmed from his love of his fatherland.[90]

So ended the life of a Chinese patriot. How many other Chinese, less famous and talented but equally dedicated to the defense of their fatherland, were forced by the KMT's intolerance of criticism to follow the same route no one will ever know.

To sum up, the war brought many important changes to China. Shanghai was no longer the principal publishing center; after the fall of the foreign settlements in December 1941, all the Chinese papers not subservient to Japan closed down. In Free China, the brief interlude of real freedom and general agreement ended with the loss of Hankow in October 1938. Prepublication censorship was restored. Claiming wartime privileges, the government demanded complete conformity and absolute power. All papers gave in except for the *New China Daily*. Although vestiges of censorship may be found in many magazines, and the banning of books went on as merrily as before, arrests of editors and suspension of newspapers and periodicals became much rarer. While most of the intellectuals realized the danger of rocking the boat and kept mum on politics, the bureaucracy proliferated, and

profiteering, corruption, and inflation reached an unprecedented
level. Sensing grave danger to the nation's future, a few bold men
offered constructive criticism, but they were either silenced as was
Ma Yin-ch'u, or driven into the Communist camp as was Tsou T'ao-
fen. China finally won the war with the help of the United States,
but the KMT government deteriorated seriously and actually
became a wartime casualty.

Chapter VII

THE AFTERMATH OF THE WAR, 1945-1949

In August 1945, when Japan surrendered unconditionally, China's dream of emerging as a truly independent nation was finally realized. Since all foreign powers had relinquished their extraterritorial privileges and settlements during the war, all vestiges of her semicolonial status disappeared. For a short while, Chinese publications were filled with expressions of joy.

Jarring notes began to appear, however, even before the capital was officially moved back to Nanking on May 1, 1946. The conduct of many KMT officials in areas formerly under Japanese occupation was a national disgrace, and the danger of civil war loomed again on the horizon. The arrival of General George C. Marshall in January 1946 could not stop the resumption of the conflict. On January 29, 1947, American efforts at mediation were officially announced to have failed, and the bitter disappointment at the renewal of internal strife found expression in many sections of the Chinese population, who were weary of war and wanted a political settlement of the KMT-CCP dispute. In spite of their misgivings about communism, their desire for peace made them more sympathetic to the CCP proposal for a coalition government. Meanwhile, the economic situation worsened rapidly. American aid had only lined the pockets of those in power, and inflation ran out of control. As a result of economic disasters, the initial successes scored by the much better equipped KMT troops on the battlefield soon turned into defeats. With the failure of the "gold yuan" policy late in 1948 went the last savings of the people as well as the last scant measure of their trust in the rule of Chiang Kai-shek, who had been elected on April 19 by the KMT-controlled National Assembly as the President of the Republic. KMT forces suffered defeats everywhere. On October 1, 1949, the new People's Central Government of the People's Republic of China was formally installed at Peiping (now renamed Peking). Deserting China's suffering millions, KMT government

160

officials, along with their minions, relatives, and favorite followers, found refuge in Taiwan.

During those four years, there were very few real Communist publications in the government-controlled areas.[1] The general discontent among the people was the result of government corruption and inefficiency and the consequent skyrocketing inflation. It had little to do with ideology or theory, and could not be attributed to Communist agitation. On matters concerning the cessation of the civil war and the establishment of a coalition government, the middle-of-the-road Democratic League pleaded more eloquently and convincingly than the Communists. It was branded by KMT officials as a spokesman for the CCP, and was outlawed on October 28, 1947. The Communist *New China Daily* continued publication in Chungking in spite of repeated harassments and attacks on its premises. It stayed open throughout 1946, when liberal newspapers and magazines were closed down by government orders in quick succession. As one writer pointed out, with an army backing it, the *New China Daily* alone could enjoy the "greatest degree of freedom" unknown to other publishers.[2] The government adopted the same policy toward it as during the war, namely, allowing it to be printed but not to be read. In distribution, it faced increasingly difficult problems. After the failure of Marshall's mission in January 1947, the KMT did not have to make any more pretense of trying to work with the Communists. On February 27, therefore, the Garrison Headquarters in Chungking ordered the CCP to suspend all activities by midnight. On March 6, the CCP delegation in Nanking, headed by Chou En-lai, returned to Yenan; so did the last group of the paper's staff three days later.[3]

Publications in Communist-held Areas

In the Communist-held areas beyond the jurisdiction of the KMT government, the control of the press was almost complete; but such effective control was at first the result of supervision by local cells rather than open intervention from above. Before the Communists began to take over larger cities in 1948, they had

operated chiefly in rural areas, where the illiteracy rate was very
high and printing presses were seldom available. Communist papers
in their own regions did not really begin to take shape until the
war years, when small newspapers appeared behind the Japanese
lines under extremely difficult conditions.

Springing up out of necessity, these newspapers reported the
policy and guidelines of the CCP, in order to tell party members
how to perform such tasks as organizing the masses. Their chief
purpose was to instruct or to prepare their readers for action, not
to enlighten the mind or to formulate public opinion. Consequently,
they were different from the newspapers in Western democratic
countries in many ways. There were no advertisements, headlines
in large type, or light reading matter, and their news value was
virtually nonexistent. Each newspaper had its own area of distribution and its own reading public. It might be published once in
two or three days. Before news agencies were formed to serve a
larger area, a paper was usually confined to a small district and run
by an army or guerrilla fighting unit. Its chief source of information
was an old radio set. Few papers owned type fonts or a printing
press, and most of them were lithographed or mimeographed. The
newspapermen had to use their ingenuity to obtain paper and ink,
or they manufactured such materials in a most primitive way.
When the enemy came, they either hid their equipment or moved it
away on mule back; then, after the enemy retreated, they would
return and resume business as usual. Although generally amateurs
without experience or training in journalism, these newspapermen
were loyal Communists; many died in action as guerilla fighters,
and some lost their lives under torture for refusing to reveal to the
Japanese the whereabouts of a battered printing press. The underground papers were usually delivered at night if the carrier had to
travel on highways patrolled by the Japanese. Many of their carriers
were elementary school children. The same situation continued in
the postwar period, when the enemy became the KMT instead of
the Japanese.

Because of their ephemeral character, it is impossible to say
how many papers of this kind existed during those days. One of the

most important examples is perhaps the *Chieh-fang jih-pao* (Liberation daily), an organ of the CCP, founded in Yenan on May 16, 1941, and discontinued on March 27, 1947. Like small guerrilla papers, its chief purpose was to inform its readers of the party's policy lines. It was essentially a part of the party apparatus. No attempt was made to "sell" the paper through its news value.[4]

Book publishing in the Communist areas originated in newspaper publishing. Long party documents and materials needed for indoctrination were first issued by the papers in the form of books or pamphlets. Later, different agencies were set up to handle them as they increased in number. The center for the sale of Communist books, Hsin-hua shu-tien (the New China Book Company), for instance, began as such an agency, although it grew very quickly. When the People's Republic of China was established on October 1, 1949, the company already claimed 735 branch offices.[5] It is now the largest publisher in mainland China.

Some figures may be cited to illustrate the rapid growth of book and magazine publishing in these areas. In 1941, in the Shansi-Hopei-Shantung-Honan Border Region, there were 38 magazines. In 1945, the North China New China Book Company, the official publisher for this region, issued 124 titles, or 596,000 volumes. Among them, 128,000 volumes were works by Chinese Communist leaders and Marxist classics, and 293,000 volumes (or 36 titles, including magazines) were popular reading materials. In the Taiyueh area, 324,526 volumes were published, or about one new volume for every ten people.[6] These figures may or may not have been accurate, but they give a general idea of the intensity of Communist propaganda in these areas. Lithography and mimeography were still in use, and some works were even in handwritten form. Nevertheless, the printing technique had, on the whole, been greatly improved.[7]

Like the newspapers, many publisher-booksellers were constantly on the run during the postwar years. Their mobility may be one of the reasons why some books published by the Communists in this period carried only the names of the publisher, without the place of publication.[8]

Since, according to the guidelines of the CCP Ministry of Propaganda, bookstores should aim at propaganda and indoctrination, not profit, many bookstores had more readers than buyers. At least one bookstore even allowed readers to borrow books for home use. As there were no libraries in the countryside, these stores performed, in fact, the functions of public libraries. To help the peasants read and purchase their books, the first "cultural cooperative" was established in the Taihang area in January 1945, and the number soon increased to seventy in the Taiyueh area.[9]

The Ministry of Propaganda, under the direct and immediate supervision of the CCP Central Committee, was invested with the responsibility of regulating the press and issued broad instructions concerning the contents of all publications. Each publication was aimed at a specific section of the reading public. In 1945, for instance, 51 newspapers, 27 magazines, and 23 other publications were published in the Communist "liberated areas" in Central China. Thirty-one of them were intended for the army, 26 for educated readers, 10 for peasants and workers, 10 for party members, three for children, one for the militia, and one for students.[10] Their specific function determined their editorial policy. The party selected the editorial personnel, stressing party loyalty over journalistic skill in its selection, and trained them accordingly. As in all Communist countries including the U.S.S.R., the party editors censored their own publications. They employed the technique of "criticism and self-criticism" either openly or between themselves to improve their work. They could not disagree with Communist ideology, but they could supposedly criticize party officials as to the implementation of the party policies from the viewpoint of their ideology.[11] In other words, strategy was above discussion or criticism, but tactics, methods, and personnel were not. Compared with the censorship policies in old China or KMT-controlled areas, the stress shifted to conformity with party policy and doctrines; personal loyalty was no longer so important.

As the Communist regime became stabilized, its publishing business also became more and more centralized. In February 1949, a Publishing Committee was set up by the CCP Ministry of

Propaganda, which soon sent guidelines to all the branch stores of
New China Book Company throughout the country. Its first job
was to promulgate standard readings for all policy documents,
Marxist and Leninist classics, and the works and speeches of CCP
leaders. Stereotypes from which approved editions could be printed
were sent to its branch offices in different areas. The originally
independent and highly decentralized New China Book Company
thus became controlled by one central authority.[12]

Punitive Censorship and Other Methods

In areas controlled by the government, every issue revolved
around the dispute between the KMT and the CCP, including, of
course, that of freedom of speech and of the press. The end of the
Sino-Japanese War brought at first a measure of freedom to the
Chinese press. With the repeal of wartime censorship regulations on
October 1, 1945, prepublication censorship and news censorship
were abolished in Free China. In areas recovered from the Japanese,
news censorship was discontinued six months later, in March 1946.[13]
The wartime subterfuge of making general statements without
specific details was thus no longer necessary. There was a sharp
decrease in translations and writings about foreign countries, as
more exposés of official corruption and demands for peace and
democracy could now appear in print. Liberal and dissenting
publications began to report social upheaval and student unrest.
The resumption of the civil war, however, soon made the government feel that severe repression was once more necessary. All
publications and activities demanding peace, unity, and a democratic government were suspected as Communist-inspired.[14] The
Publication Law of 1937, which remained in effect in spite of the
fact that the "constitutional" government came into being in 1948,
was often invoked along with other laws, such as the Martial Law,
to silence enemies and potential enemies.

Although not many books came out because of the unstable
social and economic conditions,[15] the postwar years saw the
publication of many periodicals and newspapers,[16] particularly
those owned and run by the various branches of the government

and KMT officials. Immediately after the war, many newspapers sprang up in areas formerly occupied by the Japanese. In Peiping, for instance, the number of newspapers increased from two on V-J Day to more than thirty by the end of September. Thousands of KMT officials, who took the first planes to these areas to take over enemy properties, also seized the newspapers. After the promulgation of the Provisional Regulations for Regulating News- papers in Formerly Occupied Areas in September 1945, many of the mushrooming newspapers were soon suspended or discontinued because of financial difficulties. In November, only five such papers were found in Peiping.[17] Instead, KMT and government agencies began to publish newspapers of their own. The VIPs, one writer pointed out, would simply take possession of an office building and a set of printing equipment, and there would grow up a newspaper.[18] The KMT Central Headquarters had its organ, the *Central Daily News,* established in 12 cities, plus 23 newspapers under its supervision. Provincial KMT offices owned 27 papers. KMT offices at the district level ran half of all the papers in China. There were more than 40 such papers in the province of Kiangsu and 78 (one for each district) in Hunan. The army controlled 229 papers, not including those which were not available to the general public.[19] In the northeastern provinces, almost every army division had its own paper.[20] In 1946, of the 17 papers in Mukden, "not a single one was not connected directly or indirectly with the govern- ment." Ten of the 15 dailies in Chengtu and all papers except 6 tabloids in Soochow fell into this category.[21] In 1947, except for one Soviet-registered daily, one privately-owned daily, and perhaps two privately-owned evening papers, all the others (16 dailies and 4 evening papers) in Shanghai belonged with the so-called "bureau- cratic journalism." Ten of the 13 papers in Peiping (not including several army papers unavailable in the market), 7 of the 9 larger papers in Chungking, 7 of the 8 in Kunming (not including the tabloids), 12 of the 14 in Changchun, and 4 of the 7 in Nanchang belonged to either the Party, the Youth Corps, the Army, or the KMT officials. The only two papers in Hofei, Anhwei, belonged to the Party, and so did the four papers in Canton. In Taiwan, "the

government, the Party and the military monopolized all the newspaper business."[22] There were numerous complaints that all papers
were "of the same color."[23]

Toward newspapers or magazines which would not capitulate
at once, several methods appeared to have been used. One was to
set up papers and magazines with names similar to those of the
dissidents. In Kunming during 1946, therefore, there was the
progovernment *Min-chu jih-pao* against the *Min-chu pao,* a paper
of the Democratic League. There were also the progovernment
magazines *Min-chu* (Democracy), *Shih-tai* (the Times), and *Hsin
Chung-kuo chou-pao* (the New China weekly), against *Min-chu
chou-k'an* (the Democratic weekly), *Shih-tai p'ing-lun* (the Times
review) and *Chung-kuo chou-k'an* (the China weekly), all Democratic League magazines. In Chungking, the progovernment *Hsin-
hua shih pao* (the New China times) was founded to counteract
Hsin-hua jih-pao (the *New China Daily*), the CCP organ.[24] The
purpose of such a move was evidently to confuse unwary readers.

Another method was the age-old practice of bribery, the only
difference being that, instead of outright gifts, the government
would allow those who were cooperative to buy foreign exchange
at the nominal official rate, or give them loans at low interest. This
method obviously achieved some results, as even the *Ta-kung pao*
warmed toward the authorities for a while when given the privilege
of buying U.S. $200,000 at the official rate, and an obstinate
opponent, such as the *China Times* in Shanghai, declined rapidly
for lack of funds.[25] As the price of paper began to skyrocket after
the end of 1946, many periodicals were forced either to reduce
their space or cease publication. In February 1947, the government
allowed publishers a certain amount of paper once every three
months, but only the approved ones could get foreign exchange at
the official rate and buy the paper abroad. Dissenting publishers
complained that the KMT newspapers always got the lion's share,
and some even believed that the government deliberately permitted
increases in the price of paper in order to eliminate unfriendly
publications.[26] This situation lasted for about two years, until
around the end of 1948.

A third method was to buy the stocks of a publishing house and thereby obtain control. *Shun pao* and *Hsin-wen pao,* the only two reputable Chinese-language newspapers left in Shanghai under Japanese occupation, had to accept the government's investment in 1946 and practically became government organs.[27] The government now also had large holdings in both the Commercial Press and the Chung Hwa Book Company, two of the largest publishers in China. Wang Yun-wu, general manager of the Commercial Press, was made the Minister of Economic Affairs, and a KMT official took over his position at the press.[28] The seven publishers who were permitted to publish textbooks during the war continued their lucrative business. Whether the textbooks they issued during these days would be regarded as satisfactory in a Western democratic country is of course questionable.[29]

Although the "bureaucratic newspapers" were wealthier in terms of premises, printing equipment, funds, manpower, and other special privileges, they grew poorer and poorer in the quality of their news reporting. As one writer in Mukden complained, all such papers were required to reproduce Central News Agency dispatches and had no independent position in their editorials. Some did not even have editorials.[30] The Central News Agency, too, grew larger and larger, but became worse and worse in reputation, since it could not report any news disadvantageous to the Party and the government, and consequently could not give truthful accounts. On February 10, 1946, for instance, a fist fight broke out in Chungking during a big celebration of the successful completion of the Political Consultative Conference. Many people were injured, including several reporters. Forty-two reporters protested on the next day the biased account of the incident issued by the Central News Agency, to which the Agency gave a feeble reply. More than 140 reporters found the response unsatisfactory and lodged another protest, which the Agency simply ignored.[31]

Another illustration of the inadequacy of the Central News Agency took place on July 2, 1946, when *Wen-hui pao* in Shanghai printed an "eye-witness account" of a general ordering his soldiers to open fire on a group of protesting middle school students in

Hsuchow, Kiangsu. More than ten students died, the account said, and more than twenty were wounded. The American-owned *China Weekly Review* in Shanghai commented that, if the story was true, the government ought to investigate it at once. Yet the Central News Agency, which had an office in Hsuchow, simply kept silent, and so did other papers in Shanghai.[32]

Even in transmitting foreign news, the government news agency was not always reliable. In February 1946, for instance, it issued a translation of President Truman's statement on China that differed in many important ways from its original, as the Chinese government did not want the people to know that Truman hoped for a coalition government in China. Its obvious quibbling not only gave the *New China Daily* another opportunity to jeer at the agency, but caused even a usually progovernment magazine to publish a "supplementary explanation" in order to correct the translation.[33]

The above examples are sufficient to show how important news items were suppressed or distorted by the officials. They can also help explain why the people began to lose all confidence in the government. The few privately-owned newspapers, such as *Ta-kung pao,* gradually relied less and less on the Agency's dispatches, and the public, instead of believing newspaper reports, listened again to rumors.[34]

Toward the dissident writers and publishers, the government was relentless. To recover whatever control it gave up in the abolition of prepublication censorship, the government now employed "punitive censorship," meaning government interference after publication.[35] It would even employ illegal measures to get even with its critics, and different branches of the sprawling structure began to tackle the problem in their own ways and often take the law into their own hands. The KMT, the Youth Corps, the government at various levels, and the military all tried to impose their wills on the publishing business, with the Youth Corps and secret agents growing increasingly vociferous, and the military bent on solving every problem by force. Bureaucrats kept on passing the buck, and victims often did not know who their persecutors were. Though covering only four years, this era saw perhaps more cases of government persecution of publications than the longer previous periods because of the increased desperation of the KMT machinery and the absence of prepublication censorship.

Among the various methods used to intimidate new periodical publications, one of the most widely employed was the withholding or delaying of registration. According to the Publication Law of 1937, a periodical could begin publication as soon as the provincial (or municipal) authorities gave their approval. However, both the Provisional Regulations Governing the Applications for Registration of Newspapers, News Agencies, and Magazines in Wartime (promulgated in September 1938) and the Provisional Regulations Governing Newspapers, News Agencies, and Magazines (promulgated in April 1943) specified that no periodical literature could be published without having received a registration card from the Ministry of the Interior. On January 28, 1946, the Supreme National Defense Council passed resolutions to repeal all laws and decrees which restricted the fundamental freedoms of the people, and to revise the Publication Law. Nevertheless, the government still made registration or reregistration more difficult for unofficial publications, which often had to wait for months or even one or two years for the expected card, instead of a few weeks as specified in the Publication Law. Chin I, for instance, applied for permission to start a literary magazine in Shanghai in 1946. He filed applications three times, but he was always ignored on the grounds that his handwriting was illegible or the form was not properly filled out. His fourth effort was accepted by the Bureau of Social Affairs and forwarded to the Ministry of the Interior, but, before the registration card arrived and the magazine began its existence, it was already on the list of "banned publications." Chin I inquired of the authorities, but the Bureau said that the outlawing was ordered by the police, while the police insisted that the Bureau alone was responsible. Thus his magazine died even before it was born. *Ch'ang-yen pan-yueh-k'an*'s application for official approval was rejected in 1946 on the ground that there were already too many magazines in Shanghai. Sometimes the Bureau of Social Affairs in Shanghai would not release the registration card to an applicant even though it had arrived at the Bureau, or approve any publication unless the magazine had already proven to be reliable—a condition which could rule out all new publications.[36]

Just as in the previous years, many publications tolerated in Shanghai (which resumed now its prewar prominence as *the* publishing center in China) were not permitted elsewhere.[37] Some were secretly confiscated in the mail and the post office would not explain why. Many others were returned to the senders.[38] Also, as in previous years, printers were not allowed to print certain publications, and bookstores were not allowed to sell them.[39] Most bookstores were searched by the police. In February 1946, for instance, a censorship commission was organized in Wusih, Kiangsu. All local booksellers were required to submit an inventory list describing the contents of all publications they had in stock, some of which were consequently banned from the market. In April, fifteen liberal publications were secretly banned in Canton. In June, the KMT and the police in Canton were busy confiscating "reactionary publications," and published for official use in Kwangtung lists of newspapers and magazines supposedly serving the "other parties." In July, four bookstores in Kunming were raided. On October 1, the Bureau of Social Affairs in Chungking issued a list banning twenty magazines.[40] In August 1947, there was even a report that the police in Changshu, Kiangsu, had received instructions from the Ministry of Information to ban all "books commenting on current affairs." The report could have been exaggerated or distorted. But since so many things were done in secrecy, as one writer said, no one could be sure of anything.[41]

What disturbed the publishers most was the fact that nobody seemed to know who had authorized all the banning and confiscation. Any plainclothesmen, it appeared, could go to a bookstore and give the manager a list of outlawed publications, or simply take away whatever publications they considered subversive. They could ask the booksellers to write down the customers' (or readers') names and addresses.[42] According to Peiping Publishers Association, a plainclothesman went to a newspaper wholesaler on March 14, 1946, and "bought" at wholesale prices a large pile of newspapers and magazines. He then pulled out a gun, and left with the publications without paying for them.[43] Other plainclothesmen could warn newsstands and newspaper boys not to sell certain publications. It was not unusual for booksellers to be beaten or arrested.[44]

In Shanghai, as in other Chinese cities, many bookstores and newsstands had the same experience. Large-scale police raids began in November 1945, but soon stopped because the action aroused too many protests. Then the municipal government tried to ban all newsstands on the pretext that they interfered with the traffic and made the city look ugly. After many petitions, the authorities relented, but only on condition that the newsstands would not sell unregistered publications again. Local police frequently visited booksellers, took away magazines they did not like, or simply tore them up into pieces on the spot. The municipal government promised to give receipts for publications confiscated by the police, but the promise was often forgotten.[45] *Chou-pao* complained repeatedly about the confiscation of its copies on the newsstands, together with those of some other magazines, by agents under unknown authorities. On August 3, 1946, as its forty-eighth issue was to come out, the police sent a truck to its distributor and confiscated all copies. When the editors inquired, they were directed to the Bureau of Social Affairs. The Bureau referred them to the municipal government, which passed the matter on to the Ministry of the Interior, which in turn said that the responsibility lay with the local government in Shanghai.[46] On August 28, 1946, Chang Chün-mai, a leader of the National Socialist Party, complained that Shanghai police had repeatedly warned booksellers not to sell *Tsai-sheng,* an organ of his party, and that two policemen had raided the magazine's business office, taking away over 2,000 copies without giving any reason.[47] After mid-October, the arrest of newsstand operators or confiscation and destruction of publications happened almost every day.[48]

While banning and confiscation of books had had a long history in China, they were now done more unscrupulously than ever before. In consequence, some frightened magazine publishers, such as *Wen-ts'ui* (*The Articles Digest*), used their own carriers to deliver their products.[49] To magazines with a weak financial basis, massive confiscation could deal a fatal blow. *Min-chu* (Democracy), a weekly in Shanghai which claimed to have no political affiliations, is a good example. Edited by Cheng Chen-to, it began publication on October 13, 1945. It was registered properly with the Ministry of the Interior and yet, for unknown reasons, the Bureau of Social Affairs in Shanghai held up its registration permit. About a month after it began publication, plainclothesmen who would not reveal their identity began to confiscate copies of it on the newsstands, often without a receipt. They would also warn booksellers not to sell this "banned" magazine, or would just tear it up on the spot. The editors tried to appeal to certain officials in the central government, who told them that such things could not have happened. The municipal government also denied any knowledge of such incidents. Meanwhile, readers from other towns in China complained that they could not find the magazine on their local newsstands and that the copies their friends in Shanghai had mailed to them were often returned to the senders. All that the editor could find out was that somebody in authority disliked the magazine and had issued "secret orders" to ban it. On September 28, when its fiftieth issue came off the press, the police confiscated 3,200 copies of it, and, several days later, they took away another 700 copies from its distributor and warned him not to handle the magazine any more. Many newsstand operators were arrested and/or warned that their licenses might be revoked if they should sell the magazine again. Thus an impecunious scholar's project was forced off the market.[50]

Liberal or dissenting publications often received threatening letters or telephone calls. *Chou-pao,* which had reported students' confrontations with the police in Kunming as well as in Shanghai, received many such threats in December 1945. *Hua-hsi wan-pao,* a Democratic League evening paper in Chengtu, received in November and December of 1945 at least seven anonymous letters. One of them warned it to change its stand by January 5, 1946, or face violence.[51]

Anonymous phone calls or letters were often followed by

violent actions. The premises of many papers—Communist and right-wing, as well as middle-of-the-road—all over the country, especially in Nanking and Shanghai, were damaged or smashed by all sorts of people. Often, the riot resulted from trivial causes. On December 22, 1945, *Huang-ho wan-pao* of Sian, in an article in its literary supplement, accused the Military Cadet Corps in Kunming of killing some students there. The typesetters unfortunately omitted the characters for "Kunming" in the story. On the following day, cadets from the local Military Cadet Corps smashed up the premises of the paper and carried away its director, in spite of the fact that the editors had already apologized for the error in all local papers. The director was later released, and the paper made apologies again in all local papers.[52]

On February 22, 1946, the office of the *New China Daily* in Chungking was damaged. Two days later, its branch office in Chengtu met the same fate. Both incidents took place when pro-government students were staging an anti-Soviet demonstration. On March 1, in a student demonstration in Sian, the business offices of *Ch'in-feng jih-pao* and *Kung-shang jih-pao* were damaged. The students refused to accept any responsibility for the rioting, and the papers insisted that the ruffians were actually KMT secret agents. On May 4, in an anti-Soviet demonstration in Canton, the premises of two newspapers, one bookstore, and some newsstands were destroyed. The papers claimed that the riot was directed by the local chief of police, who was also a member of the Youth Corps.[53]

On January 6 and 8, 1947, during an anti-American demonstration in Chengtu, some Youth Corps members went to the headquarters of *Hsin Chung-kuo jih-pao,* a paper of the Young China Party, injured one staff member, and destroyed its business office. A third attempt, on January 10, to destroy its printing plant was foiled by the police. In August 1947, the office of *Chin-ch'iang pao* in Tai-yuan was damaged by rioters; publication, though, was resumed in a few days. On August 13, several hundred peddlers selling chickens and ducks in Tsingtao destroyed the editorial office of *Ch'ing pao* because it had carried a letter to the editor which criticized the fowl market as being too dirty.[54]

On February 27, 1948, *Hua-pei hsin-wen* (the North China news) of Tsinan was broken into and its director injured by disabled veterans because it had published a resolution of the Provincial Bureau of Social Affairs to keep "disabled veterans and beggars off the streets." On April 23, about a hundred representatives of the National Assembly from the province of Kwangtung and overseas, under the leadership of a general, caused considerable damage to the premises of *Chiu-kuo jih-pao* in Nanking, because the paper had printed a letter from a reader criticizing Sun Fo, their favorite candidate for the vice-presidency.[55]

These were but a few examples of the lawless situation during these tumultuous years, from which the publishing business suffered most acutely. An incomplete account of the newspaper premises destroyed in a three-month period in the spring of 1947 contained more than twenty cases.[56]

Numerous newspapers and magazines were suspended temporarily or permanently. On May 24, 1946, *Hsiao-hsi* (Information), a semiweekly in Shanghai, was closed down by government order. On May 29, 77 newspapers and magazines in Peiping were closed down either because they had not been properly registered or because their "language and opinion were preposterous." In the same year, 63 periodical publications in the province of Szechwan and 46 in Kunming were closed down.[57]

Failure to register became now the government's favorite pretext for closing down magazines, and this provision was invoked more frequently than ever before. In August 1946 alone, 109 periodicals were suspended or banned in Shanghai for having failed to register, although some claimed that they had submitted applications long ago but the government had not yet given its final approval.[58] Among them was *Chou-pao,* one of the first magazines to appear immediately after the war in Shanghai. Its initial enthusiasm soon gave way to disillusionment. After it made clear its opposition to the civil war in an editorial in its tenth issue, it began to run into all kinds of trouble. The suspension order, long rumored as imminent, finally came on August 8, 1946, charging that the magazine had not been properly registered. The editors claimed that *Chou-pao* had been registered with the KMT office in Shanghai two days before it began publication. As soon as the Bureau of Social Affairs was set up in Shanghai, it submitted an application for registration on October 12, 1945, to the Bureau, which forwarded its application to the Ministry of the Interior on May 30, 1946. In its last issue, no. 49/50, the editors complained that, whereas even the *New China Daily* had been promised a "further investigation" in its application for re-registration, the government had simply turned down *Chou-pao*'s application. Without the support of a political party and the backing of guns, they said bitterly, no publication could survive in China. The Shanghai Magazine Association protested against the suspension order, maintaining that none of the views espoused by the weekly militated against the interests of the country and that the government had no grounds for suspending it. The weekly did become more critical of the government and more radical in tone in its later issues. This change in attitude, the editors said, was due to the increasing confusion in the political situation and the fury and tyranny of the "reactionary forces" in China at that time.[59]

The power struggle between the KMT and its Youth Corps led also to the destruction of some publications. In the autumn of 1946, a press committee was jointly organized in Chungking by the municipal government, the local KMT, the Youth Corps, and the military. In its first meeting, it decided to suspend sixteen newspapers, including a few related to the KMT. They were suspended, as the "rumors" went, because the local Youth Corps was more influential than the Party organization.[60] Papers of other parties friendly to the KMT might also have the same problem. In January 1947, the KMT in Hungya, Szechwan, closed down the newspapers and bookstores operated by the Young China Party.[61]

In Taiwan, after the rebellion in February 1947, five newspapers in Taipei run by the Taiwanese were closed down for having allegedly published antigovernment literature during the revolt.[62]

In Shanghai, anticipating a possible student riot on the "Anti-Civil-War Day" on June 2, 1947, the Garrison Headquarters ordered on May 24 the permanent suspension of *Wen-hui pao, Lien-ho wan-pao,* and *Hsin-min pao* under the Martial Law, because these three papers, which had reported the student movement, had "continuously printed news and opinions which were harmful to military operation, attempting to overthrow the government and disturbing peace and order."[63]

Shih yü wen (Time and Culture), a magazine in Shanghai which claimed to have no party affiliation, was suspended from December 29, 1947 to January 19, 1948 on the grounds that it "repeatedly distorted facts, spoke for the [Communist] bandits . . . intended to disturb public order." On September 21, 1948, it was closed down by the Bureau of Social Affairs in Shanghai for the same reasons. The permanent suspension order came as no surprise, since, in April 1947, only one month after its inception, copies of the magazine had been confiscated in various places. After April 1948, acts of confiscation came thicker and faster. When the editors appealed to the police, they were told that a "blacklist" had been issued by the central government in Nanking.[64]

Any criticism of military tactics would bring trouble to a publication. *Wan Wan-pao* in Changsha was closed down on February 29, 1948 because of its "preposterous opinions" which were harmful to the "bandit suppression" campaign. The charge was based on an article by a correspondent in Nanking, which described the war situation as serious.[65] On July 8, 1948, *Hsin-min pao* and Chen-li News Agency in Nanking were closed down, a decision said to have been made by Chiang Kai-shek himself. *Hsin-min pao* was owned by Ch'en Ming-te and his wife, who was a member of the Legislative Yuan. When the KMT army attacked Kaifeng in 1948, the Air Force bombed the city and allegedly killed about 60,000 to 70,000 residents. On June 25, *Hsin-min pao* printed a bill, introduced by Mrs. Ch'en and twenty-nine other legislators in the Legislative Yuan on the previous day, demanding that all bombings of Chinese cities be stopped. It then published, on June 26, an eye-witness account of the bombing written by a student who had escaped from Kaifeng. When the city was recaptured by the KMT army on June 25, all government newspapers and the Central News Agency insisted that stories about heavy civilian casualties in the bombings were untrue. In two editorials, printed on July 1 and July 8, the *Central Daily News* attributed the anti-bombing proposal to Communist influence, and denounced *Hsin-min pao*'s stand as an attempt to pinion the Air Force. In the suspension order from the Ministry of the Interior, the paper was accused of subversive activities and ordered suspended permanently in accordance with Article 32 of the Publication Law.[66]

A paper could also come to an end if it appeared to hamper the government's attempt to win more American aid. Immediately after the arrival of James Y. C. Yen and an American official in Chungking on February 7, 1949, with the purpose of allocating U.S. $27,500,000 earmarked for the rehabilitation of Chinese villages, prices in Chungking rose suddenly to an unprecedentedly high level. On February 14, *Shang-wu jih-pao*, on the basis of information obtained from an official in the Central Bank, attributed the phenomenal price increase to the hoarding of gold and cotton by the Joint Commission on Rural Reconstruction, which was headed by Dr. Yen. In an editorial the next day, the paper maintained that the speculative activity of the Commission had threatened to precipitate inflation and asked that Dr. Yen be punished. In order that the government could continue to "receive American aid," a high provincial official, who was also the chairman of the paper's board of directors, said publicly that there had been errors in reporting and apologized to Dr. Yen. He and the director of the paper promised also to resign. The announcement infuriated the paper's reporters and editors, who demanded that they be told exactly what mistakes they had made and declared that they were willing to be held legally responsible if they could be proven wrong. The decision of all the staff members to resign marked the end of a paper which had had a life span of over thirty years.[67]

Not all the papers were truthful in their reports during these days, however. Confused and worried readers eager to learn the true facts fell prey again to rumors as well as to tabloids specializing in sensational stories, such as *Jen pao* in Nanking. When President Chiang Kai-shek announced his retirement in January 1949, and Vice-President Li Chung-jen became the acting president, many high officials left Nanking with their valuable belongings. On February 1, *Jen pao* printed a story that Nanking's chief of police had attempted to leave the city on the previous day with a huge amount of money but had been stopped by a police inspector. It turned out that the story was not completely true, and, on the next day, about twenty to thirty plainclothesmen destroyed the paper's premises. The chief of police accused the paper of violating the Martial Law. The government closed down the paper, arrested two editors, and required the paper to apologize to the chief of police.[68]

To no one's surprise, many newspapermen and writers were arrested, or simply "disappeared" in these years. Among the better-known cases was the arrest of Yang Tsao and several other journalists, on July 12, 1945, in Fukien. Yang, a leftist journalist, was summoned to the Fukien provincial government office by telephone, and was arrested as soon as he got there. No one could find out what his crime was, not even the USIS, for which he had been working. The military authority announced that he had given away military secrets. Until he died on January 11, 1946, in a Hang-chow prison, he did not have an open trial. His death provoked protests from some Chinese as well as American journalists.[69]

Another sensational, though puzzling, story was that of Li Fu-jen, editor-in-chief of *Min-chung tao pao* in Sian. In May 1946, there were reports that, on the morning of May 1, Li was kidnaped by four men in Sian and killed in an isolated rural area. There were even vivid descriptions of his alleged gunshot wounds. But in July he suddenly appeared in Yenan and told his story. He was kidnaped in front of the provincial library in a car which belonged to the Sian municipal government. The "secret agents" pushed him from the car into the fields, shot him twice, and left him for dead, but some peasants rescued him and sent him to Yenan. He also insisted that some secret agents combed the village for him the day after he was shot.[70] There was no explanation of why the four "secret agents" had been so careless as to let him escape, or why other "secret agents" had taken so much trouble to search the village the next day.

As the KMT regime began to totter, it stepped up its harassment of the press. On June 1, 1947, in the face of student uprisings, the government ordered the arrest of many newspapermen—75 of them in Chungking, 22 in Canton, 5 in Shanghai, 7 in Chengtu, more than 10 in Kaifeng, and many others in other cities and towns. We do not know exactly how many journalists were seized on that day along with people of other walks of life. Over two hundred names were announced in the papers, but an unofficial estimate put the figure at one thousand. Many of these people were released soon afterwards. Acknowledged Communists were said to be sent to Communist-held areas.[71]

Many students connected with newspapers were also arrested. For instance, Li Kung-i, a Peking University student who worked as an editor for *P'ing-ming jih-pao* in Peiping, was arrested on October 2, 1947. This fact was not made public until the paper asked Hu Shih, then President of Peking University, to rescue him. In February 1948, Teng T'e and eight other Peking University students were seized by the police. Teng's alleged crime was his editorship of a radical campus handwritten paper posted on walls.[72] Since many such arrests were never made known to the public, accurate statistics may never be available.

During these years, liberal intellectuals and students who were disillusioned with both major parties and hoped for the emergence of a third party suffered most from the government's suppression. An examination of the gradual change in attitude in the liberal magazines, which claimed to have no party affiliations, may give readers a good idea of the mood of the time as well as how the punitive censorship worked. *Chou-pao* and *Min-chu* were good examples, but a better one may be *The Observer*.

K'uan-ch'a (*The Observer*) began publication on September 1, 1946, in Shanghai. At this time, many Chinese intellectuals had become disillusioned with Chiang Kai-shek's regime and felt vaguely that a drastic change was bound to come. They yearned to reform the social system of China and to make the country democratic, independent, peaceful, united, and affluent, but they had no concrete ways or means of achieving these objectives. Out of this feeling of helplessness and frustration, *The Observer* was born.[73] A highbrow liberal magazine intended for the intellectuals, especially the young, it was edited by Ch'u An-p'ing, a professor of Fu Tan University in Shanghai, who had been an editor of the literary supplement for the *Central Daily News* before the war. Among its special contributors were such distinguished names as Hu Shih, Ma Yin-ch'u, Feng Yu-lan, and Fu Ssu-nien. In its early stages it printed many essays of an academic or political nature and sometimes ventured a little criticism. It printed, for instance, three articles by Fu Ssu-nien in the March 1, 1947 issue, attacking T. V. Soong and H. H. Kung. This issue disappeared immediately afterwards from the market, where it was reportedly bought up by "somebody."[74] Realizing the futility of such an approach, *The Observer* shifted its emphasis in its later stages to the correspondence columns, particularly its reports on military operations.

The weekly's anti-civil-war stand and its revelation of social unrest, student protests, and the government's suppression won enthusiastic support from readers, but soon drew fire from the authorities. In December 1946, it was banned in Changsha.[75] Its circulation dropped from 10,000 to 7,000 in February 1947 because of government intervention.[76] In October 1947, Ch'u published his criticism of William C. Bullitt's recommendation for more American aid to China, which he maintained would aid only the government, but not the nation.[77] From then on, the "rumor" that the weekly was to be suspended began to circulate.

On March 20, 1948, Ch'u was called to the press section of the Shanghai municipal government and shown a notice from the Ministry of the Interior. It was a warning to the magazine for having "expressed radical opinions, distorted facts, and helped the [Communist] bandits."[78] The weekly was equally critical of the Communists, however, believing that both major parties worshipped militarism, and had left the poor and humble people in the lurch— hence the Communists did not like it either. On April 27, for instance, the Soviet-registered *Shih-tai jih-pao* in Shanghai reported that the government had increased *The Observer*'s paper ration, and hinted that the magazine had changed its stand to cooperate with the government. The report, Ch'u insisted, was erroneous and a malicious slander.[79]

Meanwhile, the weekly's situation went from bad to worse. According to Ch'u's report in July 1948, its distribution had repeatedly been blocked. In some places it had been banned; elsewhere copies of it had been confiscated and dealers threatened. The "Observer Series" published by the magazine also had become "prohibited books" and were always confiscated at the post office. An advertisement inviting applications from prospective employees in September clearly shows that the management knew its end might come at any time.[80] On September 28, the chief of staff of the Ministry of National Defense ordered all troops, schools, and hospitals not to read it. A postal employee in Canton was dismissed as a result of his defense of the magazine, which had been marked for confiscation by postal censors there.[81] In November, its size had to be reduced from sixteen pages to twelve because the publisher had not been able to buy any paper in the past eight weeks.[82]

On December 21, 1948, reporters of the *Ta-kung pao* in Shanghai told the editors of the weekly that the suspension order from the Ministry of the Interior was already in the hands of the Shanghai municipal government, but Ch'u had left for Peiping ten days earlier. On December 23, the complete text of the suspension order appeared in a local evening paper. Finally, on December 24, three representatives from the police, the Bureau of Social Affairs, and the Garrison Headquarters came with the suspension order, and took away 5,000 copies of its vol. 5, no. 18. Two days later, a dozen secret agents arrived, with guns in hand. Nine of the staff members were carried away, and the rest of them were placed under house arrest. For a short while, sympathetic friends, readers, and booksellers hoping to find out what had been happening were allowed to enter the premises, but not to leave. Over sixty people were at one time detained there. Most of them were released after a few days. The others were released on bail on January 26, 1949.

The nine employees who had been taken away by the secret agents were interrogated incessantly, as the agents wanted to obtain information about the author of an article on the decisive battle of Hwai-Hai and about Ch'u An-p'ing, who had denounced the failure of the gold yuan policy as having depleted many people's life savings. For a long time, the government had been casting a suspicious eye on the magazine's accurate military reports, which were suspected as having been derived from Communist sources. The report on the famous battle of Hwai-Hai, a factual account of a disaster that the government wished to hide from the people, had been written on the stationery of the Ministry of National Defense. The author analyzed the strategic errors made by the KMT army, and criticized General Claire Chennault's proposition to use the "Flying Tigers" to bomb the Communists as unlikely to help military efforts but liable to cause heavy casualties among the civilians. The identity of the author was never revealed to the KMT authorities, and he soon fled to Hong Kong.

By January 28, 1949, seven of the nine members were released on bail. The other two were sent to the Garrison Headquarters in Shanghai on that day, and to the Garrison Headquarters in Nanking on April 3. They learned then that the arrests were made by the personal order of Chiang Kai-shek. On the night of April 23, the KMT army withdrew secretly from the capital while the Communist troops were still many miles away from the northern bank of the Yangtze River. In the confusion, the prison doors were thrown wide open and the two prisoners regained freedom.[83]

Defiant Demands for Freedom of the Press

Amid all the persecutions, freedom of the press was as lively an issue in these four years as it had ever been. In spite of all its highhanded measures, the KMT government was careful to pay lip service to the freedom of the press, in order to create the impression that China had a democratic government. Just as in the pre-war period, scarcely any important conference would adjourn without first asserting the fundamental freedoms of the people. On January 10, 1946, for instance, at the Political Consultative

Conference, Chiang Kai-shek made four promises to the people, the first of which was freedom of speech, of the press, and of assembly. Whenever there was any "rumor" of suppression, the authorities would always reassert their devotion to these fundamental liberties.[84] When criticism of government measures mounted after the abolition of prepublication censorship, the government obviously became infuriated. It still seemed to believe that criticizing a high official was criticizing the government, and that pleading for the cessation of the civil war was subversive and must be silenced.[85]

Journalists and writers, on the other hand, were no longer in a mood to engage in academic discussions with the government, as they had done before the war. They attacked the Publication Law for outlawing all publications which were "calculated to overthrow the National Government." After all, the government and the country were two different things, and criticizing government policies did not mean disloyalty to the country. Besides, censorship was designed to protect the personal interest of the privileged few and "give a few officials too much freedom in doing whatever they please." It should not be tolerated in a democratic society.[86] The old saying that to stop the mouths of the people is more difficult than dealing with a river in flood was repeatedly quoted. The dissenters, in short, became now more and more vociferous, militant, and defiant.

In September 1945, magazine publishers in Chungking, Chengtu, and Kunming declared that prepublication censorship could no longer be tolerated after the war, and simply refused to submit manuscripts for censorship.[87] Then there were the "twenty-one demands" by twenty-three newspapermen in Chengtu to the Political Consultative Conference in January 1946, asking for "*absolute* freedom of speech and the press," and opposing the KMT's "monopoly" of the publishing business and properties taken over from the Japanese.[88] Thirty-five publishers in Chungking requested the same Conference to discuss the repeal of the Publication Law, since the Penal Code had already made provisions for all offenses listed in it. They also wanted the government to do

away with the registration of publications, and to denounce publicly any illegal retention or confiscation of publications. On March
18, 1946, the Peiping Publishers Association made six demands for
civil liberties, including the carrying out of Chiang Kai-shek's "four
promises," the repeal of the Publication Law, and the abolition of
the registration of publications, as well as all other measures like
postal bans which restricted people's freedom. Similar demands
came from Shanghai, Canton, and other cities in northern as well
as central China.[89] They accused the government of using illegal
means and force to impose its will on the people. Some maintained
that there would not be any point in arguing with the government,
since the pen could not compete with guns.[90] "The channel for
public opinion had been stopped." People who could not express
their opinion in words often resorted to action, and history showed
that only stupid, corrupt, and incompetent regimes had been afraid
of public opinion, and that such regimes had not escaped their
doom.[91] After all, "one cannot burn all books and bury alive all
scholars." In their cynicism and desperation, they accepted the
numerous suspension orders defiantly, and advocated an attitude
of "wait and see" until the arrival of the "bright days" when there
would be freedom for all.[92]

As we look back, this brief period may be called one of the
most tragic in Chinese history. It began with bright hopes and
triumph; it ended in utter confusion and defeat. The innumerable
forces propelling the nation toward such a dramatic denouement
need not concern us here. A study of the publications of this
period, however, clearly corroborates one of the most important
factors pointed out by keen observers: that the traditional Confucian teaching of social stratification and conformity had completely lost its hold on the people. Every group or profession, not
just students, could now rise in protest, and the number of liberal
editors, publishers, and writers who had braved death and imprisonment to advise, criticize, or argue with the authorities reached an
annual average many times higher than before. The KMT government, on the other hand, was seemingly blind to the unmistakable

signs of social upheaval. Having enjoyed almost absolute power during the war years, it entirely forgot the people who had given it the mandate and the vestiges of idealism which had animated it during its earlier years. The methods it used to control the press included not only all the devices known in the previous periods and further expansion of the bureaucratic structure, but also the delaying or withholding of registration and the refusal to supply paper at a reasonable rate. None of these methods worked, and, as the KMT breathed its last in mainland China, it resorted to unabashed persecution—a situation aggravated by the multiplicity of known or secret agencies. The liberal critics, who started after the war with good will toward the government, hoping for increasing democracy and prosperity, were either silenced or driven to the Communist camp. The astounding victories on the battlefield scored by the Communist army were admittedly due more to "political" than to "military" factors.

Chapter VIII

CONCLUSION

The controlling structure of a society, whether it be a political, religious, or economic order, stands in a special relation to the printed word. Publications spontaneously generated or skillfully promoted that support the order and rally people behind it can greatly strengthen the control. On the other hand, publications explicitly or implicitly in opposition may weaken it. Any established order tends to fear changes, and censorship is but a product of such apprehension. The various regimes during these five decades in China, ranging from the Manchu government, which never pretended to be free and democratic, to the KMT government, which wished to appear democratic but actually upheld authoritarianism, realized the power of the printed word and allowed no criticism of the government or of any government officials. Their theory was aptly expressed by an English judge who tried to justify the restrictions current in England in 1704:

> This is a very strange doctrine to say that it is not a libel reflecting on the government, endeavouring to possess the people that the government is maladministered by corrupt persons . . . To say that corrupt officers are appointed to administer affairs is certainly a reflection of the government. If people should not be called to account for possessing with an ill opinion of the government, no government can subsist. For it is very necessary for a government that the people should have a good opinion of it. And nothing can be worse to any government than to endeavour to procure animosities as to the management of it; this has always been looked upon as a crime, and no government can be safe without it.[1]

With perhaps the sole exception of Ch'en Tu-hsiu, who, in 1919, advocated absolute freedom of the press unrestrained by any law,[2] Chinese writers and publishers, by and large, granted in principle the necessity of some sort of regulation of printed matter in the interest of the state, but deplored the extension of such restrictions to include all dissenting discussions. Realizing that China had not had a long democratic tradition as had the West, they were not yet prepared to adopt complete freedom, but hoped, as William Walwyn had said in 1644, "that the Press may be free for any man that writes nothing highly scandalous or dangerous to the state."[3] Their views were quite close to those of Sir William Blackstone and Lord Mansfield: namely, that freedom of the press consists in printing without any previous licenses, but subject later to the consequences of the law. They also learned from experience, especially in the 1920s, that radical leftists could be as intolerant as the reactionary right, and that freedom of the press was often used as a pretext by a political party to advance its own cause. Once in power, it would not readily give the same freedom to its real or imaginary political enemies.

In operation, the number of controlling devices used by the various Chinese regimes increased steadily. An examination of the clauses of the four publication laws (1906, 1914, 1930, 1937), not to mention many other relevant laws and regulations, clearly shows that they were all designed to suppress political dissent and punish individuals involved in the making and distribution of undesirable reading matter. Religious and moral issues were obviously not their objectives. Each new publication law, a product of its time, surpassed its predecessors in its emphasis on suppressing political opposition, especially in newspapers and magazines that discussed affairs of the state, and social, economic, or political ideas.

To sum up, the methods of control or suppression used by the various Chinese regimes included the following, with different political and economic situations in different periods accounting for different emphases.

A. Previous restraints:
    1. Publication laws and other rules and regulations which specified among other things what could or could not be printed, and the penalties to be imposed on offenders.

2. Registration of publications, publishers, printers, book-sellers, etc.
3. Surety bonds against libel or other offending publications.
4. Prepublication censorship.
5. Compulsory disclosure of ownership.
6. Discrimination in access to news sources and facilities.
7. Prohibiting the publication of certain news items.

B. Postpublication penalties:
1. Discrimination and denial in the use of communication facilities for distribution:
   a. The mails.
   b. Other channels of transportation.
   c. Newsstands and other local commercial distributors.
2. Seizure and destruction of offending materials by the police, the post office, and other agencies.
3. Buying up all copies of offending publications.
4. Raiding bookstores and newsstands.
5. Requiring bookstores to submit inventory lists to make sure that no offensive publications could be sold.
6. Publishing lists of prohibited books.
7. Postpublication criminal penalties for objectionable reading materials—the most frequently used form of governmental control.
8. Postpublication correction of libels and other misstatements.
9. Interference with public buying and reading through extensive seizures of publications from their possessors.
10. Interference with importation of reading materials—restraints imposed through the customs.
11. Persecution of authors:
    a. Arrests and imprisonment.
    b. Kidnaping.
    c. Assassination.
    d. Execution.
12. Banning books because of the political affiliations of their authors.
13. Using diplomatic means to persecute offensive publications or publishers.
14. Threatening to confiscate the properties of overseas Chinese

merchants in their native land, regulating student activities in China, and stopping payment of scholarships to Chinese students abroad—chiefly used in the last years of the Ch'ing dynasty.

15. Threatening publishers and smashing publishers' and printers' premises.
16. Temporary or permanent suspension.
17. Denial of entry permit or request for departure to objectionable foreign correspondents.
18. Warning publishers indirectly by circulating rumors of the authorities' displeasure, and directly by messages from the government.

C. Other means of control:
1. Promoting favored books or ideas, such as Confucianism.
2. Granting special privileges to favored publishers:
   a. Franchise to publish textbooks.
   b. Granting low-interest loans.
   c. Permission to purchase foreign exchange at the nominal official rate.
   d. Preferential distribution of low-cost paper needed by publishers.
   e. Issuance of licenses on a discriminatory basis—i.e., giving priority to favored publishers and publications.
3. Subsidizing secretly favored authors and publishers.
4. Bribing dissenting authors and publishers:
   a. Money.
   b. Official positions.
   c. Special privileges.
5. Setting up official presses, news agencies, and distribution agencies by the party in power for the dissemination of counter-propaganda.
6. Investing heavily in private publishing concerns and thereby obtaining control of their publishing policy.
7. Buying off hard-to-control publishing concerns.

A study of the English book trade during the Tudor period before 1586 shows that the English authorities were almost equal in tactics of suppression to the twentieth-century Chinese. Some methods of control were developed by the Puritan government in the seventeenth century and adopted by the restored Stuarts, such as using the official newspaper as a practicable method of regulation as well as an effective means for the dissemination of propaganda.[4] The practice of secretly subsidizing publications in order to propagandize the government's policy was well-known in the eighteenth century, and may still be found today in one form or another all over the world. It appears that, once the principle of restraint is accepted, the proliferation of possible tactical devices to impose it recognizes no divisions of culture or time.

On the whole, the methods employed by the various Chinese regimes could not be compared with those in the Soviet Union, because the Chinese governments did not have the organization or the economic power that characterized Soviet Russian methods. The state did not own all the presses, and the loyalty required by the Chinese authorities was not so much ideological as personal. Nor could the methods be compared with those practiced in the United States, because the Chinese constitutions did permit the enactment of laws to restrict people's freedom, and advertisements never played a major role in the publishing world there. They were comparable perhaps only to those in England in the eighteenth century or earlier, as has been discussed before. Although the Chinese had had a long civilization, the Chinese ruling classes were relatively inexperienced at large-scale control of the press. For over two thousand years, Confucianism had dominated Chinese thought, and the institution of absolute monarchy had never been questioned. The early invention of block-printing in China had not resulted in the mass production of books, and reading and writing had remained the privilege of a select few. Except for the large-scale book-burning by the First Emperor of the Ch'in dynasty (221-209 B.C.), literary persecutions in earlier centuries had involved only a limited number of dissenting scholars and their families. The influx of Western ideas and the introduction of Western methods of printing, accompanied by foreign invasions and interferences, created an unprecedented situation after the late nineteenth century with which neither the moribund Manchu government nor the semiliterate warlords knew how to cope. Despite their crude and sometimes brutal methods, their efforts at press control were not very effective. The warlord years were, in fact, the most free period in modern China because the semiliterate warlords had no systematic ideology of their own, and usually did not persecute any dissenting opinions unless their own interests were threatened. The succeeding KMT government, however, was fully aware of the importance and influence of printed propaganda. It sought not only the suppression of undesirable reading materials, but also the promotion of official or friendly publications. Theoretically devoted to the Three People's Principles of Sun Yat-sen, which prescribed a short period of one-party rule that became, in fact, indefinitely prolonged, the KMT government was yet conscious of the new winds of democracy that had swept over the world. It tried to present an image of popular government, democracy, and the concomitant value of free expression, and yet at the same time it would not tolerate any challenge to, or criticism of, its dominance. This contradiction was too apparent and too painful for Chinese intellectuals to accept. They heard freedom promised but were punished for the mildest expression of dissent. Although the KMT regime was much more effective in press control than its predecessors, its policy achieved in the end the reverse of its goal.

A few generalizations can be drawn from this study. The first is obvious to all. As we have shown in numerous examples, government control of the press is usually exercised in inverse ratio to the security the government enjoys. George Bernard Shaw has put it well in his preface to *St. Joan:* "The degree of tolerance obtainable at any moment depends on the strain under which society is maintaining its cohesion." Frederick Siebert has also observed, when writing about freedom and restraint in the Anglo-American tradition as it developed from Caxton to 1776, that "the area of freedom contracts and the enforcement of restraints increases as the stresses on the stability of the government and of the structure of society increase."[5]

The second general conclusion may sound like a truism but is often ignored by governments that underestimate the will or intelligence of their own people. A government that wants to be supported by favorable public opinion has to enjoy general approval. Voluntary cooperation by the people is possible only when the people understand the reasons for government control. Under the threat of Japanese invasion, for instance, voluntary compliance was generally high, and regulations were not so difficult to enforce in China. After the Sino-Japanese War, when Chinese intellectuals were required to suffer the same poverty and suppression for reasons they could not understand, discontent and defiance to the government broke the dikes.

The third generalization is also common knowledge in Western democratic countries. A free press is necessary to the healthy growth of a nation. The KMT government, for instance, was not without some idealism before the Sino-Japanese War. Corruption, though common, was sometimes punished and the bureaucracy was not so unwieldy as to hamper operations. The absence of overt criticism during the war enabled the government to extend its bureaucracy rapidly, and embezzlement among both the civil and military services became almost a matter of course. When the war ended, the ruling class was already so corrupt and inefficient that the collapse of the regime on the Chinese mainland was inevitable. To prevent absolute corruption by absolute power, constant criticism by the people is a necessity.

The fourth but not so universally recognized generalization to be drawn from this study is that, whereas censorship does not always succeed in eliminating the kind of writings it is principally aimed at, it can severely restrict the free play of mind and imagination and thereby hamper a nation's intellectual development. As Milton has written in his *Areopagitica,* censorship "will be primely to the discouragement of all learning, and the stop of truth, not only by disexercising and blunting our abilities in what we know already, but by hindering and cropping the discovery that might be yet further made both in religious and civil wisdom." The censors of the KMT government had only very partial success in suppressing Communist propaganda because a determined and well-organized enemy could often elude their watchful eyes. Constructive criticism and liberal thought, on the other hand, were effectively smothered.

The fifth generalization, apparently unknown or unacceptable to many people in power, is that censorship often defeats its own ends. Unless the basic reasons that have caused grievances are removed, highhanded repression may obtain results that are opposite to those desired. To ban a publication often merely draws public attention to it. Relentless persecution of a moderate critic can drive him into the enemy camp. A government that does not allow the public to learn the truth about its political opponents may make the people sympathize more readily with its opponents and regard the government as the apparent villain. Prevented from learning the real facts, the public may turn to rumors which could be much more harmful to the government than the truth. In any event, dissatisfaction with the status quo is a common state of mind, and attempts to prevent its expression will turn unhappiness into indignation and ordinary malcontents into determined revolutionaries. The many examples described in this study are enough to show the ultimate futility of using force to bring about uniformity in thought and expression.

An anecdote from ancient Chinese history illustrates this whole subject and suggests a suitable ending to the discussion. When Duke Wu of Chou was waiting to pounce upon the tyrannical emperor of the Shang dynasty, he sent his agents to find out how things were in the capital. They came back with the report that the bad ministers were prevailing over the good ones. The Duke of Chou did not act. Their second report from the capital said that the good ministers were leaving. He still did not act. Finally the report came in that people dared not even complain any more. Then he knew it was time to strike, and he became the first emperor of the Chou dynasty in B.C. 1122.[6] Unfortunately, the truth grasped by the Duke of Chou was no longer understood by the nation's rulers more than three thousand years later, when history repeated itself in China.

NOTES

Abbreviations Used in the Notes

Chang A, B, C, D   Chang Ching-lu, *Chung-kuo hsien-tai ch'u-pan shih-liao*
(Source materials of the history of contemporary Chinese
publishing; Peking, 1954-1959). In four series: A, B, C, D.

HHKM   Chung-kuo shih-hsueh hui (Chinese Historical Society),
ed., *Hsin-hai ko-ming* (The 1911 revolution; Shanghai,
1957).

HTPL   *Hsien-tai p'ing-lun (Contemporary Review).*

KKWSN   *Chung-hua-min-kuo k'ai-kuo wu-shih nien wen-hsien*
(Documents commemorating the fiftieth anniversary of
the founding of the Republic of China; Taipei, 1964).
Series I.

KWCP   *Kuo-wen chou-pao (Kuowen Weekly Illustrated).*

NCH   *North-China Herald.*

PHCK   *Pao-hsueh chi-k'an* (Journalism quarterly).

PHYK   *Pao-hsueh yueh-k'an* (Journalism monthly).

STCK   *Shang-hai t'ung-chih kuan ch'i-k'an (Journal of the
Gazette Bureau of Shanghai).*

STPP   *Shih-tai p'i-p'ing (Modern Critique).*

TLPL   *Tu-li p'ing-lun* (Independent review).

Introduction

1.   *Ch'üan-kuo chung-wen ch'i-k'an lien-ho mu-lu, 1833-1949* (A union
catalog of Chinese periodicals in China, 1833-1949), comp. Peking
Library (Peking, 1961), lists 19,115 titles (not including the Chinese

195

Communist Party papers or those published in the Communist-held areas). Since relatively few magazines were published in the nineteenth century, my estimate is in fact a rather conservative one.

2. Cf., for instance, Eugene W. Sharp, *The Censorship and Press Laws of Sixty Countries* (Columbia, University of Missouri, 1936). In this book, the only Chinese publication law included is the one promulgated in 1930 (pp. 38-39).

3. The Kuomintang (Nationalist Party) emerged from the reorganized Tung meng hui (Revolutionary Alliance) in 1912. In 1914, it became Chung-hua Ko-ming-tang (Chinese Revolutionary Party), which was reorganized in 1919 into the present Chung-kuo Kuomintang (Chinese Nationalist Party).

I. Publication Laws and Regulations in Modern China

1. Su Ch'e (1039-1112), *Luan ch'eng chi* (Shanghai, 1929), 41:10b-11b.

2. Lü Kuang and P'an Hsien-mo, *Chung-kuo hsin-wen fa kai-lun* (A general survey of the press laws in China; Taipei, 1965), p. 4. Literary persecution was under way in the reign of Che Tsung; see Hu Ch'iu-yuan, *Yen-lun tzu-yu tsai Chung-kuo li-shih shang* (Freedom of speech in Chinese history; Taipei, 1958), p. 24.

3. *Sung hui-yao chi kao* (History of institutions in the Sung dynasty; 1809 edition), Penal Code, IIB. The *hsiao pao* (small paper) and the *chao pao* (morning paper) were both run by petty officials as sidelines and available for general distribution. In fact, as early as in June 1040, the Jen Tsung Emperor prohibited the printing and sale of works which might contain information on national security.

4. Chang Shih-yuan, *Ch'u-pan fa chih li-lun yü shih-yung* (The theory and practice of the publication laws; Taipei, 1957), pp. 14-15; Chu Ch'uan-yü, *Sung-tai hsin-wen shih* (History of journalism in the Sung dynasty; Taipei, 1967), pp. 179-218. Many references can be found in *Sung hui-yao chi kao*, Penal Code, especially in chüan 19392, 21778, 21779.

5. Ch'ang-sun Wu-chi (d. 659), *T'ang lü su i* (Commentaries on laws and statutes of the T'ang dynasty; Shanghai, 1937), chüan 17.

6. Tou I (d. 966), *Sung hsing t'ung* (Penal code of the Sung dynasty;

Taipei, 1964), 18:10b-12. In his explanation of this law, Tou I pointed
out the danger posed by the large crowds gathering usually at nighttime
around the sorcerers, who pretended to be deities. Edicts threatening
severe punishment to such rabble-rousers were issued in A.D. 740, 927,
and 958.

7. Ibid. Also *Ming lü chi chieh fu li* (Collected commentaries and precedents
   of the laws and statutes of the Ming dynasty; Peking, 1908), 18:6b-7b.

8. This law was included in the Penal Code of the Ch'ing dynasty in 1644.
   It was revised and/or expanded later also in 1740, 1757, 1759, 1801, 1812,
   and 1815. *Ta-Ch'ing hui-tien shih-li* (Laws and statutes of the Ch'ing
   dynasty; 1899), 780:1-2b. The statute "Possessing Prohibited Books and
   Studying Astrology without Permission" also provided punishment for
   those who possessed prohibited books. Ibid., 767:2b-3.

9. Kuo-chia tang-an chü Ming Ch'ing tang-an kuan (National Archives—
   Ming-Ch'ing Bureau), *Wu-hsü pien-fa tang-an shih-liao* (Source materials
   of the Reform Movement of 1898; Peking, 1958), pp. 453-454. *Te-tsung
   Ching huang-ti shih-lu* (Veritable Records of the Kuang-hsü Emperor;
   Taipei, 1964), 422:7b.

10. Full text of all the four publication laws (1906, 1914, 1930, 1937) and a
    few relevant regulations promulgated in the first half of the twentieth
    century are reprinted in Ko Kung-chen, *Chung-kuo pao-hsueh shih*
    (History of Chinese journalism; Shanghai, 1935), pp. 334-369; Lü Kuang
    and P'an Hsien-mo, pp. 133-170; and Chang C, pp. 487-520. No other
    references to the publication laws and regulations will be given except
    for those which cannot be found in the above works.

11. The Manchu government, in its last struggle to stay in power, promul-
    gated on Nov. 3, 1911, a nineteen-article constitution known as the
    "Chinese Magna Carta." It mentioned nothing about freedom of speech,
    publication, and assembly, although the Constitutional Outline promul-
    gated in 1908 had stated in Article 2 that Chinese "subjects may have"
    such freedoms "within the scope of law." P'an Shu-fan, *Chung-hua-min-
    kuo hsien-fa shih* (Constitutional history of the Republic of China;
    Shanghai, 1935), p. 323. Twenty-seven days later appeared the Repub-
    lican Articles of Confederation. Full text of all the constitutions promul-
    gated in the five decades under discussion (1911, 1912, 1914, 1923, 1931,
    1947) are reprinted in Lo Chih-yuan, *Chung-kuo hsien-fa shih* (Constitu-
    tional history of China; Taipei, 1947), pp. 473-562. The articles on
    freedom of the press in the various constitutions are on pp. 477-478,

487, 504, 524, 531, 551-552. No other references to the Chinese
constitutions will be given.

12. *Chung-hua min-kuo fa-kuei ta-ch'üan* (A comprehensive collection of
     Chinese laws and regulations; Shanghai, 1936), I, 1067-68, gives the
     full text of both the Organization Charter of the Censorship Commission
     and the Rules. "Standards for Censoring Propaganda Materials"
     mentioned in the Rules was approved by the KMT Central Executive
     Committee on May 31, 1932 (ibid., V, 889). The Censorship Commission
     was established in Shanghai on May 25, 1934, but disappeared when all
     seven censors were dismissed on July 4, 1935 on account of the *New
     Life Weekly* case. This case will be discussed in Chapter V.

13. On July 12, 1935, a revision of the Publication Law of 1930 comprising
     some stricter regulations was passed by the Legislative Yuan. Because of
     general opposition in journalistic and publishing circles, that revision was
     not enforced. The Revised Publication Law of 1937 was promulgated
     instead.

14. English translation of the full text in *China Handbook, 1937-1943,*
     comp. Chinese Ministry of Information (New York, Macmillan Co.,
     1943), pp. 61-64. Italics mine.

15. English translation of full text in *Chinese Year Book, 1943,* comp.
     Council of International Affairs (Bombay, Thacker & Co., 1943), pp.
     680-683. The Regulations were revised slightly in 1942 to incorporate
     censors' suggestions.

16. That the editors were not allowed to indicate any deletions or revisions
     was actually nothing new. Regulation no. 8 of the Regulations for News
     Censorship, issued in 1929 by the Peiping-Tientsin Garrison Headquarters,
     for instance, specified the same. See "Hsin-wen nien chi" (Journalism in
     1928), *PHYK* 1.4:92-93 (1929).

17. English translation of full text in *China Handbook, 1937-1943,* pp. 127-
     129.

18. Tu Chung-yuan, publisher-editor of the *New Life Weekly* in Shanghai.

19. For more rules and regulations enforced in the early 1930s, see the 1933
     volume of *Chung-hua-min-kuo fa-kuei hui-pien* (A collection of laws and
     regulations of the republic of China), comp. Bureau of Compilation,

Legislative Yuan (Shanghai, 1934), III, 386-392; and its 1935 volume (Shanghai, 1936), IV, pt. 4, 71-76, 100-111. There were also relevant postal and customs regulations as well as laws in the criminal and civil codes.

II. The Twilight of the Ch'ing Dynasty, 1900-1911

1. Chang Chih-tung, for instance, promoted *Shih-wu pao.* Cf. Ko Kung-chen, p. 170. After 1898, however, conservatives were anxious to suppress all progressive publications.

2. In 1900, there were less than 100 Chinese students in Japan. The number became 500 in 1902, 8,000 in 1905, and 13,000 in 1906. O. Edmond Clubb, *Twentieth Century China* (New York, Columbia University Press, 1964), p. 35. Hsiao Enchang, "Chinese Students Abroad," *Educational Review* (April 1928), pp. 153-154, gives the figures of 10,000 in 1903 and 15,000 in 1906.

3. *Te-tsung Ching huang-ti shih-lu,* 428:8ab, 458:11ab. For Liang's comments on the first edict, see *Ch'ing-i pao* (*China Discussion*), no. 2:7a (20th day of the 11th moon, 1898).

4. *Su pao* (Feb. 28, Mar. 3, Mar. 6, 1903), pp. 7, 25-26, 43. In 1899, Chang Chih-tung requested the Japanese government to ban the *Ch'ing-i pao. Kuo-wen pao* in Tientsin commented satirically that Chang, who had promoted *Shih-wu pao,* could not defend his position if he should attempt to suppress *Ch'ing-i pao.* See *Ch'ing-i pao,* no. 14:1ab (1st day of the 4th moon, 1899).

5. Advertisement in *Hsin-min ts'ung-pao* (New citizen), no. 28, no. 29, or no. 30 (1903). In its no. 1 (1902), *Hsin-min ts'ung-pao* advertised the reprint of 3,000 copies of *Ch'ing-i pao* (100 issues, 1898-1901). The prepublication subscribers (purchasers of the "stock certificate") enjoyed a 20 per cent discount.

6. Yang Yü-ju, *Hsin-hai ko-ming hsien chu chi* (The 1911 Revolution; Peking, 1957), p. 10.

7. *Kuo-min jih-jih pao* (*China National Gazette;* Aug. 15 and 19, 1903), pp. 84, 126.

8. Feng Tzu-yu, *Ko-ming i-shih* (Anecdotal history of the 1911 Revolution;

Shanghai, 1947), II, 163-170; also his *Chung-kuo ko-ming yun-tung erh-shih-liu nien tsu-chih shih* (History of the Chinese revolutionary movement, 1885-1911; Shanghai, 1948), p. 93.

9. *HHKM,* II, 438-459. Feng Tzu-yu, *Ko-ming i-shih,* II, 154-157. Two more issues, though bearing the imprint of Paris, were secretly published in Japan after the ban. Hu's article in *Min pao* (the *Minpao Magazine*), no. 3:12-14 (1906).

10. Wu Yü-Chang, *Hsin-hai ko-ming* (The 1911 Revolution; Peking, 1961), pp. 90-97. On June 22, 1908, the Japanese socialists and anarchists held a meeting in Tokyo, and clashed with the police over a red flag. Many were arrested. See also *HHKM,* II, 252-254.

11. Feng Tzu-yu, *Chung-kuo ko-ming . . .* , p. 137.

12. There were many such examples as *Kuo-min pao* in Tokyo (1910), and *Tung-t'ing p'o* (The waves of the Tungting Lake) by Hunan students in Japan.

13. Feng Tzu-yu, *Chung-hua-min-kuo k'ai-kuo ch'ien ko-ming shih* (Revolutionary history before the founding of the Republic of China; Chungking, 1944), I, 160-163; his *Ko-ming i-shih,* I, 71; III, 235; and his *Chung-kuo ko-ming . . .* , p. 40. The paper was moved to Canton in 1911, and was suppressed by Lung Chi-kuang in August 1913 as a result of the failure of Ch'en Chiung-ming's independence movement for Kwangtung.

14. Feng Tzu-yu, *Ko-ming i-shih,* III, 235-236. *KKWSN,* Ser. I, X, 507.

15. Feng Tzu-yu, *Ko-ming i-shih,* II, 256-258; V, 245-250. Chü's own account of the incident did not explain clearly what the lawsuit was about. He did not seem to know what was going on until the deportation order was executed. Through the help of the Revolutionary Alliance in Singapore, Chü and the business manager were allowed to leave the ship there, instead of being delivered to the Manchu officials in Kwangtung as the order originally specified. Chü was later to become the president of the Judiciary Yuan in the KMT regime.

16. Feng Tzu-yu, *Hua-ch'iao ko-ming tsu-chih shih-hua* (History of overseas Chinese revolutionary organizations; Taipei, 1954), p. 45. Sun Fo was later to become the president of the Legislative Yuan in the KMT regime.

17. For a bibliography of this case, see Michael Gasster, *Chinese Intellectuals and the Revolution of 1911* (Seattle, University of Washington Press, 1969), pp. 263-268.

18. In spite of the title, the pamphlet had nothing to do with the military, although it advocated the overthrow of the Manchu dynasty and the wholesale slaughter of the entire Manchu race. Cf. Tsou Jung, *Ko-ming chün* (The revolutionary army; Shanghai, 1958), pp. 2, 4. Even at that time many revolutionaries, including Ts'ai Yuan-p'ei, thought the pamphlet was too violent. See Ts'ai's "Shih ch'ou Man" (On anti-Manchuism) in *Su pao*. For Tsou's reputation as a political thinker, see Ch'en Hsü-lu, *Tsou Jung yü Ch'en T'ien-hua ti ssu-hsiang* (The ideals of Tsou Jung and Ch'en T'ien-hua; Shanghai, 1957), p. 15.

19. In the imperial days of China, emperors' names were taboo. The official translation gives the phrase *hsiao-ch'ou* as "petty thief." A more appropriate translation would be "a despicable fellow" or "a clown."

20. *Times* (London), July 13 and 31, 1903.

21. Chang Jo-yin, "Chung-kuo hsin-wen chi-che tsui-ch'u ti hsi-sheng che— Shen Chin" (The first martyr among Chinese journalists—Shen Chin), *Hsin jen-shih* (New cognizance), no. 2:96-97 (Sept. 20, 1936). Cf. also Ch'en Hsü-lu, p. 30; *KKWSN*, X, 331. There was a story that Shen was beaten to death because the authorities thought they had caught K'ang Yu-wei. See *Kuo-min jih-jih pao* (Aug. 12 and 13, 1903), pp. 57, 68.

22. *Times* (London), Aug. 5, 6, 7, 13, 14, 29, 1903. The French government concurred in September in the refusal to surrender the prisoners.

23. Justice Holmes speaking for the unanimous Supreme Court (in Schenck *v.* U.S., 1919): "The question in each case is whether the words used are used in such circumstances and are of such a nature as to create a clear and present danger that they will bring about the substantive evils that Congress has a right to prevent. It is a question of proximity and degree." Quoted in Zechariah Chafee, *Free Speech in the United States* (Cambridge, Mass., Harvard University Press, 1948), p. 81.

24. John Stuart Mill believes that "even opinions lose their immunity, when the circumstances in which they are expressed are such as to constitute their expression a positive instigation to some mischievous act." His *Essay on Liberty* (New York, P. F. Collier & Sons, 1909), p. 260. Cf.

also Zechariah Chafee, *Government and Mass Communication* (Chicago, University of Chicago Press, 1947), pp. 48-49.

25.   *Times* (London), Aug. 14, 1903.

26.   Telegrams dated June 29-July 15, 1903, in Tuan Fang's file. Reprinted in *HHKM*, I, 411-424.

27.   For the origin and growth of the settlements and the Mixed Court in Shanghai, see A. M. Kotenev, *Shanghai: Its Mixed Court and Council* (Shanghai, North-China Daily News and Herald, 1925), pp. 3-4, 13-16, 25, 27-29, 35, 47, 51, 54, 85-86, 108-109. The business district was largely in the International Settlement; the French Concession was largely residential.

28.   Ibid., pp. xi, 85. According to the treaties, the Chinese government had jurisdiction over the Chinese subjects. The extension of the power of the Mixed Court had no legal foundation, since extraterritorial jurisdiction did not apply to cases involving only the Chinese.

29.   Suggested to the Diplomatic Corps in Peking on July 23, 1903. Ibid., p. 111; *Times* (London), July 28, 1903.

30.   For the verbal contest between the counsel and the Assessor, see North China Daily News, *The Shanghai Sedition Trial* (Shanghai, 1904), pp. 5-6. The Chefoo Convention in 1876 affirmed what was provided by the treaties and stated clearly that the assessor was not a co-judge. He would merely observe, not administer, justice. The assessor in this case actually acted as a presiding judge.

31.   The prosecutor repeatedly referred to "what we should call in England seditious libel," while the defense counsel insisted that "this case is being tried under Chinese law." Then they shifted positions completely. The prosecution applied the Chinese law to throw the onus of proving the defendants' innocence on the shoulders of the defense. The defense counsel, following the tradition of English law, reminded his learned colleague that "every one is deemed innocent until he is proved guilty." Ibid., pp. 2-7.

32.   Y. C. Wang, in his "The *Su Pao* Case," *Monumenta Serica* 24:128 (1965), praised Yuan Shu-hsun for his "outstanding ability" in connection with this case. Wang obviously followed the evaluations of Yuan made by

Yuan's colleagues and superiors. Cf. *HHKM*, I, 458. For the circumstances in which Yuan made the assurance, see Wei Kuang-t'ao's telegram
to Tuan Fang, dated July 8, 1903 (ibid., pp. 419-420). Yuan seemed to
have fallen into the trap and given the assurance without specific instructions from his superiors. The case could not have grown out of such
proportion, had Yuan not ignorantly given an assurance which he had no
intention or ability to honor. Among the officials, Chang Chih-tung
seemed to be the only one who could see the legal problems involved in
the case, and knew that the treaties had not provided the Shanghai
Municipal Council with *locus standi* in jurisdiction over the Chinese. See
his telegram to Tuan Fang on July 21 (ibid., pp. 427-428, 432).

33.   Cf. *KKWSN*, X, 584; *HHKM*, III, 12.

34.   North China Daily News, *The Shanghai Sedition Trial*, p. 27.

35.   *KKWSN*, X, 584-587. The pamphlet was first published by the Ta T'ung
      Book Co. in Shanghai with the financial assistance of some revolutionaries.
      By far the largest edition was the one printed in San Francisco in 1903
      (11,000 copies). Cf. also Feng Tzu-yu, *Ko-ming i-shih*, II, 52-57; III, 184;
      his *Chung-hua min-kuo . . .* , III, 22; and Ch'en Hsü-lu, p. 33.

36.   A. M. Kotenev, in his *Shanghai: Its Municipality and the Chinese*
      (Shanghai, North China Daily News and Herald, 1927), p. 82, says that
      "the history of the modern [Chinese] press is closely bound up with the
      extraterritorial privileges enjoyed by foreigners in China." Yao Kung-ho
      also attributed the prosperity of the newspapers in Shanghai to foreign
      protection. See his *Shang-hai hsien-hua* (Anecdotal history of Shanghai;
      Shanghai, 1925), II, 110.

37.   Feng Tzu-yu, *Chung-hua min-kuo . . .* , I, 140.

38.   Ko Kung-chen, p. 157. Hu Tao-ching, "Shang-hai ti jih pao" (Dailies in
      Shanghai), *STCK* 2:261-262 (1934).

39.   Hu Tao-ching, "Shang-hai hsin-wen shih-yeh chih shih ti fa-chan"
      (Historical development of the press in Shanghai), *STCK* 2:976 (1934).

40.   Feng Tzu-yu, *Chung-hua min-kuo . . .* , I, 129; his *Ko-ming i-shih*, I,
      135-136; II, 85-86. Feng said that the paper got into trouble because
      it had criticized the Manchu government for its failure on the diplomatic
      front. According to *Shih pao* in Shanghai (March 28, 1905), the critical

letter the paper had carried on March 23 led to its demise. See Hu Tao-ching, "Shang-hai ti jih-pao," *STCK* 2:262. Also *HHKM,* II, 383-384; *NCH* (Apr. 7, 1905), pp. 52-53.

41. Feng Tzu-yu, *Ko-ming i-shih,* II, 92-93; III, 316-321. *NCH* (Aug. 7, 14, 21, 28 and Sept. 11, 1903), pp. 342-343, 406-409, 441, 521-522, 533, 632. See Chang Yün-chia, *Yü Yu-jen chuan* (Life of Yü Yu-jen; Taipei, 1958), pp. 40-42, for Yü's escape to Shanghai, when a collection of his allegedly "seditious" poems got him into trouble in his home province. He founded *Shen-chou jih-pao* (*National Herald*) in Shanghai in April 1907. For a seditious libel suit against it after Yü had left, see *NCH* (July 24 and 31, 1909), pp. 221-230, 289. Yü was later to become the president of the Control Yuan in the KMT regime.

42. Feng Tzu-yu, *Ko-ming i-shih,* II, 93-94; Chang Yun-chia, pp. 57-58. For a more detailed account of the case, see *NCH* (Nov. 27, Dec. 4, 11, 18, 24, 31, 1909), pp. 476, 498, 537, 622-623, 661, 702-703, 714, 737-738, 775, 793, 803-804); also *NCH* (Jan. 7, 14, 28, 1910), pp. 26, 85, 188, 194-195. Foreign interference was in fact quite common in these years. For other papers published elsewhere that were closed at the request of foreign authorities, see Ko Kung-chen, pp. 174-175; *NCH* (May 27, 1910), pp. 490-491.

43. Feng Tzu-yu, *Ko-ming i-shih,* II, 94; III, 346-350; Chang Yun-chia, pp. 60-61.

44. *Ch'ing-i pao,* no. 43:10b (1st day of the 4th moon, 1900).

45. *HHKM,* II, 187. *Han-chih* (The Chinese flag) also claimed that the two cases led to the promulgation of the Regulations Governing Newspapers in the same year. I doubt this claim because of the time element. Chinese scholars, except perhaps Feng Tzu-yu (see his *Ko-ming i-shih,* III, 108-109), usually attributed *Ching-hua jih-pao* (Peking dialect daily) to P'eng I-chung, and *Chung-hua pao* to Hang Hsin-chai. Cf., for instance, Ts'eng Hsü-pai, *Chung-kuo hsin-wen shih* (History of Chinese journalism; Taipei, 1966), I, 265; Ling-hsiao-i-shih, "Sui-pi" (Random notes), in *KWCP,* vol. 8, no. 47 (1931), quoting P'eng's autobiography. *Ching-hua jih-pao* itself, however, gives Hang as its proprietor. There are also different versions about the cause for the suspension of the two papers. Ko Kung-chen, p. 174, says that *"Chung-hua hsin pao"* (should be *Chung-hua pao*) was suppressed and its editors, Hang and P'eng, were deported to their native towns because it had reported the plunder by a grand

councillor's guards. *Min-hsü pao* (Sept. 13, 1909) reported that *Ching hua pao* was closed because it had offended the authorities. A contemporary newspaper in Taiwan said that the cases were connected with the arrest of a Taiwanese, who was mistaken for Dr. Sun Yat-sen, on the premises of *Ching-hua jih-pao.* Quoted in Ts'eng Hsü-pai, p. 302; or Chu Ch'uan-yu, *Pao-jen, pao-shih, pao-hsueh* (Journalist, history of journalism, and journalism; Taipei, 1966), pp. 123-127. *Ching-hua jih-pao* reported briefly in its issue of September 1906 (no. 727, p. 6), that officials had been to its premises on the evening of September 2 to arrest "Dr. Sun Yat-sen," and that many rumors arose as a result. Although the paper promised a more detailed account of this incident, I could not find any in the following issues. Its no. 739 is the last issue I have read.

46. Feng Tzu-yu, *Chung-kuo ko-ming . . . ,* p. 164.

47. *HHKM,* V, 3; Yang Yü-ju, p. 19.

48. *Hsin-hai ko-ming hui-i lu* (Recollections of the 1911 Revolution; Peking, 1962), II, 49.

49. Feng Tzu-yu, *Chung-kuo ko-ming . . . ,* pp. 227-228.

50. Ko Kung-chen, p. 174.

51. Feng Tzu-yu, *Ko-ming i-shih,* V, 45-46.

52. *Hsin-hai ko-ming hui-i lu,* I, 218.

53. Ts'ao Ya-po, *Wu-ch'ang ko-ming chen-shih* (The true history of the 1911 Revolution; Shanghai, 1928), p. iv. *Hsin-hai ko-ming hui-i lu,* II, 75-78; *HHKM,* I, 553. While a student in Japan, Ch'en was an editor of the *Min pao* and author of several pamphlets. In *Shih-tzu hou* (The roar of a lion), serialized in *Min pao,* he satirically alluded to the *Su pao* case.

54. Feng Tzu-yu, *Ko-ming i-shih,* V, 47.

55. Ibid., V, 46-47. *Hsin-hai ko-ming hui-i lu,* IV, 188-191.

56. Cf. Ko Kung-chen, p. 174. For the cases involving *Hu-pei jih-pao* in Hankow, see also *NCH* (Feb. 13, 1909), p. 383; for *Kuo pao* and *Chung-yang ta-t'ung pao* in Peking, see *NCH* (Sept. 25 and Oct. 2, 1909),

pp. 722, 752; for *Kung-yen pao* in Peking, see *NCH* (Aug. 28, 1909 and
May 6, 1910), p. 335; for *Pei-fang pao* in Tientsin, see *NCH* (May 20,
1910), pp. 454, 455; for *Shen-ching pai-hua pao* in Peking, see *NCH*
(Dec. 18, 1909); for *Yen pao* in Peking, see *NCH* (Dec. 31, 1909),
p. 797.

57. *NCH* (Aug. 14, 21, and 28, 1909).

58. Roswell S. Britton, *The Chinese Periodical Press, 1800-1912* (Shanghai,
     Kelly & Walsh, 1933), p. 4.

59. *Ch'ing-i pao* 43:12b (1st day of the 4th moon, 1900).

60. *Hsin-min ts'ung-pao* 32:65 (25th day of the 5th moon, 1903). In 1722,
     London Journal entered the service of the English government, which
     had concluded that the simplest way to deal with the paper was to buy
     it off. Yet it was already apparent early in the eighteenth century that a
     newspaper written, edited, and published by government appointees
     could not compete for public favor with the privately edited and financed
     newspapers. See Frederick Seaton Siebert, *Freedom of the Press in
     England, 1476-1776* (Urbana, University of Illinois Press, 1952), pp.
     339-340, 328.

61. *HHKM*, I, 444. The telegram was dated July 22, 1903.

62. English translation of Viceroy Chang Jen-chün's memorial in *NCH*
     (Mar. 18, 1910), pp. 604-605. Ts'ai found in April 1908 that "the
     newspapers of Shanghai bring destruction to the government." To
     remedy this situation, "he proposed *tout court* to buy up the Shanghai
     vernacular press." See ibid. (p. 591); also ibid. (Jan. 7, 14 and Feb. 25,
     1910), pp. 27, 84, 435. Hu Tao-ching, "Shang-hai ti jih-pao," *STCK*
     2:257; Yao Kung-ho, II, 111. Subsidization of newspapers was most
     common in England under the long administration of Robert Walpole.
     Cf. Siebert, p. 328.

63. Ko Kung-chen, p. 173; Yao Kung-ho, II, 119-120.

64. Speaking of the papers the government did not like, Chang admitted
     that "it is hardly possible that they could all be bought up and pro-
     hibited from speaking." He recommended that all these officially-
     managed papers "shall without exception revert to the commercial

management and the subsidies issued shall be returned." *NCH* (Mar. 18, 1910), p. 604.

65.   Britton, pp. 3-4.

66.   Yang Yü-ju, p. 10.

67.   *HHKM*, II, 251-252.

68.   A list is quoted in Ko Kung-chen, p. 171. A postal ban was imposed on three papers in Tientsin in 1909; see *NCH* (Jan. 9, 1909), p. 81. In 1910, Viceroy Yuan Shu-hsun forbade the entry of all Chinese newspapers from Hong Kong into Canton on account of their unfavorable comments on the official administration; see *NCH* (Apr. 8, 1910), p. 88.

69.   *Ch'in-ting hsueh-t'ang chang-ch'eng* (Rules for the schools by imperial orders; Shanghai, 1904), 3:16ab, 15b, 18 ("Restrictions for Schools," nos. 9, 8, 12). Cf. also Ko Kung-chen, pp. 169-171. For enforcement of these regulations in Nanking, see *Kuo-min jih-jih pao* (Aug. 9, 1903), p. 40.

70.   Upon the Superintendent's order, students of Kiangsi Academy burned Liang Ch'i-ch'ao's *Yin-ping shih wen-chi* (Collected essays of Liang Ch'i-ch'ao), *Su pao*, and *Hsin-min ts'ung-pao*. See ibid., p. 37.

71.   For instance, Nanyang Academy in Shanghai in 1902. For other cases, see *Su pao* (Apr. 30 and May 8, 1903), pp. 364-365, 416); *Kuo-min jih-jih pao* (Aug. 20 and 22, 1903), pp. 141, 160-161.

72.   Kao I-han remembers that his teacher's description of *Min pao* as an object of fear aroused instead his curiosity. He tried hard to obtain a copy of it as soon as he arrived at a new school. *Hsin-hai ko-ming hui-i lu*, IV, 434.

73.   Cf. *Kuo-min jih-jih pao* (Aug. 15, 18, and 19, 1903), pp. 89-90, 118, 129.

74.   The intendant of Anking, Anhwei, for instance, required a written statement from booksellers promising not to sell progressive books and magazines. Those who had sold or read such publications were frightened. See ibid. (Aug. 9, 1903), pp. 39-40.

75. Subscribers to the reading club in Wuhu, Anhwei, for instance, paid 20 cents a month. Those who could not afford the fee might be exempted. Ibid. (Sept. 23, 1903), p. 190. Government officials were interested in controlling these reading clubs. A viceroy made a large contribution to one of them in order to influence its acquisition policy. Ibid. (Sept. 21, 1903), pp. 169-170.

76. Cf. *Hsin-hai ko-ming hui-i lu,* II, 76; IV, 434. In 1907, nine members of the Society for Daily Improvement were arrested and the society was banned by the authorities. Yang Yü-ju, p. 12.

77. Howard W. Winger, "Regulations Relating to the Book Trade in London, from 1357 to 1586," Ph.D. dissertation (Graduate School for Library Science, University of Illinois, 1953), p. 244.

III. The Growing Pains of the New Republic, 1912-1927

1. Feng Ai-ch'ün, *Chung-kuo hsin-wen shih* (History of Chinese journalism; Taipei, 1967), p. 227. Sa K'ung-liao, *K'o-hsueh ti hsin-wen kai-lun* (A systematic survey of journalism; Hong Kong, 1946), p. 34. For a good discussion of the revolution, see Mary C. Wright, ed., *China in Revolution: The First Phase, 1900-1913* (New Haven, Yale University Press, 1968), pp. 1-63.

2. Feng Ai-ch'ün, pp. 227-238. *Tsui-chin chih wu-shih chi (The Past Fifty Years, in Commemoration of the Shun Pao's Golden Jubilee;* Shanghai, 1923), III, 24.

3. Feng Ai-ch'ün, p. 244.

4. On Oct. 9, 1912, Peking police questioned officers of fourteen papers for having published a news item that displeased Yuan. One editor was jailed for refusing to reveal the source of his information. Hu Tao-ching, "Shang-hai hsin-wen . . ." *STCK* 2:986. Cf. Ko Kung-chen, pp. 184-185; Feng Ai-ch'ün, p. 245, for more anti-Yuan papers that were suppressed.

5. For this and other cases see Wang Wen-pin, ed., *Pao-jen chih lu* (The road of the journalists; Shanghai, 1938), pp. 2-3. *Ta-han pao* in Hankow was closed in 1913 by Yuan's lackey and its editor imprisoned until after Yuan's death. Two KMT papers in Changsha were closed in 1913. See Feng Ai-ch'ün, pp. 237-238. Liu Kai, "Hsin-wen chi-che yü tao-te" (Journalists and integrity), *Chia ying (The Tiger),* 1.2:13-14 (June 10, 1914)

6. *Hsin-wen pao* (Shanghai, Aug. 5, 1913), quoted in Hu Tao-ching, "Shang-hai hsin-wen . . . ," *STCK* 2:987. For the proclamation of Chinese police in Shanghai forbidding people to read or sell *Min-ch'üan pao, Min-li pao,* and *Min-ch'iang pao,* all of which were KMT papers in the settlements, see Ko Kung-chen, p. 188.

7. Feng Ai-ch'ün, p. 236. *Chen-tan min pao* was founded after *Min-hsin pao* was suppressed by Li Yuan-hung in 1912 for a personal attack on him.

8. Ko Kung-chen, p. 185.

9. Chu Ch'uan-yü, *Pao-jen . . . ,* p. 34. Liang's article in *Ta Chung-hua (The Great Chung Hwa Magazine),* 1.8:1-18 (Aug. 20, 1915).

10. Liu Ch'eng-yü, "K'uei-ping chih chien T'ai-yen hsien-sheng chi-shih," (Mr. Chang Ping-lin in 1913-1916), *Min-chu cheng-chih* (Democracy), no. 4:98-99 (April 1945).

11. For instance, *Shen-chou jih-pao* in Shanghai. See Chin Hsiung-pai, *Min-kuo cheng-hai sou pi* (Anecdotes of government officials in republican China; Hong Kong, 1964), p. 22. *Kuo-min hsin pao* in Hankow, which was eventually closed by the Revolutionary Army in 1927 (Feng Ai-ch'ün, p. 237). K'uang Hsiao-an reported that almost all journalists in Canton were bought over by Yuan. See his "Wo chih hsin-wen chi-che t'an" (My experience as a journalist), *KWCP* 2.23:18-22 (June 21, 1925).

12. Chang Tsung-ch'ang sent troops to *Chien pao* in Mukden. The journalists fled to the roof, and promised not to publish any more anti-Yuan writings. Wang Hsin-wu, *Hsin-wen ch'üan li ssu-shih nien* (Forty years as a journalist; Taipei, 1957), p. 97.

13. After Yuan became the emperor on Dec. 23, 1915, he ordered all papers to use his new reign title as of Jan. 1, 1916. All papers published in areas under his control complied, but those in the foreign settlements in Shanghai did not. Under the threat of a postal ban, they later yielded by inserting the new reign title in very small type. Hu Tao-ching, "Shang-hai hsin-wen . . . ," *STCK* 2:990; Ko Kung-chen, p. 186; Chin Hsiung-pai, p. 38.

14. Chin Hsiung-pai, p. 41. Li Ch'eng-i, *San-shih nien lai chia kuo* (My country

in the past thirty years; Hong Kong, 1961), p. 134. The paper began
publication on Sept. 10, 1915, and was bombed on Sept. 11 and Dec. 17.
For the first bombing, see *The New York Times* 2.14:6 (Sept. 12, 1915).

15. Ko Kung-chen, p. 186. In Peking, the Japanese-owned *Shun-t'ien shih pao*
     printed a special pro-Yuan edition only for Yuan's perusal. See Hu Cheng-
     chih, "Chung-kuo wei-shen-mo mei-yu yü-lun" (Why there is no public
     opinion in China), *KWCP* 11.2:2 (Jan. 1, 1934).

16. Ko Kung-chen, p. 186.

17. Feng Ai-ch'ün, p. 245.

18. "Pen chih hsuan-yen" (A declaration by this magazine), *Hsin ch'ing-nien*
     7.1:1-4 (Dec. 1, 1919).

19. Chang A, p. 144. Wang Che-fu, *Chung-kuo hsin wen-hsueh yun-tung shih*
     (A history of the new literary movement in China; Hong Kong, 1965),
     pp. 54, 59.

20. For a Chinese translation of the message and people's reaction to it, see
     Hsin ch'ing-nien 7.6:1-29 (May 1920).

21. Chang A, pp. 46-47.

22. "Shen-mo hua" (What kind of language is this), *Hsin ch'ing-nien* 6.4:446
     (Apr. 15, 1919).

23. *Wu-ssu ai-kuo yün-tung tzu-liao* (Source materials of the May Fourth
     Movement; Peking, 1959), pp. 170, 820. At that time, warlords every-
     where were very hostile to students and newspapers; cf. ibid., pp. 171-
     173.

24. Martial law was employed to suppress *I-shih pao*, because it had pub-
     lished a telegram by military personnel. Ibid., pp. 819-821. The paper
     was founded on Oct. 10, 1915 by Vincent Lebbe, a Belgian (later
     naturalized Chinese) Catholic bishop in Tientsin. In 1925, Peiyang
     warlords imprisoned its general manager for seven months and controlled
     the paper until 1928, when the Northern Expedition was successfully
     completed. Yuan Ch'ang-ch'ao, *Chung-kuo pao-yeh hsiao-shih* (History
     of Chinese journalism; Hong Kong, 1957), p. 89.

25. *Wu-ssu ai-kuo yun-tung tzu-liao,* pp. 158-159, 177-178. The Japanese Minister to China protested to the Chinese Ministry of Foreign Affairs that the two papers carried on May 2 an article by a member of the Committee on Foreign Affairs, "A Warning to the Citizens," which opposed handing over Tsingtao to Japan, and that *Kuo-min kung pao* published also on May 19 an announcement by students saying: "It has been a long time that Japan has brought calamity to China."

26. For the above cases, see ibid., pp. 819-820, 822, 849.

27. All copies of *HTPL*'s no. 15 were detained at the post office in Peking, and copies of its no. 108 at the post office in Nanking. See the announcements in *HTPL* 1.16:2 (Mar. 28, 1925); also in vol. 5, no. 111 (Jan. 22, 1927), inside front cover.

28. The detained issue was no. 79/80, copies of which were later mailed again with its no. 81/82. See its "Important Announcement," no. 81/82:2 (July 25, 1926); no. 83:2 (Aug. 1, 1926).

29. Lu Hsün, "K'o ssu tsa kan" (On the detention of *Yü ssu*), *Yü ssu* (Brief discourses), no. 154:266-272 (Oct. 22, 1927).

30. Chang A, pp. 7-16.

31. The issue was published on Jan. 15, 1927. On p. 103, at the beginning of the blanks, there is a notation: "This article is deleted." On p. 120, there is another large blank space with a notation: "An announcement of this magazine is deleted." See the inside front cover of vol. 5, no. 111 for the editor's explanation.

32. Hu Shih, "Yen-lun tzu-yu" (Freedom of speech), *Pao hsueh* (Journalism), 4:2-3 (March 1953). Chang A, p. 48.

33. "Shih-shih tuan-p'ing" (Brief comments on current affairs), *HTPL* 1.16:2.

34. Hu Cheng-chih, "Chung-kuo wei-shen-mo mei-yu yü lun," *KWCP* 11.2:3.

35. The issues involved were vol. 1, nos. 15, 16, and 17. No. 15, which was seized by the police, was later released as the editor announced in

HTPL 1.19:2 (Apr. 18, 1925). See also the announcement in ibid. 1.18:2 (Apr. 11, 1925).

36. "T'ung-chi Wu Chih-hui wen-ti ko wen-chien" (Regarding the order for the arrest of Wu Chih-hui), *Ch'en pao fu-chien* (Literary supplement to *Ch'en pao*), no. 155 (July 6, 1924).

37. Chang A, pp. 50-54. Hu Shih, "Chi Chang Kuo-kan ti i-feng hsin" (A letter to Chang Kuo-kan), *Ch'en pao fu-chien*, no. 155:2. The two books referred to were *Ai-mei ti hsi-chü* and *Ai ti ch'eng nien.*

38. Li Ch'un-t'ao, "Shang-hai hui-shen kung-t'ang ti 'fen-shu cheng-ts'e'" (Shanghai Mixed Court's policy on book-burning), *Ch'en pao fu-chien,* no. 43:3 (Feb. 27, 1925).

39. Ibid.

40. Ibid., p. 4. Chang A, p. 48. *Mei-chou p'ing-lun* was suppressed because of an article commenting on the desirability of having China's judicial and educational systems free of politics.

41. Li Ch'un-t'ao, *Ch'en pao fu-chien,* no. 43:3.

42. Both were published in 1919 in Shanghai. *Chang Tsung-hsiang* was first advertised in *Min-kuo jih-pao* in Shanghai on May 7-11 as a forthcoming book. On June 22, there was an advertisement of its sixth edition.

43. Hu Shih, "Chi Chang Kuo-kan . . . ," *Ch'en pao fu-chien,* no. 155:2.

44. The political situation in China was in great confusion during this period. After the death of Yuan Shih-k'ai, there was no longer a strong man around whom China might be united. The central government controlled no more territory than Peking and its surrounding areas, though internationally it was recognized as representing China. The rest of China was divided among the warlords—the local leaders with independent armies of their own, usually military governors, who did not always take orders from the Peking government. From 1916 to 1927, there were dozens of warlords, each fighting the other for more land or money as the feudal lords in Europe had done. Some of them were later eliminated and some joined the KMT government in Nanking.

45. During Chang Hsün's twelve-day occupation of Peking in July 1917,

14 papers were closed. Tuan Ch'i-jui closed 8 Peking papers which displeased him on March 4, 1918, and 6 in September 1918, including
Ch'en-chung pao which revealed a secret loan he had arranged. Two
months later, the paper appeared under a new title, *Ch'en pao,* but it
was closed in 1919 because of its attack on Tuan's clique. Feng Ai-ch'ün,
pp. 254, 256.

46. "Shih-shih tuan-p'ing," *HTPL* 4.80:21 (Jan. 19, 1926). Han Lu, "Hsien-
hua" (Random talks), *HTPL* 4.89:208-209 (Aug. 21, 1926).

47. Wang Hsin-wu, pp. 292-293; Kung Te-pai, *Kung Te-pai hui-i lu* (Kung
Te-pai's memoir; Hong Kong, 1963-1964), I, 93.

48. Newspapers received "gratuities" from Ts'ao K'un, who bribed all
parliamentarians to have himself elected as the president in 1923. In the
summer of 1925, 300 newspapermen in Peking received gratuities varying
from 300 yuan to 600 yuan. Some newspapermen sat in the Ministry of
Finance and would not leave until their demands for money were
satisfied. Wang Hsin-wu, pp. 164-165, 295-298. Po T'ao, "Pei-ching
chih hsin-wen chieh" (Journalists in Peking), *KWCP* 2.3:10 (Apr. 12,
1925).

49. Yü Jen, "Pei-ching pao-chieh tsui-o chi" (The sins of the journalists in
Peking), *Ku-chün* (The lonely soldier), 1.6:2-4 (March 1923). Wang
Hsin-wu, pp. 294-295. Pai T'ao, *KWCP* 2.3:9-10. Ch'eng Ch'i-heng and
Jung Yu-ming, eds., *Chi-che ching-yen t'an* (Journalists' personal
experiences; Kweilin, 1943), pp. 145-146.

50. "Cheng-chü ta-pien chung chih Shang-hai yü-lun" (Public opinion in
Shanghai during the political crisis), *KWCP* 1.15:7 (Nov. 9, 1924).
According to "Shih-shih tuan-p'ing," *HTPL* 4.92:261 (Sept. 11, 1926),
journalists dared not express their opinions. To please the powerful,
some even published news stories contrary to the facts, and often even
contradictory to what they said elsewhere on the same page.

51. Lin Yutang, *The History of the Press and Public Opinion in China*
(Chicago, University of Chicago Press, 1936), p. 169.

52. Kung Te-pai, I, 114. He was arrested on February 21, 1926, and was
released one week later. For his other arrests and suspensions of his
papers, see ibid., I, 97-98, 102, 111-112, 115, 127.

53.   Ibid., p. 89.

54.   Ibid., pp. 90, 125-126. Li Ch'eng-i, p. 137. "Shao P'iao-p'ing shih-lueh"
      (Life of Shao P'iao-p'ing), *PHCK* 1.1:146 (Oct. 10, 1934).

55.   Ch'eng She-wo, "Chi-che ssu-shih nien" (Forty years as a journalist),
      Pao hsueh 5:87-88 (October 1953).

56.   "Pei-ching chih-an" (Peace and order in Peking), *KWCP* 3.18:25 (May 9,
      1926). Yuan Sheng, "Che suan shen-mo shih-chieh" (What kind of world
      is this), *Ku-chün chou-pao* (The lonely soldier weekly), no. 85:5 (Aug.
      15, 1926).

57.   Li Chien-hua, "Ai P'iao-p'ing chih ssu" (On the death of Shao P'iao-p'ing),
      Hung-shui (The flood), 2:376-377 (1926).

58.   Hu Cheng-chih, "Ai P'iao-p'ing" (In memory of Shao P'iao-p'ing),
      KWCP 3.17:4-5 (May 9, 1926).

59.   Kung Te-pai, I, 90-91.

60.   Li Ch'eng-i, pp. 135-136. "Hsin-wen chieh pei-nan che shih-lueh" (Lives
      of martyred journalists), *PHCK* 1.2:162 (1935). Lin was arrested on
      August 6 at 2 A.M., and shot at 4:40 A.M. For an account of this case
      given by Lin's daughter, see Lin Wei-chün, "Lin Pai-shui hsien-sheng
      chuan" (Life of Mr. Lin Pai-shui), *Chuan-chi wen-hsueh* (Biographical
      literature), 14.5:44-46 (1969). Though Miss Lin defended her father as
      a very upright man who "did not want any government subsidy or
      [financial] assistance from his friends," she described their very luxurious
      life in Peking without explaining how her father had risen from poverty
      to such wealth.

61.   Hu Cheng-chih, "Wu-hu Lin Shao-ch'üan hsien-sheng chih ssu" (On the
      death of Lin Shao-ch'üan), *KWCP* 3.31:3 (Aug. 15, 1926). Hu and Lin
      founded *Hsin she-hui pao* in 1920. Soon afterwards, Hu went to Shang-
      hai to found the Kuo-wen News Agency. After *Hsin she-hui pao* was
      suppressed for having offended certain of the authorities, the title of the
      paper was changed to *She-hui jih-pao*. See also "Shih-shih tuan-p'ing,"
      HTPL 4.88:181 (Aug. 14, 1926), for a protest at Lin's execution.

62.   Ch'eng She-wo, *Pao hsueh* 5:89. The version given by Lin Yutang, pp.

170-171, was somewhat different from Ch'eng's own. The KMT was considered "Red" at that time.

63. Yu Jen, *Ku-chün* 1.6:1.

64. "Ko-ti hsin-wen shih-yeh chih yen-ko yü chin-k'uang" (The history of newspapers in various cities), *PHCK* 1.2:95-96 (1935).

65. "Hsin-wen chieh pei-nan che shih-lueh," *PHCK* 1.3:217-218 (1935).

66. *NCH* (Aug. 8, 1925), p. 121.

67. "Ko-ming jih-chih" (Diary of the Revolution), *Hsin ch'ing-nien,* no. 5:1 (July 25, 1926). *NCH* (July 18, 1925). See "Ko-ti hsin-wen . . . chin-k'uang," *PHCK* 1.2:111-112, 114 for other persecuted papers in Kiangsu and Chekiang.

68. Chang B, pp. 441-442.

69. Chang A, pp. 37-43. *Hsin wan-pao* (*New Evening Post,* Hong Kong, May 7, 1968), p. 5.

70. Chang B, p. 431. See also ibid., pp. 425-444 for other persecution cases in Hunan.

71. Ibid., pp. 435-436. There were many such cases. In April 1924, for instance, *Feng-t'ien tung pao* in Mukden was suspended one week for its anti-Japanese attitude, although the Japanese pressured the Chinese authorities for its permanent suspension. Ch'en Tu-hsiu, "Huan-ying *Feng-t'ien tung pao* fu-k'an" (On the reissuance of *Feng-t'ien tung pao*), *Hsiang-tao* (*Guide Weekly*), no. 64:513 (May 7, 1924).

72. Five journalists were killed by the warlords in the South (Feng Ai-ch'ün, p. 253). For the persecution of journalists in Ch'iung-yai, Kwangtung, see Chih Chien, "Ch'iung-yai i-p'ieh" (A bird's-eye view of Ch'iung-yai), *KWCP* 3.2:11 (Apr. 4, 1926); in Amoy, see "Ko-ti hsin-wen . . . chin-k'uang," *PHCK* 1.2:99-103.

73. K'uang Hsiao-an, *KWCP* 2.23:20-21.

74. Meng Tieh, "San-min-chu-i chih pu-t'ung wu-ch'ih" (The irrationality

and shamelessness of the Three People's Principles), *Ping-yin* (The year of 1926), no. 2:1-4 (1926). Also his "P'ing-min tzu-chiu chih chen ching-shen" (The true spirit of the people's self-salvation), ibid., pp. 5-11.

75. Pai Yü, "Liu-pieh yu-ch'iang ti t'ung-chih" (A farewell to armed comrades), *Ko-ming chün* (The revolutionary army), no. 9:19 (Dec. 25, 1925).

76. Cf. T'ao Meng-ho, "Yen-lun tzu-yu" (Freedom of speech), *HTPL* 1.19:5-7 (Apr. 18, 1925).

77. Kao I-han, "Tu Mi-erh ti tzu-yu lun" (After reading Mill's "On Liberty"), *Hsin ch'ing-nien* 4.3:215-216 (Mar. 15, 1918).

78. Kao I-han, "Tui-yü chih-an ching-ch'a t'iao-li ti p'i-p'ing" (A critique of the police regulations), *Hsin ch'ing-nien* 7.2:15-23 (Jan. 1, 1920).

79. Ch'en Tu-hsiu, "Yueh-fa ti tsui-o" (The defects of the constitution), *Hsin ch'ing-nien* 7.2:157-158; and his "Fa-lü yü yen-len tzu-yu" (The law and the freedom of speech and the press), ibid. 7.1:114-115 (Dec. 1, 1919).

80. Wang Shih-chieh, "Che chi-chung fa-ling huan pu fei-ch'u ma" (Why not rescind these laws and regulations), *HTPL* 3.61:4-6 (Feb. 6, 1926); his "Ching-chih yü fa-chih" (The rule by the police and the rule by the law), *HTPL* 1.21:8-10 (May 2, 1925). "Shih-shih tuan-p'ing," *HTPL* 1.6:3 (Jan. 17, 1925); ibid. 1.16:2-3 (Mar. 28, 1925).

81. Wang Shih-chieh, "Che chi-chung fa-ling . . . ," *HTPL* 3.61:6. "Shih-shih tuan-p'ing," *HTPL* 3.55:2 (Dec. 26, 1925). Ch'eng Fu, "Chang Shih-chao chih ch'ü liu" (On Chang Shih-chao), *KWCP* 2.20:3-4 (May 31, 1925); also his "Hsueh-che p'o-ch'an" (The disappearance of academic integrity), *KWCP* 2.24:3-4 (June 28, 1925).

82. Kao I-han, "Ko-ming chün yu yen-lun tzu-yu" (The revolutionary army and the freedom of speech and the press), *HTPL* 3.64:4-5 (Feb. 27, 1926).

83. Cf. also T'ien Sheng, "Chung-kuo chih hsin-wen hsueh" (Journalism in China), *KWCP* 2.6:13 (Feb. 22, 1925); Ko Kung-chen, p. 378.

84. Wei Ying, "Yen-lun chieh ti pu-p'ing ming" (All should have the same

freedom of speech), *Hsiang-tao,* no. 53/54:419-420 (Feb. 20, 1924).

85.   "Fan Kuo-min ko-ming che ti min-ch'üan hu-sheng" (The counter-revolutionaries' clamor for democracy), *Hsiang-tao,* no. 175:1806 (Oct. 12, 1926).

86.   During the warlord period, *Eastern Miscellany* at one time published two different editions of comments on current affairs: one intended for the North, and one for the South. Chang A, p. 86n.

87.   Kotenev, *Shanghai: Its Mixed Court . . . ,* p. 111.

88.   For instance, on May 20, 1912, Tai Chi-t'ao wrote an editorial in *Min-ch'üan pao* criticizing the Chinese Ministry of Finance for accepting loans from the Four Power Consortium. Tai denounced President Yuan, Prime Minister Hsiung Hsi-ling, and two other government officials as traitors and called for their execution. As a result, he was arrested on May 22 by the Shanghai Municipal Police and charged with unlawfully soliciting, encouraging, and persuading his readers to murder the four officials. He was found guilty by the Mixed Court on June 13 and fined. *NCH* (May 25 and June 15, 1912), pp. 567, 805. Hu Tao-ching, "Shanghai ti jih-pao," *STCK* 2:279. Tai was later to become the president of the Examination Yuan in the KMT regime.

89.   Kotenev, *Shanghai: Its Municipality . . . ,* pp. 82-83.

90.   Shanghai Municipal Council, *Report for the Year of 1919* (Shanghai, Kelly & Walsh, 1920), pp. 87a, 88a.

91.   Kotenev, *Shanghai: Its Municipality . . . ,* pp. 83-84. Under this ordinance, *Kuo-min jih-pao* was not permitted to publish in the French Concession in 1926. In December 1933, *Wen-hsueh* (Literature) was fined. See Hu Tao-ching, "Shang-hai hsin-wen . . . ," *STCK* 2:1004-05.

92.   *NCH* (May 17 and Aug. 2, 1919), p. 286.

93.   In favor, 269, including 138 Japanese in a block vote; opposed 159. *Tsui-chin chih wu-shih chi,* III, 3; Y. P. Wang, *The Rise of the Native Press in China* (Shanghai, 1924), p. 43.

94.   Shanghai Municipal Council, *Report for the Year of 1921* (Shanghai, Kelly & Walsh, 1922), pp. 58a, 61a.

95. "Chang Hu shih tui-yü wu-sa an chih t'an-hua" (Mr. Chang Hu's talk on the May Thirtieth Incident), *KWCP* 2.25:10 (July 5, 1925). Cf. also "P'ing-lun kuo-min yun-tung i-chü kung-p'ing hua" (A fair comment on the National Movement), *KWCP* 2.27:17 (July 19, 1925).

96. The police raided *La Jeunesse*'s printing plant and took away all manuscripts of its vol. 8, no. 6; see the editor's note in *Hsin ch'ing-nien* 4.1:2 (May 1, 1921). From vol. 9, no. 1, it moved to Canton and became even more radical. On April 7, 1926, Ch'uang-tsao she (The Creation Society) was raided and staff members were arrested because it was rumored that the KMT local headquarters was situated there. Ch'üan P'ing, "Ch'u-pan pu ti hsin yü pu-hsin erh shih" (Two fortunate and unfortunate incidents in the publishing department), *Hung-shui* 2.11/12:577-578 (1926).

97. Y. P. Wang, p. 37.

98. Kotenev, *Shanghai: Its Mixed Court . . .* , pp. 169, 175.

99. Chang Ching-lu, *Tsai ch'u-pan chieh erh-shih nien* (Twenty years in the publishing business; Hankow, 1938), pp. 107, 118-121.

100. Chang A, pp. 68-74 give a partial list of Communist books (171 books) in 1921-1927; pp. 86-102 give a list of 641 magazines (covering 1919-1927), of which 11 were CCP organs, 4 were publications of Communist cells.

101. Ibid., pp. 61-66. *Guide Weekly* began publication in Shanghai on Sept. 13, 1922. After the premises were raided by the police on Dec. 9, 1924, it moved to Hangchow. See the announcement in *Hsiang-tao*, no. 95:800 (Dec. 17, 1924). Judging from the address given in the magazine, it presumably then moved to Peking, Canton, Kaifeng, and Hankow.

102. Chü Yuan, "Chung-kuo jen ti yen-lun tzu-yu yü wai-kuo jen ti cheng-fu" (Freedom of speech and the press for the Chinese under a foreign government), *Hsiang-tao*, no. 61:490-491 (Apr. 16, 1924). *Tsui-chin chih wu-shih chi*, III, 3-4. Cf. also Kotenev, *Shanghai: Its Municipality . . .* , pp. 84-89. Chü Yuan was one of Ch'ü ch'iu-pai's many pen names.

103. Kotenev, *Shanghai: Its Municipality . . .* , pp. 191-192. Bertrand Russell's works in English were among those seized by the police. The Japanese translation of *Das Kapital*, however, was left intact, probably because

the foreign police could not read Japanese and thus did not know what it was. Li Ch'un-t'ao, *Ch'en pao fu-chien*, no. 43:4.

104. Kotenev, *Shanghai: Its Municipality* . . . , pp. 196–197.

105. Ibid., pp. 198–199. Hu Tao-ching, "Shang-hai hsin-wen . . . ," *STCK* 2:1008.

106. Ibid. Kotenev, *Shanghai: Its Municipality* . . . , pp. 199–202.

107. Ibid., pp. 202–203. Many arrests were made during these days. On June 17, for instance, a newspaper boy was arrested for selling *Kung-li jih-pao*. On June 28, the printer for *Jo-hsueh jih-pao* was arrested. Hu Tao-ching, "Shang-hai hsin-wen . . . ," *STCK* 2:1013.

108. Ibid. 2:1009, 1011, 1013. Hsiu Lu, "Shen-mo shih Ch'eng-yen" (What are these "Sincere words"), *Tung-fang tsa-chih* (*Eastern Miscellany*) special issue (July 1925). Hu Cheng-chih, "Ching-mu ti pei-ai" (The silent sadness), *KWCP* 2.21:1 (June 7, 1925).

109. Hu Tao-ching, "Shang-hai hsin-wen . . . ," *STCK* 2:1009. *NCH* (July 18 and Aug. 1, 1925), pp. 34, 97.

110. *NCH* (Sept. 19, 1925), p. 401; (Oct. 3, 1925), p. 29. *Shang-hai pao* was moved to the International Settlement from the French Concession after the French police forbade its publication.

111. *NCH* (Sept. 19, 1925), p. 401; (Oct. 17, 1925), p. 114. Chang A, pp. 230–236.

112. "Ch'u-pan chieh chih tzu-yu yun-tung" (The freedom movement of the publishing business), *KWCP* 2.13:1–2 (Apr. 12, 1925). *NCH* (Sept. 26, 1925), p. 446; (Oct. 3, 1925), p. 29.

113. *NCH* (Dec. 12, 1925).

114. Wu Ming, "Shang-hai yin-shua ch'u-pan chieh hou-huan wei i" (The endless troubles for the printing and publishing business in Shanghai), *Tung-fang tsa-chih* 31.9:12–15 (May 10, 1924).

115. "Shih-shih tuan-p'ing," *HTPL* 1.4:3 (Jan. 3, 1925).

116. *Times* (London, Aug. 14, 1925). Clubb, p. 129.

117. Ch'en Han-sheng, "Lin-shih pao fo-chiao" (Eleventh hour efforts), *HTPL* 3.53:17 (Dec. 12, 1925). Chang Ching-lu, *Tsai ch'u-pan chieh erh-shih nien*, p. 126.

IV. The Kuomintang Regime Before the War, 1927-1937 (1)

1. Cf. Chang B, pp. 8-17 for a list of 151 social science books published in 1929. Most of them were on Marxism, socialism, Soviet Russia, and dialectical materialism, though some Japanese writers were also included.

2. Wang Yao, *Chung-kuo hsin wen-hsueh shih-kao* (Draft history of modern Chinese literature; Shanghai, 1951), I, 144. Wang Che-fu, pp. 82, 410-412, 424.

3. Liang yu t'u-shu kung-ssu (Good Friend Book Company) and Shen-chou kuo kuang she in Shanghai were warned by hoodlums in 1933. *Lu Hsün ch'üan-chi* (Complete works of Lu Hsün), ed. Lu Hsün hsien-sheng chi-nien wei-yuan hui (Lu Hsün Memorial Committee; Shanghai, 1938), V, 456-460.

4. The Creation Society was closed down in 1929. Chang B, p. 52; Chang A, pp. 191, 134. Shen-chou kuo kuang she was sealed up in February 1934. *Hsin-sheng chou-k'an* (New life weekly), 1.3:45 (Feb. 24, 1934). Chao Nan-kung of T'ai Tung Book Co. was imprisoned three times for publishing leftist books. Chang A, p. 43.

5. Lu Hsün, *Lu Hsün ch'üan-chi*, IV, 271.

6. *Ch'ien-shao* (*The Outpost*), vol. 1, no. 1 (Apr. 25, 1931). The entire issue was devoted to the "Seven Martyrs." For more information, see Hsia Tsi-an, *Gate of Darkness* (Seattle, University of Washington Press, 1968), pp. 163-233; Ting Ching-t'ang and Ch'ü Kuang-hsi (comps.), *Tso-lien wu-lieh-shih yen-chiu tzu-liao pien-mu* (A catalog of research materials on the five martyrs of the League of Left-Wing Writers; Shanghai, 1962).

7. Chang B, p. 45. Shen Ts'ung-wen, "Ting Ling nü-shih pei-p'u" (The arrest of Miss Ting Ling), *TLPL*, no. 52/53: 12-13 (June 4, 1933). Due to the many conflicting rumors circulating at the time, it is difficult to

say exactly how long Ting Ling was imprisoned. "Wo ho kung-tang tou-cheng ti hui-i" (Memories of my struggles with the Communists), reprinted in Wang Chang-ling, *Chung-kung ti wen-i cheng-feng* (Chinese Communists' Setting-literature-in-order movement; Taipei, 1967), pp. 120-122, gives the following account: Ting Ling and her husband were arrested in April 1933 in Shanghai and sent to Nanking. Soon afterwards, they recanted. They were allowed to live in a hotel and then in a friend's house in Nanking, but were watched all the time by the police and were not allowed to go out. They were moved to Mokanshan, Hangchow in summer, "accompanied" by a couple. That winter, when they returned to Nanking, they regained freedom.

8. Wang Yao, I, 144. According to Chang B, pp. 44, 55, he was shot to death when resisting arrest.

9. Chang B, p. 55.

10. Edgar Snow, "The Ways of the Chinese Censor," *Current History* 42:384 (1935).

11. *Mao Tun wen-chi* (Works of Mao Tun; Peking, 1958), I, 431-432.

12. Wang I-an, "Chi A Ying" (On A Ying), *Tsa-chih* 10.6:90 (March 1943).

13. Hsü Ching-sung's postscript in *Lu Hsün ch'üan-chi pu-i* (A supplement to the complete works of Lu Hsün), ed. T'ang T'ao (Shanghai, 1948), p. 380.

14. In 1930, 1931, and 1934. Chang B, p. 55.

15. *Lu Hsün ch'üan-chi*, IV, 197. Cf. ibid., V, 446.

16. Ibid., IV, 424. Hsü Ching-sung, "Yen-chiu Lu Hsün wen-hsueh i-ch'an ti chi-ko wen-t'i" (The problems in the study of the literary heritage left us by Lu Hsün), *Chou-pao* (Weekly), no. 4:13 (Sept. 29, 1945). For some of the pseudonyms Lu Hsün used, see *Lu Hsün ch'üan-chi*, IV, 443; V, 236, 479.

17. The five "bandit suppression" campaigns were launched in January, May, and July, 1931, and April and October, 1933. The sixth campaign, scheduled to be launched in December 1936, did not take place because of the Sian Incident.

18. The preface in *Yin Fu hsuan-chi* (Selected works of Yin Fu; Peking, 1951), pp. 8, 11. *The Outpost,* which commemorated the execution of seven members of the Left-Wing Writers League in 1931, was printed at a legitimate printing shop by a few comrades at dead of night with all window shutters down. To avoid arousing the suspicion of the police, the printer did not put the title on the cover; this job was done by hand by the editors after they had carried the copies home.

19. The following is a partial list of some fake titles which I have come across:
      Hung-ch'i (Red flag): nos. 6, 7, 8, 9, and 11 (Dec. 25, 1928, Jan. 2, 9, 16, 30, 1929), *K'uai-lo chih shen* (The goddess of happiness); no. 10 (Jan. 23, 1929), *I ku ch'ing-ch'eng* (The ravishing beauty); no. 12 (Feb. 7, 1929), *Hung Ni ku-niang yen-shih* (The love history of Miss Hung Ni); nos. 13, 14, 15, and 16 (Feb. 14 and 21, Mar. 8 and 16, 1929), *Ching-chi t'ung-chi* (Statistics of finance, compiled by the Shanghai Bank Weekly; no. 13 dated Feb. 19, no. 14 dated Feb. 26); no. 17/18 (Apr. 13, 1929), *Ch'u-pan chieh* (The publishing world), no. 78, published by the Commercial Press, Shanghai, August 1928; no. 19 (May 1, 1929), *Wu-i t'e-k'an* (May 1 special issue); no. 22 (May 21, 1929), *Ch'u-pan chieh,* no. 22 (Shanghai, Commercial Press, May 21, 1929).
      Hung-ch'i chou-pao (Red flag weekly): nos. 12, 16 and 21 (July 1, Sept. 10, and Oct. 25, 1931), *Shih-yeh chou-pao* (Industrial weekly), published by the Shanghai Industrial Weekly, issue numbers and dates of publication unchanged; nos. 49 and 51 (Sept. 1 and Nov. 1, 1932), *Ch'ao* (The tide); no. 50 (Sept. 10, 1932), *Hsin sheng-huo* (New life), by Yen Tun (Shanghai, Ta Chung shu-chü, 1932); no. 52 [?] (Nov. 10, 1932 [?]), *Hsin sheng-huo* (New life), ed. by I Min (Shanghai, Sheng-huo she, 1932).
      Lieh-ning ch'ing-nien (Leninist youth): vol. 2, no. 2 (Oct. 20, 1929), *Ch'ing-nien pan-yüeh-k'an* (Youth semi-monthly); vol. 2, no. 16 (June 30, 1930), *Ch'ing-nien hsün-k'an* (Youth), published once every ten days.
      Pu-erh-sai-wei-k'o (Bolshevik): vol. 3, no. 1 (Jan. 15, 1930), *Hsin shih-tai kuo-yü chiao-shou shu* (New times Chinese reader), vol. 1, Commercial Press; vol. 3, no. 2/3 and no. 4/5 (Mar. 15 and May 15, 1930) used the same title as no. 1, but changed the volume numbers to 2 and 4/5; vol. 3, no. 6 (June 15, 1930), *Chung-kuo wen-hua shih* (Cultural history of China), compiled by Ku K'ang-po (n.p., 1928).
      I am grateful to Mr. Patrick Tseng of the Library of Congress Orientalia Division for making this information available to me. For more examples of this kind, see Chang D, pp. 107, 139-141.

20. Chang B, pp. 18-21.

21. "Pen-k'an ch'i-shih" (An announcement), *Hung-ch'i*, no. 11:30 (Jan. 30, 1929).

22. Shih I, "Chi Wen-i hsin-wen" (On literary news), *Tu-shu yü ch'u-pan* (Reading and publishing), 2.1:23-25 (Jan. 15, 1947).

23. Ai Ssu-ch'i, "Wo tsen-yang hsieh-ch'eng *Che-hsueh chiang-hua* ti" (How I wrote the discourses on philosophy), *Hsin jen-shih*, no. 4:216-218 (Oct. 20, 1936). Ai's book was banned on Feb. 20, 1936 (Chang B, p. 249). Mu Hsin, ed., *Tsou T'ao-fen* (Hong Kong, 1959), p. 150, tells us that Tsou T'ao-fen used in his essay "Ch'ün" (The group) the word "group" to stand for the word "class."

24. Edited by Chung-kuo li-shih yen-chiu she (Chinese Historical Research Society), and published by Shen-chou kuo kuang she. The editor explained the incident in terms of the class struggle. This method had been used in other lands. In early seventeenth-century England, a popular method was to obtain a license for the book proper and then to insert the questionable matter in a dedication or introduction. This evasion was remedied in the Star Chamber Decree of 1637 (Siebert, p. 144).

25. Chiang Chao-chi, "I-chiu-san-ssu nien wo-kuo hsin-wen shih-yeh liao-k'an" (A bird's-eye view of Chinese journalism in 1934), *PHCK* 1.2:44 (January 1935). The methods used in censorship varied at different places. In Shanghai, news examiners were appointed at first by the Garrison Commander of Greater Shanghai. All proof sheets had to be passed by them before going to the press room. Sometimes changes were made after the stereotypes had been set, necessitating the use of a chisel and hammer to carve out the condemned news items and leaving a blank on the printed sheet, nicknamed the "skylight." See "The Futility of the Press Censorship," *People's Tribune*, n.s. 2:240 (1932). The News Censorship Bureau was established in the International Settlement in Shanghai in 1933. For news censorship in Peiping and Tientsin, see Sa K'ung-liao, "Yu Hua-pei hsin-wen chien-ch'a t'an-tao hsin-wen chien-ch'a wen-t'i" (On news censorship), *PHCK* 1.2:12. Cf. also Ch'ing Seng, "Pao hsieh lu" (Miscellaneous notes on newspapers), *PHYK* 1.4:102-106 (1929); Huang Liang-meng, "Hsin-wen nien-chi" (Chronicle of journalism), ibid., pp. 92-93.

26. The text is reprinted in "Hsin-wen shih-yeh chih fa-ling kuei-chang" (Laws and regulations concerning journalism), *PHCK* 1.1:169-171 (October 1934). See ibid., pp. 171-178 for other regulations governing newspapers. According to Article 9.5 of the Revised Regulations Governing the News Censorship Procedures in Nanking, newspapers were not allowed to leave any blanks to indicate passages or words which had been deleted by censors. See also Sa K'ung-liao, *PHCK* 1.2:12.

27. "She-lun," *Ta-kung pao* (*L'Impartial*) (May 22, 1931). Sa K'ung-liao, *PHCK* 1.2:12; Ma Hsing-yeh, "Yen-lun tzu-yu yü cheng-fu ti hsin-wen cheng-ts'e" (The freedom of speech and the government's press policy), 14.12:5 (Mar. 29, 1937).

28. Wang Wen-pin, p. 169.

29. "She-lun," *Ta-kung pao* (Apr. 25, 1930); Lo Ch'eng-lieh, *Hsin-min pao she-lun* (Editorials of *Hsin-min pao;* Nanking, 1936), I, 362, 364.

30. Ma Hsing-yeh, *KWCP* 14.12:4.

31. "She-lun," *Ta-kung pao* (Jan. 25, 1935; Aug. 3, 1931; May 29, 1933).

32. Ibid. (Oct. 30, 1934); Sa K'ung-liao, *PHCK* 1.2:12-13.

33. Sa K'ung-liao, *PHCK* 1.2:13-14.

34. Cf. Hu Shih, "Wo-men yao-ch'iu wai-chiao kung-k'ai" (We demand open-handed diplomacy), *Ta-kung pao* (Dec. 29, 1935); Lin Yutang, pp. 139ff, 176.

35. Wang Wen-pin, pp. 169-171. In Nanking, the news censorship was once extended to the long distance telephone. Correspondents of Shanghai newspapers were required to make telephone calls at the Nanking Telephone Administration in the presence of an official listener. This particular form of news censorship was soon removed because of various difficulties involved ("The Futility of the Press Censorship," *People's Tribune,* n.s. 2:240-241).

36. "She-lun," *Ta-kung pao* (May 27, 1930; May 28, 1931).

37. "The Law and the Freedom of the Press," *People's Tribune,* n.s. 2:277 (1932), calls the Emergency Law Governing Treason and Sedition

"certainly one of the most tyrannical ever devised." Text of this law is reprinted in *KWCP* 8.11:5-6 (Mar. 23, 1931); the regulations for its application in ibid., no. 13:6 (Apr. 6, 1931). Ch'en Tu-hsiu was arrested on Oct. 15, 1932 and prosecuted in 1933 under this law. The trial of Ch'en and nine others was the first public trial given to known Communists. Ch'en and three others were convicted, on Apr. 26, 1933, of betraying their country by their writings. The offensive passages, being banned, were not quoted even in court. See "She-lun," *Ta-kung pao* (Apr. 27, 1933); "Ch'en Tu-hsiu an k'ai-shen chi" (The trial of Ch'en Tu-hsiu), *KWCP* 10.17:1-18 (May 1, 1933).

38. *Nei-cheng nien-chien* (Yearbook of Chinese internal affairs) comp. Nei-cheng-pu nien-chien pien-chi wei-yuan hui (Yearbook of Chinese Internal Affairs Compilation Committee, Ministry of the Interior, Shanghai, 1936), II, 1065-66.

39. Hsiang Kung, "T'u-shu shen-ch'a pien-li chien-t'ao" (On the convenience offered by pre-publication censorship), *Jen yen* 1:434 (1934).

40. *Lu Hsün ch'üan-chi,* V, 237, 480.

41. Chang B, pp. 50-51.

42. Lin Yutang, pp. 163-164.

43. Chang B, p. 51; Hsü Ching-sung, *Chou-pao,* no. 4:13; Wang Yao, I, 284.

44. Cf. *Lu Hsün ch'üan-chi,* IV, 477, 497, 514; V, 290, 317, 333, 393, 429, 481. This edition was published by Lu Hsün ch'üan-chi ch'u-pan she (Complete Works of Lu Hsun Press).

45. Chang Ching-lu, *Tsai ch'u-pan chieh . . . ,* pp. 141-142.

46. "Wo-kuo ko-ti hsin-wen-chieh ta-shih jih-chih" (Important events in Chinese journalism), *PHCK* 1.1:157 (1934); 1.2:173 (1935).

47. "She-lun," *Ta-kung pao* (Apr. 24, 1930). In "Pien-chi hou-chi" (Editor's postscript), *TLPL,* no. 181:19 (Dec. 15, 1936), Hu Shih said that the Dec. 4, 1936 issue of *Ta-kung pao* was seized. In April 1936, *Ta-kung pao* began publishing a Shanghai edition, as a result of the postal ban imposed on the paper in the winter of 1935 (Yuan Ch'ang-ch'ao, p. 85).

48. Hu Shih, "Pien-chi hou-chi," *TLPL,* no. 86:19-20 (Jan. 21, 1934); no. 95: 20-21 (Apr. 8, 1934). The editors suspected that Fu Ssu-nien's article on Henry P'u Yi was responsible for the detention of its no. 91.

49. "Pien hou" (The editor's notes), *Tu-shu tsa-chih* (Readings), 3.5:6 (May 1, 1933). The editors at first intended to use "Chan-ch'ang" (The battle-field) for the title of the magazine but, fearing police interference, decided on this less suspicious title. See ibid. 1.9:9 (Dec. 10, 1931).

50. "Chien-ch'a hsin-wer. yu yen-ko ch'i-lai" (News censorship has become stringent again), *T'ai-p'ing-yang kung-pao* (The Pacific), 1.4:46 (Aug. 1929). The real title of the monthly was probably *T'ai-p'ing-yang ch'ih-se chiu-chi-hui kung-pao* (Pacific Red Relief Association bulletin), which was given inside the publication.

51. Huang Liang-meng, *PHYK* 1.4:89.

52. Tsou T'ao-fen, "Hsiao yen-lun" (Brief comments), *Sheng-hou* 7:142 (1932).

53. "I-chou chien-p'ing" (Brief comments on the events in the past week), *KWCP* 11.23:1-2 (June 11, 1934). Snow reported (*Current History* 42:381) that "during 1934, there were in North China 110 cases of suspension or total suppression of publications of various kinds, while the toll in Southern cities was also heavy."

54. "Wo-kuo ko-ti . . . ," *PHCK* 1.1:153; 1.2:173. For other such cases in Nanking, Peiping, Nantung, and Taiyuan, as well as cities under regional militarists, such as Chengtu, see ibid. 1.1:153, 156; no. 1.2:175; "Ko-ti hsin-wen . . . chin-k'uang," *PHCK* 1.2:106; and "Futility of the Press Censorship," *People's Tribune,* n.s. 2:243.

55. When the suspension order reached the weekly on Apr. 3, 1935, the cover for its vol. 2, no. 10 (Apr. 6, 1935) had already been printed. The notation "Publication resumed on May 18" was then superimposed in red on the cover. On p. 181 of this issue, the editor said that it had been suspended, but gave no explanation for the punishment.

56. These cases will be discussed in more detail in Chap. VI.

57. Hu Shih, "Yen-lun tzu-yu" (Freedom of speech), *Pao-hsueh,* no. 4:3 (1953); Wen Tsai-tao, "Pi-huo chi-lueh" (Writings which bring calamities

to their writers), *Tsa-chih* 13.3:111 (June 1944); *Jih-pao so-yin* (Index to newspapers), 6:506 (1936/1937). Cf. also T'ao Hsi-sheng, "Pei-p'ing erh san shih" (Two or three anecdotes in Peiping), *Chuan-chi wen-hsüeh* 1.7:12 (December 1962); Ch'in Te-shun, "Chi-Ch'a cheng-wei-hui shih-ch'i ti hui-i" (When I was with the Hopei-Chahar Political Council), ibid. 2.1:21 (January 1963). On Dec. 8, 1936, 14 literary magazines were closed down by government orders (*Jih-pao so-yin* 6:506).

58. Wang Hsin-wu, pp. 421-422.

59. Kung Te-pai, II, 179.

60. Ko Ta, "Yen-lun tzu-yu yü chin-shu wen-t'i" (Freedom of the press and the prohibited books), *Ch'en pao fu-chien*, no. 289:4 (June 5, 1929).

61. "Ko-ti hsin-wen . . . chin-k'uang," *PHCK* 1.2:105.

62. Chang B, p. 59.

63. "Pien hou," *Tu-shu tsa-chih* 3.3/4:1-5 (Mar. 20, 1933).

64. In December 1935, the Kwangsi provincial government gave orders to ban "reactionary" books. In May 1936, "reactionary" magazines were banned in Southwest China. See *Jih-pao so-yin* 4:3261 (1936); 5:364 (1936).

65. Chang B, pp. 173-189, 191-196, 205-254; Chang C, pp. 145-164, 164-172; Chang D, pp. 153-160, 161-176, 177-180. The 1929-1936 list claimed to have 309 titles, and the August 1936 list 676 titles, but actually they gave only 307 and 662 titles respectively.

66. Some prohibited books are not included in Chang. For instance, Ts'ao Ya-po's *Wu-ch'ang ko-ming chen-shih* was banned soon after its publication in 1928. A corner was cut off from each of the several hundred remaining copies to be sure that they could not be sold again. (Tso Shun-sheng, *Chung-kuo chin-tai shih-hua* [*Familiar Talks in Modern Chinese History;* Taipei, 1967], II, 157). *Ch'ing shih kao* (Draft history of the Ch'ing dynasty) was banned in February 1937 (*Jih-pao so-yin* 6:506). For other examples see Wen Tsai-tao, *Tsa-chih* 13.3:109; T'ao Hsi-sheng, "Chung-ta i hsueh-ch'i" (A semester at Central University), *Chuan-chi wen-hsüeh* 1.5:8 (October 1962).

67. The 1931 list, for instance, included anti-Chiang Kai-shek books

by his then political rivals, such as Wang Ching-wei and Hu Han-min.

68. See Chang B, pp. 230, 231, 240, 247, 249, 251, 253 for these examples.
     In 1930, Ch'ü Ch'iu-pai published in Moscow a pamphlet entitled *Zhonguo
     Latinhuadi Zemu* (Chinese Latinized alphabet). The scheme, which was
     designed by Ch'ü with the assistance of Kolokolov for the needs of the
     Chinese minority in the U.S.S.R., was first called Latinxua (Latinization)
     and later designated as Sin Wenz (Hsin wen-tzu according to the Wade-
     Giles system, or New Language). It was developed in the U.S.S.R., but
     was abandoned in that country about 1939. The Latinxua movement
     began in China in 1934, and was promoted by Lu Hsün, Kuo Mo-jo,
     T'ao Hsing-chih, National Salvation Association, activists in the student
     movement of mid-1930s, and many others. For the promotion and
     suppression of Sin Wenz in China, cf. John de Francis, *Nationalism and
     Language Reform in China* (Princeton, N.J., Princeton University Press,
     1950), pp. 115-120.

69. Chang B, p. 229. "She-lun," *Ta-kung pao* (Feb. 17, 1931), commented
     on the government's absurd efforts in outlawing the Chinese lunar New
     Year's Day. According to Wu Shih-ch'ang, "Lun tang ti chih-yeh hua"
     (On professional politicians in the KMT), *Kuan-ch'a* (The observer),
     2.2:9 (Mar. 8, 1947), Hu Shih said that, in the prewar years, the govern-
     ment seemed to put an all-out effort into abolishing the lunar calendar.

70. Such lists were not always issued openly. Of the eight lists, this is the
     only one I have been able to find in contemporary magazines. See
     KWCP, vol. 11, no. 11, unnumbered page (Mar. 19, 1934); *Hsien-tai
     ch'u-pan-chieh* (Contemporary publishing world), no. 22:8-9 (Mar. 1,
     1934). Wang Yao, I, 145, and Snow, *Current History* 42:383, give some
     of the names of the foreign writers included in this list.

71. For instance, Mao Tun's *Ch'un ch'an* (The spring silkworms). Hu Shih in
     an editorial postscript in *TLPL*, no. 124:18 (Oct. 22, 1934), calls this
     novel, which describes the peasants' miseries, "a most profoundly
     affecting, first-rate novel."

72. Confidential order of the Ministry of Education, No. 452; confidential
     order of the Executive Yuan, No. 4841, dated Oct. 30, 1933. Chang B,
     pp. 170-173.

73. Shen Ts'ung-wen, "Chin-shu wen-t'i" (On prohibited books), *KWCP*
     11.9:1-4 (Mar. 5, 1934); *Lu Hsün ch'üan-chi*, VI, 444-463; Wen Tsai-tao,

Tsa-chih 13.3:111-112; Hsiang Kung, "Kuan-yü chin-shu wen-t'i" (On prohibited books), *Jen-yen* 1:127 (1934). All complained that it was not a book's content, but its author, that caused it to be banned.

74. Chang B, pp. 201-205.

75. Lo Lung-chi, "Wo-ti pei-p'u ching-kuo yü fan-kan" (On my arrest), *Hsin-yueh* (New moon) 3.3:1-17 (1931); his "Shen-mo shih fa-chih" (What is rule by law), ibid. 3.11:1-17 (1931).

76. *The New York Times* (Aug. 26, 1934), 4.8:6; Kung Te-pai, II, 164-165; Chiang Chao-chi, *PHCK* 1.2:43-44; "I-chou chien" (Within this week), *Jen-yen* 1:512 (1934); Lin Yutang, pp. 168-171. It is interesting to note that Ch'eng She-wo in *Pao-hsueh,* 5:90 and his *Pao-hsueh tsa-chu* (Notes on journalism; Taipei, 1956), pp. 154-156, merely touched upon this case, although he described in detail his arrest by Chang Tsung-ch'ang.

77. "The Futility of the Press Censorship," *People's Tribune,* n.s. 2:242-243.

78. In 1933, the central government ordered all local governments and military units to protect journalists. "Hsiao yen-lun," *Sheng-huo* 8:718 (1933), said that the order was given because too many journalists had been imprisoned or executed by the military without due process of law in the past few years.

79. Both cases in *Sheng-huo* 5:645 (1930).

80. "Wo-kuo ko-ti . . . ," *PHCK* 1.2:175.

81. *NCH* (Aug. 12 and 19, 1936), pp. 267, 315.

82. Huang Liang-meng, *PHCK* 1.4:86-88.

83. "The Futility of the Press Censorship," *People's Tribune,* n.s. 2:243.

84. *Hsin-wen pao* (Shanghai, Feb. 5, 1933), quoted in *KWCP* 10.6:4-5 (Feb. 13, 1933); *Shih-lun ts'ung-k'an* (A collection of essays on current affairs; Canton, 1933), ser. I, pp. 80-82; Tsou T'ao-fen, "Hsiao yen-lun," *Sheng-huo* 8:97 (1933); T'u Jan, "Wang-yuan-ching yü hsien-wei-ching" (Telescope and microscope), *Sheng-huo* 8:149 (1933); "Hsin-wen-chieh . . . ," *PHCK* 1.3:218.

85. The use of assassins by unknown sources could seriously hurt China's national interest. On May 2, 1935, Yang En-p'u of *Kuo-ch'üan pao,* which spoke for the Japanese, was injured by an assassin and died of wounds three days later. On May 3, Pai Yü-huan of *Chen pao,* another pro-Japanese paper, was assassinated. Both papers were published in the Japanese Concession in Tientsin. Alleging that the assassins were Chiang's secret agents, the Japanese military pressured the Chinese government into signing on June 10 the Ho-Umetsu Agreement, in accordance with which the Chinese government had to withdraw all KMT headquarters as well as the Chinese army from Hopei and Chahar, and outlaw all anti-Japanese movements and propaganda there. See Kung Te-pai, II, 84.

86. Madame Sun Yat-sen declared in *Ta-mei wan-pao* (*Shanghai Evening Post and Mercury*) that Yang's assassination was connected with the aid to Ting Ling. Tsou T'ao-fen, "Hsin-hsiang" (Letters to the editor), *Sheng-huo* 8:92 (1933). Pai Hung, "Chi Yang Hsing-fo," *Tsa-chih* 15.4:58-60 (July 1945); Lin Yutang, p. 174. Chang B, p. 55.

87. Kung Te-pai, I, 188; Wang Yao, I, 145; Chang B, p. 55. Snow says (*Current History* 42:385) that Shih was "allegedly leader of a group of constitutional democrats opposed to the Fascist dictatorship." According to Yeh Chün-i, "Teng Yen-ta i-shih" (Anecdotes of Teng Yen-ta), *Tsa-chih* 11.3:25 (June 1943), and Tung Ta-tsai, "Huang Yen-p'ei lun" (On Huang Yen-p'ei), ibid. 12.6:29 (September 1944), Shih's assassination was connected with the publication of Madame Sun Yat-sen's denunciation of Chiang Kai-shek because of the execution of Teng Yen-ta in November 1931.

88. "What's Wrong with the Press in China," *People's Tribune,* n.s. 3:16 (1932). Cf. also A Mei, "Nei-ti pao-kuan chi-che" (Journalists in interior China), *Hsin-sheng chou-k'an* 2:129 (1935); Chieh Fu, "Ts'ung tu-hui hsin-wen . . . fan-chan" (The danger and development of journalism in interior China), *PHCK* 1.2:81-82 (1935).

89. Kuo Ming, "Ch'i-jih jih-chi" (A diary for seven days), *Jen-yen* 1:366 (1934).

90. "What's Wrong with the Press in China," *People's Tribune,* n.s. 3:13.

91. Wang I-an, *Tsa-chih* 10.6:90; Mu Hsin, p. 159.

92. Wang I-an, *Tsa-chih* 10.6:89; Chang B, pp. 56, 59n. Lu Hsün said (*Lu*

Hsün ch'üan-chi, IV, 272-273) that many publishers and bookstores were closed down in 1930 by government orders for having published or sold leftist publications. Some of them later resumed business and handled safer books such as bilingual editions of works by Robert Louis Stevenson, Oscar Wilde, and others.

93.   Chang I-wei, "Hua-pei hsin-wen chieh" (Journalism in North China), *PHYK* 1.2:67 (1929); "Ko-ti hsin-wen shih-yeh chih shih-k'uang" (Conditions of journalists in various localities), *PHCK* 1.3:140-141 (1935).

94.   Wang Wen-pin, pp. 203-204. *The New York Times* reported on Nov. 8, 1933, 14:3, about the KMT's plan for issuing weekly bulletins containing "authentic reports of latest international and domestic happenings": "Chinese newspapers which publish news items other than those officially authorized will be punished by fines or suspension of publication."

95.   Chao Tse-ch'eng, "Lun Chung-yang she" (Central News Agency), *Wents'ui,* no. 34:13-14 (June 13, 1946).

96.   Huang Liang-meng, *PHCK* 1.4:90.

97.   *Shih-shih hsin pao* (*China Times,* Shanghai, Mar. 10, 1930), reprinted in *KWCP* 7.10:6-7 (Mar. 17, 1930).

98.   "She-lun," *Ta-kung pao* (Apr. 7, 1930).

99.   Ssu Fang, "Li-ti ch'üan-wei" (Authority and military force), *Jen-yen* 1:427-428 (1934); Chang K'o-piao, "Pi-huo" (Writers' calamities), ibid., p. 467. However, not all people protested in such ways as these militant groups. In 1934, for instance, citizens in Yangchow were enraged by the vile and indiscriminate attacks on their city in I Chüntso's *Hsien-hua Yang-chou* (Idle tales about Yangchow). The case was peacefully settled. The author and the publisher, Chung Hwa Book Company, formally apologized to the people of Yangchow and agreed to destroy the stereotypes of the book. Most contemporary writers felt that such a silly book was not even worth refuting. One writer used this case as an example to show that censorship usually succeeded only in giving free publicity to the books it wished to ban. Cf. Wen Tsai-tao, *Tsa-chih* 13.3:103; Chih T'ang, "Tu chin-shu" (On reading prohibited books), *TLPL,* no. 166:14 (Sept. 1, 1935); Ts'ao Chü-jen, "Hsien-hua

Yang-chou," *Jen-chien shih* (In the world), 1.10:25 (1934).

100. Lin Lan, ed., *Hsiao Chu-pa-chieh* (The Piggy; Shanghai, 1932), pp. 1-10. The Pig is a character in *Hsi yu chi* (translated by Arthur Waley as *The Monkey*). Lou's article in *Nan-hua wen-i* (South China literary Magazine) 1.14:59-63 (July 16, 1932).

101. "Shang-hai ch'ing-chen tung-shih-hui lai-han" (A letter from the Shanghai Islamic Association), *Nan-hua wen-i* 1.18:79-80 (Sept. 18, 1932). The issue was obviously behind its publication schedule, as was often the case with Chinese magazines.

102. Hu Shih, "Wu-ju hui-chiao shih-chien chi ch'i ch'u-fen" (On the Piggy case), *TLPL,* no. 27:6-10 (Nov. 20, 1932); Hu Shih, "Ching-ta Chiang Shao-yuan hsien-sheng" (A reply to Mr. Chiang Shao-yuan), *TLPL*, no. 29:22 (Dec. 4, 1932). Chiang's protest to Hu in *TLPL*, no. 29:21-22.

103. It was called "a novel" in *NCH* (Nov. 9, 1932), p. 212, or just a story by others.

104. *NCH* (Nov. 9 and 16, 1932), pp. 212, 242, 243. The inside cover of *Nan-hua wen-i,* vol. 1, no. 19 (Oct. 1, 1932) carries the magazine's apology to its readers that it was forced to cease publication as of that issue. Obviously this issue also came out behind schedule.

105. Chiang Shao-yuan's letter to Ch'en Shu-yung in *TLPL,* no. 31:18 (Dec. 18, 1932).

106. There was some criticism that the government seemed to be harsher towards Pei Hsin Book Company than towards *Nan-hua wen-i,* the editor-in-chief of which was the Minister of Railways. (T'u Jan, *Sheng-huo* 7:966 [1932].) Some were resentful that other writers would have to lose their royalties due to the closing of the publishing firm. (Wen Tsai-tao, *Tsa-chih* 13.3:103.)

107. Hu Shih, *TLPL,* no. 27:10; his "Fu-ta Chiang Shao-yuan hsien-sheng" (Another reply to Mr. Chiang Shao-yuan), *TLPL,* no. 31:19 (Dec. 18, 1932).

V. The Kuomintang Regime Before the War, 1927-1937 (2)

1. Cf. Harold S. Quigley, *The Far East* (Boston, World Peace Foundation,

1938), pp. 138-144. By an almost identical agreement, the rendition of the Mixed Court in the French Concession took place on July 31, 1931. This agreement was renewed on Apr. 1, 1933.

2. *Shang-hai shih nien-chien, 1937* (Yearbook of Shanghai), comp. the Gazette Bureau of Shanghai (Shanghai, 1938), p. T71.

3. Shun Te, "Wei k'an-wu ch'ing-ming" (A plea on behalf of the magazines), *Jen-yen* 2:402 (1935); *NCH* (July 24, 1935). Also in 1935, the Chinese police with the assistance of the Settlement police in Shanghai conducted a series of raids in the Settlement and seized no less than 33,000 lunar calendars. The First Special District Court on Sept. 3 ordered the confiscation of 10,000 calendar blocks seized in a Chinese printing shop (*NCH,* Sept. 4, 1935).

4. Fu Ssu-nien, "Ch'en Tu-hsiu an" (Ch'en Tu-hsiu case), *TLPL,* no. 24:2 (Oct. 30, 1932); Tsou T'ao-fen, *Ching-li* (My experiences; Shanghai, 1938), pp. 159-190.

5. Chi-lin i fen-tzu, "Pu-hsü Chung-kuo jen ai-kuo" (Chinese are not allowed to be patriotic), *Sheng-huo* 6:1145-46 (1931). *The New York Times* (Aug. 13, 1933), 4.2:5.

6. Hu Tao-ching, *STCK* 2:281-282.

7. *Sheng-huo* 8:317 (1933). *I-shih pao*'s editorial on April 12 showed its disapproval.

8. Snow, *Current History* 42:385-386; *The New York Times* (Mar. 13, 1935), 9:6; Li Shu-ch'ing, "Ti-pu hsueh-sheng kan-yen" (On arresting students), *TLPL,* no. 143:6 (Mar. 25, 1935). Cf. also *TLPL,* no. 143:22, the editor's postscript.

9. "She-lun," *Ta-kung pao* (Mar. 17, 1934); Hu Shih, "Wo-men yao-chiu . . . ," *Ta-kung pao* (Dec. 29, 1935). At the time when Hu wrote the article, the contents of the Tangku Truce, which had been signed in May 1933, had still not been made public.

10. *The New York Times* (Aug. 12, 1934), 4.8:6.

11. I Shui, "Hsien-hua huang-ti," *Hsin-sheng chou-k'an* 2:312-313 (1935). Reprinted in *Chou-pao,* no. 5:6-9 (Oct. 6, 1945).

12. The censors were dismissed in July, and the ill-fated Censorship Com-
     mission disappeared. For a more detailed description of this case, see
     NCH (July 3, 10, 17, 24, 1935), pp. 15, 60, 89-90, 100, 140; *The New
     York Times* (July 4, 1935), 5:3; (July 5, 1935), 7:2; (July 6, 1935), 4:2;
     (July 10, 1935), 1:2; (Sept. 1, 1935), 4.5:8; "I-yueh lai chih Chung-
     kuo . . ." (Important national and international events in the past
     month), *Shen pao yueh-k'an* (Shun pao monthly) 4.8:120-121 (1935).
     According to Ai Han-sung (Chang B, p. 148), Tu was assured by govern-
     ment officials, including the Mayor of Shanghai, that nothing would
     happen to him if he would only appear before the court. Judging from
     the fact that the defense made no attempt to justify the article and the
     accused was visibly surprised at the court's decision, we may conclude
     that there might have been some sort of "understanding" between the
     prosecution and the defense before the trial. When the sentence was
     read, a number of Chinese students in the courtroom were enraged.
     They shouted slogans and staged a peaceful anti-Japanese demonstration.
     The judge and the Japanese observers had to retire in a hurry. The
     Chinese papers did not give any details of the demonstration. The report
     in *NCH* (July 17, 1935), p. 100, says that the pamphlets which were
     scattered in the courtroom bore such slogans as "Down with the
     Fascist Kuomintang," "Down with Traitor Chiang," "Abolish Censor-
     ship," "Down with the Imperialists' Running Dogs," etc.

13. *NCH* (Aug. 14, 1935), pp. 249, 264. *The New York Times* (Aug. 4,
     1935), 1:7; (Aug. 5, 1935), 3:1; (Aug. 6, 1935), 11:1.

14. Chu Kuang-yü, "Tui-yü hsiu-cheng ch'u-pan fa-an ti kan-hsiang" (On
     the revision of the Publication Law), *Cheng lun* (Righteous discourses),
     no. 38:6 (Aug. 1, 1935); Li Tsu-ch'eng, "Yen erh pu lun" (Reports
     without comment), *Jen-yen* 2:416 (1935); "She-lun," *Ta-kung pao*
     (June 11, 1935); Chang B, pp. 153-154; Lo Ch'eng-lieh, pp. 384-387;
     NCH (July 24, 1935), p. 140; Ch'ang Sheng, "Tu Chung-yuan an i chun
     shang-su" (Tu Chung-yuan is allowed to appeal his case), *Jen-yen*
     2:581.

15. *NCH* (July 17 and 24, Aug. 7, 1935), pp. 100, 151, 238; (Dec. 4 and 11,
     1935).

16. Huai Kan, "Shih-chien ho to" (Why so many incidents), *Hsin jen-shih*,
     no. 6:324 (Nov. 20, 1936). Cf. *NCH* (Oct. 16, 1935) for the so-called
     "anti-Japanese poster incident" in Hankow. The Japanese, however,
     could not do much about the anti-Japanese literature in the foreign

press in China. On July 27, 1935, *China Weekly Review* in Shanghai commented on the *New Life Weekly* case in an article entitled "Anti-foreignism Prohibited. Editor's Appeal Denied." The Japanese papers in Shanghai denounced the weekly's anti-Japanese attitude and remarked that its editor and publisher, J. B. Powell, was trusted by Chiang Kai-shek (*NCH* [Aug. 28, 1935], p. 344). Powell was imprisoned by the Japanese, after they occupied the foreign settlements in Shanghai, from Dec. 20, 1941 to September 1943 (J. B. Powell, *My Twenty-Five Years in China* [New York, Macmillan Co., 1945], pp. 370ff).

17. *NCH* (July 31, 1935); ibid. (Aug. 14, 1935), p. 250.

18. *NCH* (Dec. 18, 1935).

19. Yang I, "Ch'ing ch'üan-kuo shang-hsia chu-i" (Attention! Everybody in the nation!), *Hsin jen-shih,* no. 2:113-114 (Sept. 20, 1936).

20. Yang Shou-ch'ing, *Chung-kuo ch'u-pan chieh chien-shih* (A short history of Chinese publishing; Shanghai, 1946), pp. 66-67; *Jih-pao so-yin* 6:506.

21. Sha Ch'ien-li, *Ch'i jen chih yü* (The imprisonment of the seven; Shanghai, 1937), pp. 133-143; Tsou T'ao-fen, *Ching-li,* pp. 157-245.

22. Cf. T'ao Ti-ya, "Kuo-chi hsin-wen hui-i yü Chung-kuo" (International conference of journalism and China), *Shen pao yueh-k'an* 2.11:54-55 (Nov. 15, 1933); T'u Jan, *Sheng-huo* 4:353 (1931); Lo Ch'eng-lieh, I, 35-37; "She-lun," *Ta-kung pao* (Mar. 27, 1930, Apr. 13, 1931, May 29, 1933, Sept. 27, 1935). Liang Shih-ch'un, "Chan-shih ti yü-lun . . ." (Public opinion in wartime and its control), *KWCP* 13.25:28 (June 22, 1936). Chinese journalists also complained that some foreign correspondents had a superiority complex about the Chinese. Cf. Wang Po-heng, "Chung-kuo chih hsi-tzu pao-chih" (Foreign press in China), *HTPL,* special issue (January 1927), pp. 94, 101. Wu T'ien-fang, "Chung-kuo tang-ch'ien . . ." (The most important problems in China's information work in foreign countries), *PHCK* 1.1:3-9 (1934).

23. *NCH* (Nov. 9 and 23, 1932), pp. 215, 284. *The New York Times* (Nov. 15, 1934), 10:3.

24. *Times* (London, Aug. 4, 1927). North China Daily News, *China's Attempt to Muzzle the Foreign Press* (Shanghai, 1929), pp. 3, 9.

25. North China Daily News, *China's Attempt*..., pp. 5, 11, 13-14, 16, 22, 30. Huang Liang-meng, *PHYK* 1.4:83-84.

26. *NCH* (Dec. 28, 1932), p. 483. Hu Tao-ching, "Shang-hai ti ting-ch'i k'an-wu" (Periodical literature in Shanghai), *STCK* 1:862 (1933).

27. "Postal Ban on Oriental Affairs," *People's Tribune*, n.s. 7:7-10 (1934); "Banned From the Mails for Telling the Truth," ibid., pp. 293-294. In the same volume, the *People's Tribune* devoted nine articles to this case, defending the government. The other seven are as follows: "The Case of 'Oriental Affairs,'" pp. 21-24; "Some Studies in Alleged Sedition," pp. 25-34; "On the Attribution of Unworthy Motives," pp. 49-50; "Mr. Woodhead's Charges of Inconsistency," pp. 55-58; "Banned from 'Oriental Affairs' for Speaking the Truth," pp. 157-158; "Esoteric Finance—Mystery of 'Oriental Affairs' Solved," pp. 195-206; "Truth and Chinese Affairs," pp. 255-258.

28. "Courtesy and Cable Censorship," *People's Tribune*, n.s. 7:350-352 (1934). *The New York Times* (Feb. 24, 1935), 4.5:6.

29. *The New York Times* (Feb. 24, 1935), 4.5:6. "Shih-p'ing" (Editorial), *Shen pao* (June 9, 1936), also complained of the Japanese news agency.

30. *The New York Times* (Sept. 18, 1934), 12:8. *China Times* received the same punishment for the same reason.

31. North China Daily News, *China's Attempt*..., p. 20. Hallett Abend, *My Life in China, 1926-1941* (New York, Harcourt, Brace & Co., 1943), pp. 22, 102-105, 114-134.

32. "The Liberty of the Press," *People's Tribune*, n.s. 3:459 (1933). "On the Attribution of Unworthy Motives," ibid., n.s. 7:49-50. *NCH* (Aug. 17, 1932), p. 256.

33. "What's Wrong with the Press in China," *People's Tribune*, n.s. 3:16-17. Cf. also North China Daily News, *China's Attempt*..., p. 25.

34. Sun Wen, *San-min chu-i* (Three People's Principles; Shanghai, 1927), p. 1. This was Dr. Sun's first lecture on the Principle of People's Livelihood. *Sun Yat-sen, His Political and Social Ideas, a Source Book,* tr. and annotated by Leonard Shih Lien Hsü (Los Angeles, University of Southern California Press, 1933), p. 422.

35. Chiang Kai-shek, "Chung-kao pen-tang t'ung-chih" (An advice to my comrades in the KMT), *Ko-ming chün,* no. 9:79 (Dec. 25, 1925).

36. Chiang Kai-shek, "Pan-hsiao ti-san-ch'i t'ung-hsüeh-lu hsü" (A preface to the yearbook of the third class, Whampoa Military Academy), ibid., p. 74.

37. Chi Lien, "Chung-kuo cheng-chih . . ." (Why Chinese politics is not on the right track), *KWCP* 9.1:1-8 (Jan. 1, 1932).

38. Lo Lung-chi, "Kao ya-p'o yen-lun tzu-yu che" (To those who deny our people the freedom of speech), *Hsin-yueh* 2.6/7:1 (September 1929). Hu Shih's articles are in ibid. 2.2:1-8 (April 1929); 2.4:1-15 (June 1929). Because of these articles, Hu was arrested for four days in 1929 (Abend, pp. 142-145).

39. Liang Shih-ch'iu, "Lun ssu-hsiang t'ung-i" (On the regimentation of thought), *Hsin-yueh* 2.3:1-10 (May 1929); his "Sun Chung-shan hsien-sheng lun tzu-yu" (Dr. Sun Yat-sen's comment on freedom), ibid. 2.9:1-10 (November 1929); and his "Ssu-hsiang tzu-yu" (On the freedom of thought), ibid. 2.11:9-11 (January 1930).

40. Lo Lung-chi, "Kao ya-p'o . . . ," *Hsin-yueh* 2.6/7:1-17; his "Kao Jih-pen kuo-min . . ." (An advice to the Japanese people and the Chinese authorities), ibid. 3.12:19 (1931). See also his "Wo tui tang-wu . . ." (My criticism of the KMT), ibid. 2.8:1-15 (October 1929), for his criticism of the KMT dictatorship, which prohibited people from freely discussing national affairs and the Three People's Principles; his "Wang Ching-wei lun ssu-hsiang t'ung-i" (Wang Ching-wei's comments on the regimentation of thought), ibid., 2.12:1-5 (Feb. 10, 1930), for his attack on Wang's theory that there could be no absolute freedom for political ideas.

41. See the many protests in Chang B, pp. 110-136, 144-145; Chiang Chao-chi, *PHCK* 1.2:44.

42. "She-lun," *Ta-kung pao* (May 12, 1931, Apr. 2, 1936, Jan. 25 and Feb. 18, 1937). Lo Ch'eng-lieh, I, 359-363. Hu Shih, "Wang Chiang t'ung-tien li t'i-ch'i ti tzu-yu" (The freedom which Wang and Chiang talked about in their circular telegram), *KWCP* 11.50:1-2 (Dec. 17, 1934). In 1932, Shanghai publishers petitioned the National Government opposing the Publication Law of 1930 and the regulations for its application.

KMT headquarters in Shanghai forbade the publication of this petition in the papers as an advertisement (Chang D, pp. 412-414).

43. Hu Shih, "Wang Chiang t'ung-tien . . . ," *KWCP* 11.50:2. Cf. "She-lun, *Ta-kung pao* (Jan. 28 and Feb. 28, 1931).

44. Cf. "She-lun," *Ta-kung pao* (Feb. 18, 1937); Kao Shih-ming, "Ch'u-pan tzu-yu yü cheng-chih an-ting" (Freedom of publication and political stability), *Cheng lun*, no. 40:5 (Aug. 15, 1935). For the Camden-Erskine-Jefferson school of thought, cf. Siebert, p. 7.

45. "She-lun," *Ta-kung pao* (Apr. 2, 1936). For the Blackstone-Mansfield theory, cf. Siebert, p. 391.

46. "Wo-kuo ko-ti . . . ," *PHCK* 1.2:184. "She-lun," *Ta-kung pao* (May 12 and 22, 1931, Dec. 12, 1934).

47. "She-lun," *Ta-kung pao* (Dec. 29, 1929).

48. *The New York Times* (Jan. 24, 1934), 6:2. Cf. also "Wo-kuo ko-ti . . . ," *PHCK* 1.3:227, and "She-lun," *Ta-kung pao* (Jan. 25, 1935), for the resolution adopted by the KMT Central Executive Committee on Jan. 24, 1935.

49. *NCH* (Nov. 20, Dec. 11 and 18, 1935). The proposal adopted by the Central Executive Committee was an aftermath of the ban imposed by the Tientsin and Peiping Public Safety Bureaus on the *Ta-kung pao* for its editorial giving advice to General Sung Che-yuan.

50. The government obviously held the Tudor-Stuart theory. According to the Tudor and Stuart kings and queens, the safety, stability, and welfare of the state depended on the efforts of the crown and therefore anything which interfered with or undermined those efforts was to be suppressed or at least controlled (Siebert, pp. 6, 34).

51. "Shih-shih hsin pao yü Chiang chu-hsi chih pien-po" (The controversy between the *China Times* and President Chiang), *Sheng-huo* 6:115-116 (1931).

52. *Wu-ssu ai-kuo yun-tung tzu-liao,* p. 820; *Sheng-huo* 7:257 (1932).

53. Ch'ien Tuan-sheng, "Tang-chih yü yü-lun" (The rule of the **party** and

public opinion), *HTPL* 6.139:7-9 (Aug. 6, 1927). This passage may remind readers of the words attributed to Lenin: "Why should freedom of speech and freedom of the press be allowed? Why should a government which is doing what it believes to be right allow itself to be criticized? It would not allow the opposition to buy lethal weapons. Ideas are much more fatal things than guns. Why should any man be allowed to buy a printing press and disseminate pernicious opinions calculated to embarrass the government?" (Quoted in Alan Barth, *Government by Investigation* [New York, Viking Press, 1955], p. 183). Su Hsueh-lin wrote in 1937 that thought control was very necessary in China and that burning books as Hitler had done was sometimes indispensable to "maintain the nation's [mental?] health." See her *Wo lun Lu Hsün* (*My Critique on Lu Hsün;* Taipei, 1967), pp. 68, 114.

54.   Hsü Ch'ing-yu, "Ssu-hsiang t'ung-i yü yen-lun tzu-yu" (The regimentation of thought and the freedom of speech), *KWCP* 14.19:13-16 (May 17, 1937).

55.   Chao Chan-yuan, *Kuo-fang hsin-wen shih-yeh chih t'ung-chih* (The control of journalism for national defense; Shanghai, 1937), pp. 52-53, 129-136, 140. Chao was not alone in holding such ideas. Among the proposals Ma Hsing-yeh made to "cultivate journalism" (*KWCP* 14.12:8), were the improvement and increasing importance of the Central News Agency, the registration of all journalists, and the training of journalists.

56.   Chang B, pp. 24-31, lists 97 books and 16 magazines published in 1930-1934 in areas under Communist control. "Pei-p'ing k'an-wu i-lan-paio" (A list of periodicals in Peiping), *Ch'ing-nien ssu-ch'ao* (Thoughts of youths), no. 3/4:21-25 (1932?), gives the titles of many communist magazines. (The real title of *Ch'ing-nien ssu-ch'ao* was probably *Chung-kuo lun-t'an* [China forum], which was published in Peiping. *Chung-kuo lun-t'an* was printed on the cover of the copy I read, but a strip of paper bearing the title *Ch'ing-nien ssu-ch'ao* was pasted over it. The semi-monthly was devoted to the discussion of Marxism-Leninism.) The large number of Communist publications on the government's lists of prohibited books and magazines attested to the futility of the government's efforts. Yen Ling-feng in "Wo yü she-hui k'o-hsueh" (I and the social sciences), *Tu-shu tsa-chih* 3.1:24, 40-44 (Jan. 1, 1933), still recommended some books written from the Marxist point of view, and the magazine often carried advertisements for such books; e.g., its announcement in vol. 3, no. 9 (Sept. 1, 1933), at the end of the issue; and vol. 3, no. 6 (June 20, 1933).

57.   Accurate official statistics on the publishing trade in China during this
      period are not available. *Shen pao nien-chien, 1936* (Yearbook of Shun
      pao; Shanghai, 1937), pp. 1285-86, says that a total of 8,148 titles were
      submitted for censorship from March 1932 to September 1935, and
      5,075 titles were registered with the Ministry of the Interior from June
      1928 to June 1935. According to Wang Yun-wu's estimate (Chung-kuo
      wen-hua chien-she hsueh-hui [China Cultural Reconstruction Association],
      ed. *Shih-nien lai ti Chung-kuo* [China in the past ten years; Shanghai,
      1937], pp. 463-479), less than 3,000 titles were published each year
      before 1932. From 1933 on, there was a great increase in the number of
      titles. In 1936, 9,438 titles were published. Hsü Wan-ch'eng says (Chang B,
      p. 424) that 939 newspapers and 1,796 magazines were published in
      1935. In 1935, there were 260 publishers and booksellers in Shanghai
      ("Shang-hai shu-tien t'ung-chi" [A statistics of bookstores in Shanghai],
      Jen-yen 2:268 [1935]).

58.   The number of magazines published in 1934 was so large that 1934 was
      nicknamed "the year of the magazines." Hu Tao-ching (*STCK* 2:1030)
      gives the reasons as: (1) more timely information, (2) cheaper to buy,
      (3) more varieties in content, (4) a place for a group of people to express
      their own views. See also Hsing Su, "Tsa-chih nien" (The year of the
      magazines), *Hsin-sheng chou-k'an* 2:63 (1935); Wang I-an, *Tsa-chih*
      10.6:90; *Shang-hai yen-chiu tzu-liao* (Source materials on Shanghai;
      Shanghai, 1936), p. 403. Yü I-ch'en, "Chung-kuo chin-jih chih ch'u-pan
      chieh" (Chinese publishing business of today), *Wen-hua chien-she yueh-
      k'an* (Cultural reconstruction monthly), 1.2:115 (Nov. 10, 1934), and
      Chang Ching-lu, *Tsai ch'u-pan chieh . . .* , p. 157, give the economic
      conditions as the chief reason.

59.   "K'ai-tsung-ming-i ti-i chang" (The very first chapter), *Tzu-yu yen-lun*
      (Free speech) 1.1:2 (1933); "Tao-ch'u tu-shih so-ko" (Manacles every-
      where), ibid., p. 3. The second article also gives the titles of several
      other "reactionary" magazines banned in November 1932.

60.   For instance, *Meng-ya* was banned after five issues came out. Its no. 6
      appeared under the new title *Hsin-lu* (New road), and its no. 7 *Wen-
      hsueh yueh-pao* (Literature, a monthly). See Feng Ai-ch'ün, p. 407.
      Hai-yen (The petrels) was actually the new title for the last issue of
      T'o-huang che (Chang D, p. 578). After *Huan chou,* a literary semi-
      monthly, was banned, *Ko pi* appeared in its place. Wang Che-fu, p. 424.
      See also Lin Yutang, p. 126.

61. Chang Ching-lu, *Tsai ch'u-pan chieh . . .* , p. 139.

62. *Shang-hai shih nien-chien, 1937* 2:R11, R24. "She-lun," *Ta-kung pao* (Apr. 30, 1936). P'ing Hsin, "Ch'u-pan chieh wang na-erh tsou" (Which way will the publishing business go), *Tu-shu yü ch'u-pan,* no. 1:4 (May 18, 1935). I Hsia, "T'ung-chih Chung-kuo . . . ," (The devils that control the thought of millions of the Chinese), *Sheng-huo* 5:615-617 (1930).

63. Li Hsuan, "Chiu-tiao ch'ung-t'an" (To play an old tune), *Jen-yen* 1:410-411 (1934). Yü I-ch'en, *Wen-hua chien-she yueh-k'an* 1.2:115.

64. Cf. "What's Wrong with the Press in China," *People's Tribune,* n.s. 3:18. In 1934, Chinese newspapers in Shanghai were ordered to submit all advertisements to the Social Affairs Bureau for examination and approval before publication. The order was designed (1) to prevent the use of the advertising columns for unlawful acts, and (2) to curb the insertion of advertisements in indecent books and pictures. (*The New York Times* [Nov. 11, 1934], 4.2:6). The government's interest, however, seemed to be in (1), but not in (2). See also Ko Kung-chen, p. 231, for the resolution against immoral and indecent advertisements adopted by the National Press Association.

65. "She-lun," *Ta-kung pao* (May 27, 1930); "What's Wrong with the Press in China," *People's Tribune,* n.s. 3:17-18; A Mei, *Hsin-sheng chou-k'an* 2:129; Chieh Fu, *PHCK* 1.2:80-83.

66. Shih Tung, "Kuan-yü pei-fang Hung-ch'i chung yu-ch'in chi-hui chu-i ti ts'uo-wu" (The Northern Red Flag's mistake in publishing the views of rightist opportunism), *Hung-ch'i chou-pao,* no. 50:34 (Sept. 10, 1932).

67. "Chung-hua su-wei-ai kung-ho-kuo lin-shih chung-yang cheng-fu kuan-yü tung-yuan tui-jih hsuan-chan ti hsün-ling" (A directive from the provisional central government of the Soviet Republic of China in regard to the declaration of war against Japan), ibid., pp. 17-18.

VI. The War of Resistance, 1937-1945

1. During the war, the Chinese government was still in the hands of the KMT under the leadership of Chiang Kai-shek, whose prestige was at an all-time high. The CCP maintained its headquarters in Yenan, but sent a delegation, headed by Chou En-lai, to Chungking. The Communists held

seven seats in the Political Council, but no other government positions. The designation "Red Army" was abolished, and the Communist forces were reorganized as the Eighth Route Army and brought nominally under the control of the National Military Council in Chungking.

2. For a list of the new literary magazines geared to the war of resistance after August 1937, see Chang D, pp. 547ff.

3. Cf. Chao Ming-heng, "The War-time Press," in *Chinese Year Book, 1938-1939* (Chungking, 1939), p. 702; and his *Ts'ai-fang shih-wu nien* (Fifteen years as a reporter; Chungking, 1944), p. 55.

4. Ta Tun, "Shu-yang yu-kan" (On the tragedy of books), *STPP* 3:3006 (1941); "She-lun," *STPP* 3:2849. This liberal magazine, published in Hong Kong, was banned in Free China in March 1939 (Chang C, p. 214).

5. Cf. Ts'ao Ching-hua, "T'ieh-liu ti chieh-fang" (The liberation of *T'ieh-liu*), *Jen-min wen-hsueh* (People's literature), 2.4:44-48 (August 1950), for the methods of control.

6. For newspapers in North China, see Chao Ming-heng, *Chinese Year Book, 1938-1939,* pp. 696-701.

7. Feng Ai-ch'ün, pp. 316-317; Chang D, pp. 307-308. In October 1937, Shanghai Municipal Council required all papers in Shanghai to register with it. Many publishing houses moved to the interior provinces later in that year. Those that remained did not publish actively, and printing costs thus fell (Chang C, p. 269).

8. Hu Sheng, "Shang-hai hsin-wen chieh tsai k'u-tou chung" (The struggling Shanghai journalists), *Ch'üan-min k'ang-chan* (War of resistance for all the people), no. 74:1066-67 (1939). *Hsin-wen tu-fa* (How to read a newspaper; Shanghai, n.d.), pp. 25-26. Chang Chih-han, "Hu-k'ou yü-sheng hua Shang-hai" (Memories of terrible experiences in Shanghai), *Hsin-wen chan-hsien* (News front), 2.2/3:31 (May 16, 1942).

9. Hu Sheng, *Ch'üan-min k'ang-chan,* no. 74:1067. Feng Ai-ch'ün, p. 317.

10. *Kuo-min cheng-fu kung pao* (Official gazette of [Wang's] National Government), no. 130:1-9 (Jan. 31, 1941). Wang Ching-wei left Chungking on Dec. 18, 1938, and signed a secret treaty with the Japanese in Shanghai on Dec. 30, 1939. His puppet regime was

established at Nanking on March 30, 1940. It superseded the so-called "Provisional Government" at Peiping (established on Dec. 14, 1937) and "Reformed Government" at Nanking (established on Mar. 28, 1938).

11. Yüan Ch'ang-ch'ao, p. 70.

12. Feng Ai-ch'ün, pp. 316-319; Chang D, pp. 310, 320.

13. Feng Ai-ch'ün, pp. 319-322. *Chung-hua min-kuo k'ai-kuo wu-shih nien shih lun-chi* (A collection of essays commemorating the fiftieth anniversary of the Republic of China), ser. I, pp. 1075-76 (Taipei, 1964). Four of the assassinated victims worked for *Ta-mei wan-pao;* see *China Handbook, 1937-1943,* pp. 700-701. For the names of the victims, see Chang Chih-han, *Hsin-wen chan-hsien* 2.2/3:26-30. See also Powell, pp. 334-341. For two victims' own reports, see Ch'eng Ch'i-heng and Jung Yu-ming, pp. 89-91, 151-169. There were always retaliations. On Aug. 9, 1941, for instance, *Chung-hua jih-pao,* Wang's organ in Shanghai, was bombed. In retaliation, Wang's men bombed *Shun pao.*

14. Feng Ai-ch'ün, p. 322.

15. Hsü Ching-sung, *Chou-pao,* no. 4:12.

16. Cf. T'ieh, "Tao shih shu" (In memory of my lost books), *Tu-shu yü ch'u-pan* 2.9:48 (Sept. 15, 1947).

17. Hsin-min-hui chung-yang chih-tao-pu, tiao-ch'a-k'o, *Chin-chih t'u-shu mu-lu, k'ang-jih chih pu* (Prohibited books—anti-Japanese section), Series I (Nanking, 1939). Also its *Kuo-ming-tang kuan-hsi t'u-shu mu-lu* (Prohibited books concerned with the KMT; Nanking, 1939).

18. Yuan Ch'ang-ch'ao, p. 70. Fan Ch'üan, "Wen-hua fan-lan yü wen-hua chien-she" (The deluge of bad literature and the cultural reconstruction), *Tzu-yu lun-t'an,* no. 1:15 (Dec. 9, 1945). For comments on Eileen Chang and her poem expressing her wish to become the third concubine of Hu Lan-ch'eng, see Wen Shang, "Ts'ung Chang Ai-ling shuo-tao chin-chih ch'ü hsiao-lao-p'o" (On Eileen Chang and the outlawing of concubinage), *Yung-sheng* (Eternal life), no. 7:100 (Dec. 10, 1945).

19. *Chan-shih hsin-wen kung-tso ju-men* (An introduction to wartime journalism), ed. Chung-kuo ch'ing-nien chi-che hsüeh-hui (Young

Chinese Journalists Association; Chungking, 1939), pp. 2-3, 271-272.
Chang Chi-luan would not accept the *New China Daily*'s suggestion to
refuse news censorship in 1938 in Hankow, as he believed that all
citizens must obey the KMT government's laws and regulations in a
national crisis. See P'an Tzu-nien et al, *Hsin-hua jih-pao ti hui-i* (A
reminiscence of the *New China Daily;* Chungking, 1960), pp. 13-14.
Wen Hua, "Chi-che tsai chin-jih" (Journalists of today), *Shih-lun fen-
hsi* (Analysis of current events), no. 26:41 (Oct. 1, 1940). T'ien Yü-
chen, in his "Tsung-tung-yuan-fa yü hsin-wen shih-yeh" (National
General Mobilization Act and journalism), *Hsin-wen chan-hsien* 2.2/3:
7-8 (May 16, 1942), declared that journalists in contributing to the
war efforts must have the determination to sacrifice personal freedom.

20.   The protests in Free China were usually mild, as writers hoped only
that the government would relax a little on its censorship policy and
practice. See, e.g., Mao Chien-wu, "Yen-lun tzu-yu yü ko-hsin cheng-
chih" (Freedom of speech and reform in government), *Hsin-wen chan-
hsien* 5.1:6 (Jan. 16, 1945); Hu Chao, "Shih-lun kai-shan pao-jen
sheng-huo" (On the improvement of newspapermen's working conditions), ibid. 5.2/3:12-13, 15 (May 16, 1945). More outspoken criticisms
probably were not given a chance to see the light in Free China, but
were apparent in Hong Kong. See, e.g., Chou Ching-wen, "Cheng-
ch'ü k'ang-chan ti yen-lun tzu-yu" (Fighting for freedom of speech
during the war), *STPP* 2:1155 (1939); Tsou T'ao-fen, "P'i-p'ing yü
min-chu" (Criticism and democracy), *STPP* 3:3015-16 (1941). Writers
felt it unfair that the KMT Party or government publications were
exempt from censorship. Why could only the ideas expressed by the
official agencies be regarded as infallible and thus guaranteed to be not
"reactionary" or "erroneous," one writer asked. See "Lun shen-ch'a
yuan-kao chi t'u-shu tsa-chih" (On pre-publication censorship, books
and magazines), *STPP* 1:142 (1938).

21.   P'an Kung-chan, "Kuo-fu hsin-pan ch'u-pan-p'in . . ." (The regulations
for the censorship of wartime publications, promulgated recently by the
national government, are now in effect), *Ch'u-pan chieh* (The publishing
world), 1.6/7:2 (August 1944).

22.   Ch'eng Ch'i-heng and Jung Yu-ming, pp. 171-173. See also *Chan-shih
hsin-wen kung-tso ju-men,* pp. 268-269. T'ien Yü-chen, *Chan-shih hsin-
wen kung-tso ti t'u-ching* (The path of wartime journalism; Chungking,
1944), pp. 28, 32, for the government's not wanting any exposé of its
weaknesses.

23. T'ien Yü-chen, *Chan-shih hsin-wen* . . . , p. 2. Huang Yen-p'ei compared all 13 newspapers in Chungking from Feb. 1 to Feb. 5, 1939, and found that 85 per cent of the news stories which appeared in two or more papers were the same on Feb. 1, 81 per cent on Feb. 2, 80 per cent on Feb. 3, 87 per cent on Feb. 4 and 5. See his "Chiu-chiu nei-ti ti wen-hua chi-min" (Save those culturally starved people in interior China), *Kuo hsin,* no. 204:1 (May 21, 1939). Chao Ming-heng in his *Ts'ai-fang shih-wu nien,* pp. 72-73, wrote about the lack of human interest stories. Liu Wen-ch'ü, "Ch'uang-tsao hsin-wen hsieh-tso ti hsin hsing" (Finding new ways to write news reports), *Hsin-wen chan-hsien* 2.2/3:24-25 (May 16, 1942), complained that news reports had become so stereotyped as to remind readers of formal classical essays penned in a most rigid style for imperial examinations.

24. Huang T'ien-p'eng, "Chan-shih pao-chih kuan-chih i-chien" (On the control of the press in wartime), *Hsin-wen chan-hsien* 2.9/10:3-6 (Jan. 16, 1943).

25. T'ien Yü-chen, *Chan-shih hsin-wen* . . . , p. 50.

26. In spite of the prepublication censorship, there were still some suspensions. Some magazines were closed down because they failed to obtain a permit for publication, such as one magazine in Chengtu in 1938, and two in Kunming in 1939. See *Chan-shih hsin-wen kung-tso ju-men,* p. 163; Ch'eng Mai, "Erh-ch'i k'ang-chan chung ti K'un-ming ch'u-pan chieh" (The publishing world in Kunming during the second stage of the war of resistance), *Kuo hsin,* no. 205/206:14-16 (June 11, 1939). In Chang D, pp. 334-363, there is a chronological list of important events in journalism for this period, which lists many suspensions. Although *Chieh-fang jih-pao,* a CCP organ in Yenan, claimed that more than 500 newspapers and magazines were closed down in 1943 (Chung T'ien, "Ch'ung-ch'ing wen-hua chieh i-p'ieh" [The cultural circle in Chungking], *Tsa-chih* 12.4:156-160 [January 1944]), it did not give a list of their titles. Compared with the prewar and especially the postwar years, there were far fewer permanent suspensions during these years.

27. "Hsin-wen chieh hsin-wen" (News about journalists and journalism), *Hsin-wen chan-hsien* 4.1/2:33 (Apr. 16, 1944).

28. *Ts'an-cheng-hui yü yen-lun tzu-yu* (The Political Council and the free-dom of speech and the press; n.p., Shanghai Magazine Co., 1941),

pp. 42-46. Ch'ang Chiang, "Ts'ui-ts'an hsin-wen chieh jen-ch'üan chih i li" (An example of the violation of journalists' human rights), *STPP* 4:3191-94 (1941).

29. The section on the *New China Daily* is based chiefly on *Ts'an-cheng-hui yü yen-lun tzu-yu,* pp. 14-31; P'an Tzu-nien et al., *passim,* esp. (in the order of our discussion) pp. 12, 13-14, 21-31, 68, 17-19, 20-21, 33, 77, 109-117, 34-35, 118-129, 121, 78, 64, 72, 60-64, 39, 2, 47-48, 50. No other reference will be given to this work in this section.

30. A Communist member of the Political Council also complained that the Chinese military authorities did not make public the battles Communist troops won and that the *New China Daily* could not get censors' approval in printing such news. Tsou Yang, *Kuo kung chih chien* (Between the KMT and the CCP; n.p., Li-shih tzu-liao kung-ying she, 1945), p. 38.

31. *Ch'ün-chung* began publication on Dec. 11, 1937, in Hankow. Following a suspension of about half a year, it resumed publication in Chungking in December 1938.

32. *Shih-shih lei pien* (Digest of current events), a monthly, was published by the Sun Yat-sen Institute for the Advancement of Culture and Education in Chungking. Ma's two articles appeared in its no. 54, pp. 46-50, and no. 57. The Chinese translation of G. Stein's article, "Fa-pi wen-t'i chien-t'ao" (On Chinese currency), appeared in *Ts'ai-cheng p'ing-lun* (Finance review), 2.3:115-121 (1940).

33. "I-ko chih-te chu-i ti t'i-i" (A proposal that is worthy of our attention), *Ch'üan-min k'ang-chan,* no. 133:2028 (1940). Ting I, "Ma Yin-ch'u feng-ming k'ao-ch'a ti ch'ien-ch'ien hou-hou" (How Ma Yin-ch'u was ordered to go to the battle front), *STPP* 4:3182-84 (1941). I was then a freshman at the National Central University.

34. Li Tui, "Hu-tsou ti shih-li" (A wild talk), *Ta-chung sheng-huo,* n.s. no. 16:375 (Aug. 30, 1941). Ying Wei-min, "Chuan-fang Liu Ya-tzu hsien-sheng" (A visit to Mr. Liu Ya-tzu), *Chou-pao,* no. 20:21 (Jan. 19, 1946). Hung P'o, "Jang wo-men tsen-yang huo che" (How can we live on), *STPP* 3:2717 (1941). Liu Ya-tzu, an early disciple of Dr. Sun Yat-sen, was later expelled from the KMT because of his allegedly leftist leanings.

35. Chang C, p. 173. On Aug. 20, 1938, fifteen publishers in Hankow, includ-ing Commercial Press and Chung Hwa Book Company, petitioned the

government to rescind the Revised Standards for Censoring Wartime Books and Periodicals, which had just been promulgated. They listed eight reasons to show that prepublication censorship was contrary to the government's professed policy of "encouraging people to make constructive criticisms," and would cause undue difficulties to the publishers. Mu Hsin, pp. 239-240.

36. Tsou T'ao-fen, *K'ang-chan i-lai* (Since the outbreak of the war), 3rd ed. (Shanghai, 1947), pp. 58, 61-63. The book was first serialized in a newspaper in Hong Kong in 1941.

37. Hsuan Chu, "T'ung-i, t'uan-chieh yü min-chu" (Unification, unity, and democracy), *Ta-chung sheng-huo (Public Life)*, n.s. no. 20:471 (1941). Chung Ming, "P'ing ssu-hsiang shang ti chüeh-tui chu-i" (On absolutism), *STPP* 3:2938 (1941). Tsou T'ao-fen, *K'ang-chan i-lai*, p. 85. *Ts'an-cheng-hui yü yen-lun tzu-yu*, pp. 27-28.

38. Chang D, p. 354. Po Yuan, "Chin-shu, chin-chi chi ch'i-t'a" (Prohibited books, taboos and others), *Tu-shu yü ch'u-pan* 2.6:15 (June 15, 1947).

39. Ts'ai I, *Chung-kuo hsin wen-hsueh shih chiang-hua* (A history of new Chinese literature; Shanghai, 1953), p. 139. Po Yuan, "T'u-shu shen-ch'a chung-chung" (On the censorship of books and magazines), *Tu-shu yü ch'u-pan* 2.7:53 (July 15, 1947). "Lun shen-ch'a yuan-kao . . . ," *STPP* 1:143. Chung Ming, *STPP* 3:2936. Ts'ao Yü in his play *Shui-pien* (The transformation) described the corruption in an army hospital. The authority in Chungking withheld its permit for performance until the producers agreed to change the setting to a private hospital. See P'u, "Shih-shih ch'ao-kuo hsiang-hsiang" (Facts are more fantastic than fiction), *Ta-chung sheng-huo*, n.s. no. 17:410 (1941).

40. Tsou T'ao-fen, "Tang-p'ai yü jen-ch'üan" (Party cliques and human rights), *STPP* 4:3094 (1941).

41. "Ta hou-fang pao-chih tsa-chih ti ming-yun" (The fate of the press in Free China), *Ta-kung* (The impartial), no. 9:140 (June 6, 1945).

42. "Pien-chi-pu ti hua" (Editor's notes), *Min-chu chou-k'an (Democratic weekly)* 1.2:22 (Dec. 16, 1944). See also "Ch'i-shih" (An announcement), ibid. 1.22:1 (May 23, 1945), which said that two short comments on current affairs had been deleted; ibid. 1.23:5 (June 2, 1945), which said two short comments had been deleted. In ibid. 2.2:5 (July 16, 1945),

the editor said that three short comments could not appear in that issue because they had been forwarded to the Central Censorship Commission in Chungking for censorship and had not been returned. An article on the democratic movement in China during the war was also in the Central Censorship Commission at the time of printing.

43. Ch'ih Ch'un-huan, "Wen-hua ch'eng chi-shih" (Writers in Kweilin), *Ta-chung sheng-huo,* n.s. no. 9:224 (1941).

44. Po Yuan, "Tu-shu . . . ," *Tu-shu yü ch'u-pan* 2.7:52.

45. "Pien-chi hou-chi" (The editor's postscripts), *Tzu-yu lun-t'an* 3.2:24 (Oct. 1, 1944).

46. "Chin-yao ch'i-shih" (An important announcement), *Min-chu chou-k'an* 1.25:3 (June 18, 1945). Cf. also "Pien-che, tso-che, tu-che" (The editor, the writer, and the reader), *Min-chu shih-chieh* (Democratic world) 2.4/5: 27 (Mar. 1, 1945).

47. Ssu Hsien, "Ch'ing-pi k'o-i yü fei-ch'ih fu-pai" (Corruption and ineffi- ciency), *Min-chu shih-chieh* 2.8/9:29 (May 1, 1945).

48. Chiang Hsing-yü, "Lun Hua Wei hsien-sheng" (On Mr. Hua Wei), *Min- chu chou-k'an* 1.14:21 (Dec. 1, 1944). Tzu Kang, "Min-chu ti-i" (Democracy comes first), ibid., 2.7:14-15 (Sept. 1, 1945). For other examples in the same magazine, see ibid. 1.22:1 (May 23, 1945), at the end of a short comment on the Nazis, "a long paragraph has been deleted"; ibid. 1.23:3 (June 2, 1945), when a column (one-third of a page) is blank; ibid. 1.26:12 (June 23, 1945), at the end of an article commenting on the suicide of a poor peasant family of four, "80 characters have been deleted."

49. "Pen-k'an kao-yueh" (To the contributors), *Chung-hua lun-t'an* (China forum), in all issues. The semimonthly began publication on Feb. 1, 1945, in Chungking.

50. Books and magazines passed by censors in Kwangsi were often banned in Hunan and Kiangsi. Han Tzu, "I-nien lai ti Kuei-lin wen-hua chieh" (The cultural circle in Kweilin in the past year), *Tsa-chih* 11.2:73 (May 10, 1943); Lu Lien-t'ang, "Wen-hua ch'eng ti ch'u-pan shih-yeh" (Publishing in Kweilin), *T'u-shu yin-shua yueh-pao* (Book printing monthly), 1.1:18 (October 1943). See also Wan Ch'eng, "Tang-ch'ien

wen-hua-jen ti o-yun" (The bad luck of contemporary writers), *STPP* 3:2907 (1941); Chung Ming, *STPP* 3:2938; Po Yuan, "T'u-shu . . . ," *Tu-shu yü ch'u-pan* 2.7:53.

51. "Pien-chi hou-chi," *Tzu-yu lun-t'an* 3.2:24.

52. Po Yuan, "Chin-shu . . . ," *Tu-shu yü ch'u-pan* 2.6:15.

53. Wang Hsin-wu, pp. 449-450. Chiang's translation was banned in June 1941 (Chang C, p. 214). For other works which could not pass the censors, see Hsü Hsien, "Kuei-lin ti tso-chia ch'ün" (Writers in Kweilin), *Tsa-chih* 12.3:185-187 (December 1943).

54. Sa K'ung-liao, *K'o-hsueh ti hsin-wen kai-lun*, pp. 1, 35. Sa was arrested in Kweilin in 1943.

55. Wan Ch'eng, *STPP* 3:2905, 2907.

56. Chang C, pp. 173-238. The two examples are on pp. 231 and 182.

57. Tsou T'ao-fen, *K'ang-chan i-lai*, pp. 55, 141-142. Cf. also ibid., pp. 218-220. *Ts'an-cheng-hui yü yen-lun tzu-yu*, pp. 33-41. Chung Ming, *STPP* 3:2938.

58. Hung P'o, "Chi-chung-ying ti ku-shih" (Tales of the concentration camps), *STPP* 4:3190 (1941). Po Yuan, "Shu tsai lü-hsing chung ti o-yun" (The dangers in carrying books around), *Tu-shu yü ch'u-pan* 2.2:35-38 (Feb. 15, 1947). Yuan I-min, "Kuei pu te" (There is no return), *STPP* 4:3185 (1941).

59. *San-shih nien-tu k'ang-chan chien-kuo kung-tso shih-chi* (An annual report on our achievements in the war of resistance and the reconstruction of the country in the fiscal year 1941), comp. Ministry of Information (Chungking, 1942), pp. 24-27, 40.

60. Cf. Ch'eng Mai, *Kuo hsin*, no. 205/206:16.

61. Wang Yun-wu, *Shih-nien k'u-tou chi* (Ten years' struggle; Taipei, 1966), pp. 38-39, 54-55. Wang said (pp. 62-64) that the fabulous progress the Commercial Press had made was due entirely to the company's self-reliance. He obviously played down the government's part. For instance, after V-J Day in 1945 when the government controlled all means of

transportation, Wang had the unusual privilege of flying back without delay to Shanghai, Nanking, and Hong Kong on company business.

62. P'an Kung-chan, "Ch'u-pan ch'ü-hsiang ti kuo-ch'ü yü chiang-lai" (The past and future of the publishing trends), *Ch'u-pan chieh* 1.1:2-3 (Dec. 15, 1943). More than 1/3 of all books and magazines were published in Chungking, and about 1/4 in Kweilin during these years. In Chungking, 10 per cent of the 166 magazines published in 1941, 21 per cent of the 220 magazines in 1942, and 16 per cent of the 259 magazines in 1943 were literature. In Kunming, of the 30-odd magazines published, 16 were on drama and literature. There were altogether 776 magazines published in Free China in 1942, and 718 in 1943. Generally speaking, more government publications were published in Chungking and more literary publications in Kweilin, where many leftist writers resided after Hong Kong fell in December 1941 (Chung T'ien, *Tsa-chih* 12.4:156). This may also explain why censorship was usually more strict in Kweilin than in Chungking. See also Ch'iu, "Pai-fen chih ssu i tien ch'i" (41.7 per cent), *T'u-shu yin-shua yüeh-pao* 1.1:2-3 (Oct. 1, 1943). Wu T'ieh-sheng, "Wo-kuo ch'u-pan chieh ti hsien-tsai yü chiang-lai" (The present and the future of the Chinese publishing business), *Hsin Chung-hua*, n.s. 2.11:27 (November 1944).

63. Kuo Mo-jo's *Ch'ü Yuan,* a play about the beloved poet-statesman (ca. 343 B.C.-277 B.C.), is a good example of this tendency. The method of discussing personalities and state matters under feigned or historical guises had also been used by the Elizabethan pamphleteers who were denied the privilege of discussing current political affairs (Siebert, p. 94).

64. Mao Tun "Hsien-tsai wo-men yao k'ai-shih ch'ien-t'ao" (Let us take a good look at our literature), *Wen-ts'ui (Articles Digest),* no. 15:14 (Jan. 17, 1946). Hung P'o, "Kuan-yü ch'u-pan wen-hua" (On the publishing business), *Tsa-chih* 11.5:28 (August 1943).

65. Mei Chih, "Hsi-pi lai-hung" (Letters from the West), *Tsa-chih* 13.3:180 (June 1944). Han Tzu, ibid. 11.2:73. Chung T'ien, ibid. 12.4:156-157.

66. *Hsin-wen chan-hsien,* vol. 4, no. 7/8 (Nov. 16, 1944). Similar examples may be found in Meng Ch'ang, "Hsin-wen tzu-yu" (Freedom of the press), *Chung-hua lun-t'an* (China forum), no. 5/6:28-32 (June 1945). Meng Ch'ang, "Tsai lun hsin-wen tzu-yu" (Another essay on the freedom of the press), ibid., no. 7/8:37 (July 1945). "Yao-chiu hsin-wen tzu-yu" (We want freedom of the press), *Min-chu shih-chieh* 2.4/5:28 (Mar. 1, 1945).

67. "Pien-che ti hua" (Editor's notes), *Min-chu shih-chieh* 1.1:55 (May 5,
     1944). "Tzu-pen chu-i yü kung-ch'an chu-i pi-hsü ch'ung-t'u ma," ibid.
     1.12:5-7 (Nov. 1, 1944), a USIS translation of Geoffrey Crowther's
     "Must Capitalism and Communism Clash?" (*The New York Times
     Magazine,* Aug. 6, 1944, p. 5), concluded that capitalism and com-
     munism could coexist. Such an article could not have been passed by
     the censors had it been written by a Chinese. At that time, censors
     would not approve any translations unless they were submitted together
     with the English originals.

68. T'ien Yü-chen, *Chan-shih hsin-wen . . .* , pp. 34, 36.

69. Sha, "Hsien-te chiu-cheng k'ung-ch'i" (We have to clear the air first),
     Yü-lun chou-pao (Public opinion weekly), 1.5:7 (Sept. 5, 1943). Cf.
     also Chung T'ien, *Tsa-chih* 12.4:158.

70. The section on Tsou T'ao-fen is based chiefly on the magazines he edited
     and his own writings, especially his "Hsiao yen-lun" (in *Sheng-huo*),
     Ching-li (from his birth to 1937), *K'ang-chan i-lai* (1937-1941). Works
     on him have also been consulted, including Mu Hsin, *Tsou T'ao-fen;
     T'ao-fen ti tao-lu* (The road of Tsou T'ao-fen), comp. Shang-hai T'ao-
     fen chi-nien-kuan (Peking, 1958); *Tao-nien T'ao-fen* (In memory of
     Tsou T'ao-fen; n.p., Ch'ün-Chung Press, 1944); *Yung tsai chui-nien
     chung ti T'ao-fen hsien-sheng* (Mr. Tsou T'ao-fen will always live in our
     memory; n.p., T'ao-fen Press, 1947).

71. Mu Hsin, pp. 61-63. Cf. Tsou's articles in *Sheng-huo,* such as "Tyrannic
     Russian Invasion" (1929), "The Two Ways of Social Revolution" (1930),
     "The Root of the Malady" (1930). When the Red Army captured
     Changsha on July 27, 1930, he lamented the "arson, murder and looting"
     brought upon the city by the Red Army.

72. Mu Hsin, pp. 71-72. This article as well as his "Our Recent Tendency"
     are in *Sheng-huo,* vol. 7 (1932).

73. Tsou T'ao-fen, "Kuan-yü le-ling t'ing-k'an ti ch'uan-wen" (On the rumor
     of the suspension of *Life Weekly*), *Sheng-huo* 6:1169-70 (1931).

74. Tsou T'ao-fen, "Tsui-hou ti chi-chü hua" (Last few words), *Sheng-huo*
     8:1017-18 (1933). Though published in the last issue of the magazine
     (vol. 8, no. 50, on Dec. 16, 1933), it was actually written in October
     1932 in anticipation of the suspension of the weekly. Tsou asserted that
     he could not understand which article of the Publication Law the weekly

had violated. (Mu Hsin, p. 89.) For a photographic copy of Tsou's own notes in connection with the postal ban and rumored suspension order in 1932, see his *T'ao-fen wen-chi* (Collected works of Tsou T'ao-fen; Hong Kong, 1957), plates at the beginning of the volume.

75. Huan Ch'eng, "Sheng-huo chou-k'an t'ing-chih yu-chi kan-yen" (On the postal ban on *Life Weekly*), *Hsin she-hui pan-yüeh-k'an* (New society semi-monthly), 3.5:93 (Sept. 1, 1932). Cf. also "Pien-chi yü tan" (The editor's notes), ibid., p. 115.

76. Mu Hsin, p. 81; *T'ao-fen ti tao-lu*, pp. 33, 175.

77. Ibid., pp. 158-159.

78. Ibid., 185-186. For the strict censorship in Hong Kong, see ibid., pp. 172-174; Tsou T'ao-fen, *Ching-li*, pp. 267-280.

79. Cf. Tsou T'ao-fen, "Tsen-yang yung-hu Chiang wei-yuan-ch'ang k'ang-chan tao ti" (How to support Generalissimo Chiang's efforts to fight to the bitter end), *K'ang-chan* (War of resistance), no. 30:2 (Dec. 23, 1937); and his "Kuo-nan chung ti yen-lun chieh tse-jen" (The responsibilities of the press during national crisis), ibid., no. 43:2 (Feb. 6, 1938).

80. Tsou T'ao-fen, *K'ang-chan i-lai*, p. 213; also ibid., pp. 61-70, 82-85 for his trouble in dealing with the censors. Often, more than half of the manuscripts submitted for censorship by the magazine could be detained by the censors (*T'ao-fen ti tao-lu*, p. 25). For a list of these confiscated publications and their permit numbers issued by the government, see *Ts'an-cheng-hui yü yen-lun tzu-yu*, pp. 38-46. In 1938, *Sao-tang pao* (*The Broom*), an army paper, refused to accept the company's advertisement giving the locations of its branch offices on a map (Mu Hsin, pp. 229-230).

81. Tsou was a man of integrity. All his life he remained incorrupt. In 1931, for instance, *Life Weekly* revealed the corruption of the then Minister of Railways, who had forced a young student to marry him. The minister failed in his attempts to bribe Tsou with a huge sum of money and an official position. Following the exposé, Tsou received many anonymous letters threatening his life, but won great admiration from many people for his honesty and courage. Cf. *T'ao-fen ti tao-lu*, pp. 89, 255-256. For his decision not to join the KMT, see his *K'ang-chan i-lai,* p. 207.

82. Tsou T'ao-fen, *K'ang-chan i-lai*, p. 204.

83. *T'ao-fen ti tao-lu*, p. 17.

84. Tsou T'ao-fen, *K'ang-chan i-lai*, p. 206.

85. For the persecution of Life Publishing Company, which was suspected of having connections with the CCP, see Tsou, *K'ang-chan i-lai*, pp. 183-230; *Ts'an-cheng-hui yü yen-lun tzu-yu*, pp. 31-46. In closing the company's branch offices, the government always used flimsy pretexts. The procedures employed, however, were different in different places, depending largely on the local authorities. When its branch office in Kweiyang was sealed off on Feb. 20, 1941, all the staff members were arrested and everything in the store was hauled away. Of the 960 titles the company published, 26 were banned, although all but two of them had been approved by the government. Of the more than 300 staff members, 43 were arrested, one of whom was killed (*Tao-nien T'ao-fen*, p. 4a). According to *Chieh-fang jih-pao*, Nov. 22, 1944, the rapid growth of the company was due entirely to the efforts of Tsou and his staff, but had nothing to do with the CCP (*T'ao-fen ti tao-lu*, p. 17). It is interesting to note that Yeh Ch'u-ts'ang himself had once fought for the freedom of the press when he was an editor in the International Settlement in Shanghai (cf. above, Chap. III). Wang Shih-chieh, the new Minister of Information, who gave Tsou equally evasive replies before his escape to Hong Kong, also had written several articles demanding freedom of the press during the warlord years.

86. "Tu-che hsin-hsiang" (Letters from the readers), *Ta-chung sheng-huo*, n.s. no. 6:142 (June 21, 1941). Cf. also the same column in ibid., n.s. no. 10:250 (July 17, 1941); no. 14:346 (Aug. 16, 1941), for Tsou's unswerving support of the KMT government and the leaders in the war.

87. *Tao-nien T'ao-fen*, p. 4a. Yang Ming, *T'ao-fen hsien-sheng ti liu-wang sheng-huo* (Mr. Tsou T'ao-fen in exile; n.p., Min-chu she, 1946), pp. 39-40.

88. Ch'en Yi's speech at a memorial service for Tsou in Yenan (*Chieh-fang jih-pao* [Nov. 24, 1944], reprinted in *T'ao-fen ti tao-lu*, pp. 2-3).

89. *Chieh-fang jih-pao* (Nov. 22, 1944), reprinted in ibid., p. 5.

90. *Yung-tsai tsui-nien chung ti T'ao-fen hsien-sheng*, p. 119.

VII. The Aftermath of the War, 1945–1949

1. Feng Ai-ch'ün, p. 333. The New China News Agency was allowed to
    operate in a few cities in 1945. On April 3, 1946, *Chieh-fang pao* and
    the New China News Agency in Peiping were raided, and 39 staff
    members were arrested (Chang C, p. 88). The Communist magazine,
    Ch'ün-chung, was published in Shanghai after the war. After it was
    suspended in 1946, it moved to Hong Kong in January 1947 ("Shih-
    p'ing," *Cheng pao,* n.s. no. 8:168 [Oct. 1, 1948]). The Soviet-registered
    Shih-tai jih-pao in Shanghai was suspended in June 1948, on the grounds
    that it "twisted military news, incited strikes among workers and
    students, and tried to sabotage the nation's financial stability." *Shih-tai*
    (Times) and *Su-lien wen-i* (Soviet literature), both published by the
    Soviet-registered Shih Tai Press in Shanghai, lived to see the Communist
    takeover of Shanghai in 1949. The government certainly disliked the
    press and, from 1945 on, the press had to obtain the paper it needed
    from the Soviet Union. These publications were available on the open
    market, but had few subscribers, because readers were afraid of leaving
    their names with a Red publisher (Chang D, p. 507).

2. Chao Ch'ao-kou, "I-ko hsin-wen chi-che yen-chung ti yen-lun tzu-yu
    wen-t'i" (The freedom of the press as a journalist sees it), *Wen-ts'ui,*
    no. 15:11 (Jan. 17, 1946).

3. P'an Tzu-nien et al, pp. 123–154.

4. Chang D, pp. 199–297. The government announced the capture of Yenan
    on March 19, 1947.

5. The North China New China Book Company, for instance, became
    independent of the *New China Daily* in 1942 (Chang D, p. 241). In
    August 1950, the New China Book Company had 1,032 branch offices,
    with over 12,000 employees (Chang C, p. 265).

6. Chang D, p. 242. For a list of newspapers in the "liberated areas" in
    1948, see Chang D, pp. 370–373. For the magazines published in the
    Shansi-Hopei-Shantung-Honan Border Areas, see "Wen-hua hsiao-hsi
    shih ling" (Cultural activities in North China), *Pei-fang wen-hua* (Culture
    in the north), 2.6:58 (n.d.).

7. The copy of *Tao-nien T'ao-fen* which I used is a carbon copy in hand-
    written form. However, the printing of the bilingual *Chin-Ch'a-Chi hua-*

pao (*Chin-Cha-Chi Pictorial*), founded on July 7, 1942, and published by the Political Department of the Shansi-Chahar-Hopei Military District, is indeed very good.

8. Some of such books were used in this study. In the notes and the bibliography, their publishers are given, preceded by "n.p."

9. Chang D, pp. 494-504, 243.

10. Chang C, pp. 379-384.

11. Chang D, p. 214. Any mistakes in selecting proper materials for publication could be criticized. This technique of criticism and self-criticism was used even in the prewar period. Cf. Chung Ch'ih, "Tsai-lun Su ch'ü kung-hui . . ." (On membership in labor unions in the Soviet areas, and a rebuttal to Comrade Ch'iu), *Hung-ch'i chou-pao,* no. 51:83 (Nov. 1, 1932). The editor of the CCP organ in Hopei admitted his mistake: he should not have printed any writings on Trotskyism, even for discussion. In an announcement in *Hung-ch'i,* no. 21:29 (1929) and no. 23:33 (1929), the editor asked readers to fill out a form giving their opinions about the magazine so that these forms might be forwarded to the CCP Ministry of Propaganda for its improvement. Cf. also Alex Inkeles, *Public Opinion in Soviet Russia* (Cambridge, Mass., Harvard University Press, 1950), pp. 184-190.

12. Chang C, p. 264. In March 1950, the Publishing Bureau approved the plans to centralize the New China Book Company. The company's Central Administration was established accordingly in the following month.

13. There was no prepublication censorship in areas recovered from the Japanese. News censorship, even after its official abolition, was later imposed occasionally at various places. Cf. Ma Hsü-lun, "Tsou-shang min-chu ti lu pa" (Let's be on the road to democracy), *Min-chu,* no. 11:1-3 (Dec. 22, 1945); K'o Shih, "Chien-ch'a chih-tu hsi-i" (On censorship), *Chou-pao,* no. 19:5 (Jan. 12, 1946). On June 1, 1947, for instance, news censorship was imposed for nine days in Tientsin (but not in Peiping) to prevent papers from reporting or commenting on the student movement. Cf. Wang Shui, "Pei-fang hsueh-yun ti yuan yuan pen pen" (Student movement in North China), *Kuan-ch'a* 2.17:19-21 (June 21, 1947); "Chi T'ien-chin ch'ien hou chiu-t'ien ti hsin-wen chien-ch'a" (The nine-day news censorship in Tientsin), ibid. 2.18:17 (June 28,

1947). Ma Hsü-lun reported the irregular news censorship in Shanghai in his "Hsieh tsai Kuo-min-tang erh chung ch'üan-hui ti ch'i nei" (When the KMT Second Plenary Congress was in session), *Min-chu,* no. 21/22: 533 (1947). "Chi-che pu-man yu-tien chien-ch'a" (Journalists are unhappy about telegraphic and postal censorship), *Kuo-hsin,* no. 437:11 (Nov. 1, 1947), reported the blackout of news on President Chiang Kai-shek's activities in Tsingtao.

14. Cf. Yeh Sheng-t'ao, "Pao-lu ti hsiao-kuo" (The effects of exposing government corruption and inefficiency), *Chou-pao,* no. 15:22 (Dec. 15, 1945). One could easily be labeled as a Communist during these years. "Hsin-wen chi-ts'ui" (Miscellaneous news), *Wen-ts'ui,* no. 20 (Mar. 14, 1946) reported that a general called Professor Ch'ien Tuan-sheng a Communist because (1) in a public speech, Ch'ien referred to Chiang Kai-shek as "Mr. Chiang" instead of "the leader"; (2) Ch'ien was "senile."

15. In 1946, 1,461 titles were published by more than 80 publishers: general, 28 (2 per cent); philosophy, psychology and religion, 92 (6 per cent); education, 87 (5 per cent); social sciences, 343 (23 per cent); arts, 38 (3 per cent); applied sciences, 145 (10 per cent); natural science, 64 (4 per cent); language, 55 (4 per cent); literature, 422 (29 per cent); history and geography, 188 (14 per cent). No monumental work was published, nor any books on public finance, sculpture, architecture, printing, folk literature, or archaeology. One-fourth of the books in education were on ball-game rules. Most of the literature books were reprints of works published in Free China during the war. The science books were poor in quality, many of them intended for middle school students. The single book on botany was a translation. There was a marked interest in English, as 37 of the 55 language books were on the English language. See *Wu-han jih-pao nien-chien, 1947* (Yearbook of the Wuhan Daily; Wuhan, 1948), pp. *chiao,* 186-189.

The publishers moved back to Shanghai in 1946. In that year, only 231 titles were published in Shanghai, 73 of which were in literature. Most of the books in this category were reprints of books first published in Free China. See *Shang-hai nien-chien, 1946* (Yearbook of Shanghai, 1946; Shanghai, 1947), p. Q1. Usually 1,000-2,000 copies were printed for each edition. See Ch'in Mu, "Wen-hua shih-yeh ti hao-chieh" (A calamity to civilization), *STPP* 5:3811 (1947). Ts'ai Shang-ssu in his "Shih-nien lai ti chiao-yü wen-hua t'ung-chih" (The control of education and culture in the past ten years), *Shih yü wen (Time and Culture)* 1:347 (1947), also complained of the limited number of books published, most of which were actually reprints under new titles. Shanghai again became the largest publishing center in China. In a 1949 list of the publishers in China and Hong Kong, 302 publishers were included. Among them, 211 were in Shanghai, 41 in Peiping, and 3 gave both Shanghai and Peiping addresses (Chang D, pp. 681-702).

16. In 1946, 984 newspapers were registered with the government. In 1947, there were 1,781 dailies and 1,763 magazines (*Chung-hua nien-chien, 1948* [China yearbook], Nanking, 1949, p. 1942). Feng Ai-ch'ün, pp. 326-329, says that in 1946, 70 papers were published in Shanghai, 44 in Chungking, 42 each in Peiping and Canton, 40 in Nanking. In 1947, 96 papers were published in Shanghai, 87 in Nanking, 68 in Tientsin, and 59 in Peiping. There were also 729 news agencies. According to Reuter's News Agency, there were 950 newspapers in China in 1947 (Ch'in Mu, *STPP* 5:3811). I question the accuracy of these figures, because, in contemporary magazine articles which listed the titles of the newspapers published then in Peiping, Chungking, Chengtu, and other cities, with a description of the background for each paper, the number of titles was much smaller. One must of course bear in mind that many newspapers had but a short life span. Shih Kang in his "Ku-ch'eng pao-yeh niao-k'an" (A bird's-eye view of the newspapers in Peiping), *Fu-nü wen-hua* (Women and culture), 2.1:14 (January 1947), said, for instance, that the newspapers in Peiping came and went in such quick succession that even the government authorities in charge of regulating newspapers could not keep an accurate account of them.

17. An I, "Sheng-li hou ti Pei-p'ing pao-chih" (Newspapers in Peiping after V-J day), *Min-chu,* no. 3:84 (1945). In Tientsin, no new newspapers sprang up. The KMT took over the only paper left there after the war, and *Ta-kung pao* and *I-shih pao* later resumed publication. In February 1946, there were only five newspapers in that city. See Lao Jung, "Pei-fang wen-hua la-tsa t'an" (Random talks on culture in the north), *Min-chu,* no. 18:474-475 (1946). In Peiping, the KMT took over two of the largest papers. There were seven papers in that city in February 1946. In Shanghai, many newspapers sprang up after V-J Day, only to be suppressed soon afterwards. It was said that no newspapers would be allowed except those connected with the KMT. See Hsueh Fan, "Wo-men hsü-yao jen-min ti pao-chih" (We need newspapers for the people), *Min-chu,* no. 13:330 (1946); Fan Ch'üan, *Tzu-yu lun-t'an,* no. 1:15. Many tabloids in Shanghai became weeklies, because newspapers could not begin publication without a permit while magazines could do so at that time after they had obtained the approval of the local Bureau of Social Affairs. See "Hsiao-pao hua chou-k'an wen-t'i tso-t'an-hui" (Why

tabloids became weeklies: a discussion), *Shang-hai wen-hua* (Shanghai culture), no. 4:15 (May 1, 1946).

18. Huo Yen, "Shen-yang chan-shih feng-kuang" (Mukden in wartime), *Shih yü wen* 1:399 (1947).

19. Feng Ai-ch'ün, pp. 331-333; Yuan Ch'ang-ch'ao, p. 73.

20. "Chi-che t'ung-hsin" (Correspondence column), *Kuan-ch'a* 2.1:17-18 (Mar. 1, 1947). The writer complained that public opinion was "formulated by guns."

21. "Chin-jih chih Shen-yang" (Mukden today), *Kuan-ch'a* 1.11:16-17 (Nov. 9, 1946); Fen P'ing, "Ch'eng-tu ti pao-chih" (Newspapers in Chengtu), *Wen-ts'ui*, no. 37:20 (July 4, 1946); Yin Yang, "Sheng-li hsin-nien chi ch'i-t'a" (A victorious New Year), *Min-chu*, no. 14:354 (1946).

22. Ch'en Lang, "Chan-hou Chung-kuo ti hsin-wen shih-yeh" (Chinese journalism after the war), *STPP* 6:3843 (1947). Tzu Kang, "Pei-p'ing chin shih" (Recent events in Peiping), *Wen-ts'ui* (Peiping), no. 17:9 (Mar. 31, 1946). Shih Kang, *Fu-nü wen-hua* 2.1:14-15. Chiang Liu, "Ch'ung-ch'ing yü-lun chieh wu-sheng le" (The silent Chungking press), *Shih yü wen* 1.22:17 (Aug. 8, 1947). Helen P. F. Shih, "Ts'ung K'un-ming pao-chih k'an Yün-nan" (Yunnan as reflected in newspapers at Kunming), *Kuo-hsin*, no. 429:8-9 (Sept. 7, 1947). "Chi-che t'ung-hsin," *Kuan-ch'a* 2.1:17-18 (Mar. 1, 1947); 2.2:18 (Mar. 8, 1947); 2.6:18 (Apr. 5, 1947). Fang Ying, "Ho-fei ch'eng hsiang" (Hofei, town and country), *Shih yü wen* 2:322 (1947). Yüan Ch'ang-ch'ao, p. 73.

23. Ho Shu, "Hsin-wen ch'üan wai" (Outside the journalistic circle), *Chou-pao*, no. 49/50:46 (Aug. 24, 1946). Tzu Kang, *Wen-ts'ui*, no. 17:9. Hu Chao, in his "K'un-ming tung hsin" (Winter in Kunming), *Min-chu*, no. 9:219 (1945), complained of the "silence" of the papers in Kunming in 1945. See also T'ing Ming, "K'un-ming tsai chuan-pien chung" (Kunming in transition), *Wen-ts'ui*, no. 36:22 (June 27, 1946).

24. Wu Han, "Lun ta-shou cheng-chih" (On the policy of using hooligans), *Chou-pao*, no. 43:6 (June 29, 1946). P'an Tzu-nien et al, p. 97.

25. Feng Ai-ch'ün, p. 338. Chao Tse-ch'eng, "Yü Wang Yün-sheng hsien-sheng lun Ta-kung pao shu" (A letter to Mr. Wang Yun-sheng commenting on the *Ta-kung pao*), *Wen-ts'ui* 2.2:19-20 (Oct. 17, 1946). Chao had

once worked for the *Ta-kung pao* during the war. The paper was awarded the "Medal of Honor for Distinguished Service in Journalism" by the Missouri School of Journalism on May 15, 1941, "for the excellence and thoroughness of its national and international news coverage . . . for the power and wide influence of its fearless and trenchant editorials; for its unusual liberal and progressive policies since its founding in 1902 . . ." (*China Handbook, 1937-1943*, p. 701). The paper's reputation declined after Chang Chi-luan's death in September 1941. Cf. also Chang Hsiao-hu, "Yen-lun yü tzu-pen" (The press and the capital), *Shih yü wen* 2.17:8 (Jan. 30, 1948).

26. Ch'u An-p'ing, "Pai pao-chih" (Newsprint), *Kuan-ch'a* 3.9:6-7 (Oct. 25, 1947). From February to April 1947, 4,000 tons of newsprint (U.S. $2,000,000) were allowed to be imported and divided equally between book and newspaper publishing. About 1,000-1,500 tons were designated for KMT newspapers. At that time, 3,700 tons were needed for Shanghai alone. Due to the imbalance in demand and supply, the price of paper rose quickly and some newspapers had to cease publication (Ch'in Mu, *STPP* 5:3810). The KMT papers in Shanghai obtained 1/8 of the total amount allowed for the entire country. See Ch'u An-p'ing, "Wo-men chien-i . . ." (We suggest that the government investigate the distribution of the newsprint and make public its findings), *Kuan-ch'a* 3.19:3-4 (Jan. 3, 1948). Yuan T'ien, "Wo-men yeh-yao p'ing-chia pao-chih" (We too want newsprint at the official exchange rate), *Wen-ts'ui*, no. 9:6-7 (Dec. 4, 1945). For the hoarding of paper by the *Central Daily News* in Nanking, see "Tu-che t'ou-shu" (Letters to the editor), *Kuan-ch'a* 2.4:2 (Mar. 22, 1947). The system lasted for about two years until around the end of 1948 (Feng Ai-ch'ün, p. 329).

27. P'an Kung-chan, formerly Vice Minister of Information, obtained the majority shares of *Shun pao*. Ch'eng Ts'ang-po, who had once been in charge of the *Central Daily News,* took over *Hsin-wen pao*. See Ch'en Lang, *STPP* 6:3843.

28. Ch'in Mu, *STPP* 5:3811.

29. In a government-sponsored civics textbook for the junior middle schools, for instance, a lesson entitled "The Country and the Leader" asserted that "to obey Generalissimo Chiang is the heaven-imposed duty of all citizens of the Republic of China." See Shih Yung, "Ch'ü-hsiao ts'an-tsa . . ." (Abolish government-sponsored textbooks which are infested with fascist ideas), *Min-chu*, no. 29:731 (1946). In a senior

middle school history textbook, Dr. Sun Yat-sen and Chiang Kai-shek were represented in such terms as if there had been no other great Chinese thinkers since the seventeenth century. See Ts'ai Shang-ssu, *Shih yü wen,* I, 346-347.

30. Huo Yen, *Shih yü wen,* I, 399. "Chin-jih chih Shen-yang," *Kuan-ch'a* 1.11:16-17.

31. "Ch'ung-ch'ing ko-pao . . ." (A letter from journalists in Chungking to the Central News Agency), *Chou-pao,* no. 24:10 (Feb. 16, 1946). Chao Tse-ch'eng, "Lun Chung-yang she," *Wen-ts'ui,* no. 34:14. The first protest was organized by the head reporter of the *New China Daily* (P'an Tzu-nien et al, p. 97). At the end of the war in 1945, Central News Agency had 43 branch offices in China and 16 overseas offices (*China Handbook, 1956-1957,* p. 214).

32. Tung Ch'iu-ssu, "Mei pao lun Hsü-chou . . ." (An American journal's comment on the massacre of students in Hsuchow), *Min-chu,* no. 39: 988-989 (1946).

33. Chao Tse-ch'eng, "Lun Chung-yang she," *Wen-ts'ui,* no. 34:14. See also Ch'iu Ssu, "Shen-mo shih-hou . . ." (When shall we have freedom of the press?), *Min-chu,* no. 24:610-611 (1946).

34. Chao Tse-ch'eng, "Lun Chung-yang she," *Wen-ts'ui,* no. 34:14.

35. Tung Shih-chin in his "Ting-chih tu i-chu ti shang-ch'üeh" (On the ritual of reciting Dr. Sun Yat-sen's will), *Wen-ts'ui,* no. 26:13 (Apr. 21, 1946), criticized the ritual of reciting Dr. Sun's will at every gathering. His postscript tells us that the article was written in 1944 but, when submitted for censorship, was retained by the censors. It could not be printed until after the prepublication censorship was abolished. Although undesirable writings had more chance to be in print, the fear of punishment did act sometimes as a deterrent to dissident publishers; cf. Chao ch'ao-kou, "I-ko hsin-wen chi-che . . . ," *Wen-ts'ui,* no. 15:9-12.

36. Ch'in Mu, *STPP* 5:3810. Ting Ching, "Pao-wei yen-lun ch'u-pan tzu-yu" (On defending the freedom of the press), *Min-chu,* no. 36:901 (1946). When Li Kung-p'u, a leader of the Democratic League, was assassinated in 1946, he had not yet heard about his application for the registration of two proposed magazines in Kunming, which he had submitted in 1944. See Kuang Wei-jan, *Chiang Chieh-shih chiao-sha wen-hua* (Chiang

Kai-shek strangulates civilization; n.p., North China New China Book Co., 1947), pp. 13-14.

37. Cheng Chen-to, "Lun min-ch'üan ch'u-pu" (The first step toward democracy), *Chou-pao*, no. 26:6 (Mar. 2, 1946). "Tu-che t'ou-shu" (Letters to the editor), ibid., no. 19:28 (Jan. 12, 1946); no. 24:23 (Feb. 16, 1946). Shao Huan, "Pu-te-i ti min-chu" (Involuntary democracy), ibid., no. 42:22-23 (June 22, 1946). Ho Shu, "Kuang-ming yü hei-an" (The bright side and the dark side), *Min-chu*, no. 28: 710 (1946).

38. "Tu-che t'ou-shu," *Kuan-ch'a* 2.17:2 (June 21, 1947); 4.20:2 (July 17, 1948). Readers in Sian and Tientsin reported that many publications sent from Shanghai were confiscated at the post offices. "Tu-che chih sheng" (Readers' column), *Min-chu*, no. 26:665 (1946).

39. Tsun Wen, "Lun cheng-hsieh-hui chung ti cheng-cheng hsing-shih" (On the power struggle in the Political Consultative Conference), *Chou-pao*, no. 24:7 (Feb. 16, 1946). Tzu Wu, "P'ing Chin ch'u-pan chieh erh san shih" (The publishing world in Peiping and Tientsin), *Min-chu*, no. 15:384 (1946). The Regulations Governing Bookstores and Printing Shops were promulgated in 1943. All bookstores and printing shops had to be registered with the local government, and were forbidden to print banned or uncensored works (unregistered works after the war). See Ting Ching, *Min-chu*, no. 36:901. Cf. also Chang C, p. 118. In 1948, in order to save paper, printers in Shanghai were not allowed to print magazines which had more pages than officially permitted. See Ch'u An-p'ing, "P'ing ch'u-pan-fa hsiu-cheng ts'ao-an" (On the draft revised publication law), *Kuan-ch'a* 3.15:10 (Dec. 6, 1947).

40. "Tu-che t'ung-hsin" (Reader's column), *Chou-pao*, no. 24:22 (Feb. 16, 1946). Yeh Ko, "Chi-o ti Kuang-chou" (Canton hungry for culture), ibid., no. 33:15 (Apr. 20, 1946). "Hsin-wen chi-ts'ui," *Wen-ts'ui*, no. 36:23 (June 27, 1946). Shanghai Magazine Association's memorandum, in Chang C, p. 125. For the names of the bookstores, see Hu Ti, "K'ung-pu chih ch'eng—K'un-ming" (A city in terror—Kunming), *Wen-ts'ui*, no. 39:3 (July 18, 1946).

41. Chiang Wen-yü, "Shuo-hua nan" (It is difficult to say anything), *Kuo-hsin*, no. 426:10 (Aug. 17, 1947). The report was originally printed in *Ta-kung pao* (Aug. 6, 1947).

42. Jen Ssu-wei, "Tu-che ti i-fen . . ." (A reader's righteous indignation—where is freedom of the press), *Min-chu,* no. 14:356 (1946), gave an eyewitness account of this procedure in Ningpo, Chekiang. Many impecunious students went to the bookstores only to stand there to read.

43. *Wen-ts'ui,* no. 3:22 (Mar. 28, 1946); reprinted in Chang C, p. 118.

44. "Hsin-wen chi-ts'ui," *Wen-ts'ui,* no. 14:14 (Jan. 8, 1946); no. 17:8 (Jan. 31, 1946). Yen Ching-yao, "Lun min-chu yü tzu-yu" (On democracy and freedom), *Min-chu,* no. 17:447 (1946).

45. Li Chu, "Lueh-lun sou-ch'a shu-pao-t'an" (On the raiding of newsstands), *Wen-ts'ui,* no. 42:8 (Aug. 8, 1946). Chang C, p. 126. Shen Yu, "Yen-lun tzu-yu tsai chin-t'ien" (Freedom of the press today), *Wen-ts'ui,* no. 44:7 (Aug. 22, 1946).

46. T'ang T'ao and K'o Ling, "Chan-pieh tu-che" (A farewell to our readers), *Chou-pao,* no. 49/50:2-3 (Aug. 24, 1946).

47. Chang Chün-mai, "Wei Shang-hai shih . . ." (A protest against the illegal banning of *Tsai-sheng* magazine by the Shanghai police), *Tsai-sheng* (Rebirth), no. 129:10 (Sept. 9, 1946). The weekly was founded in 1931, and properly registered in Hankow and Chungking. It moved to Shanghai in April 1946.

48. Chang C, p. 126.

49. "Ch'i-shih" (An announcement), *Wen-ts'ui* 2.3:30 (Oct. 24, 1946).

50. Cheng Chen-to, "Wo-men ti k'ang-i" (Our protest), *Min-chu,* no. 9:1-2 (Dec. 8, 1945); and his "Wen-hua cheng pei o-sha che" (Civilization is being strangled), ibid., no. 44:1089-94 (1946). Ma Hsü-lun, "Min-chu shih feng-chin pu-liao ti" (Democracy cannot be suppressed), ibid., no. 47:1161-63 (1946). See especially "Wo-men ti k'ang-i" (Our protests), ibid., no. 53/54:1306-16 (Oct. 31, 1946). The bitter protests included in its last issue were written by its editor as well as other writers: "All written protests by oppressed people are of no use" (p. 1311). "Those who strangulate freedom will strangulate themselves" (p. 1312). "If the government insisted on forbidding people without guns from saying things that might displease it, the result could only be forcing people to give up pens and take up arms. This is nothing but encouraging political

enemies to arm themselves" (p. 1315). "In a new society and new
country soon to come, you will enjoy all freedoms, including the revival
of *Min-chu*" (p. 1308). Protests of this kind, which could scarcely be
found in earlier periods, were quite typical of this period. For the
objective of the magazine, see "Fa k'an tzu" (Foreword), *Min-chu*, no.
1:1 (Oct. 13, 1945); "Ch'ung-hsing shen-ming wo-men ti t'ai-tu ho chu-
chang" (A reiteration of our attitude and opinion), ibid., no. 51/52:
1258-59 (1946). Its registration permit was numbered 68.

51. "P'ing-t'an" (Comments), *Chou-pao*, no. 16:3 (Dec. 22, 1945); no. 17:2
    (Dec. 29, 1945). "Hsin-wen chi-ts'ui," *Wen-ts'ui*, no. 15:6 (Jan. 15, 1946).
    Ho Man-tzu, "Huo i-ching jen ch'i-lai le . . ." (The fire is burning–Chengtu
    after V-J Day), ibid., no. 12:17 (Dec. 25, 1945).

52. Shih Yen, "Hsi-an pao-chih so tsao-shou ti feng-pao" (Newspapers in
    Sian under stormy weather), *Chou-pao*, no. 27/28:25 (Mar. 16, 1946).

53. Ch'iu Ssu, *Min-chu*, no. 24:609-610. "Wei t'e-wu tao-hui pen-pao chin-
    kao she-hui" (How secret agents damaged our premises–an open letter),
    Wen-ts'ui, no. 22:21-22 (Mar. 21, 1946). The letter from the two papers
    in Sian was dated March 2, 1946. Yeh Ko, "Min-chu ho fan min-chu . . ."
    (The struggle between the democratic and anti-democratic forces in
    Canton), *Chou-pao*, no. 39:19-20 (June 1, 1946).

54. "Ch'eng-tu Hsin Chung-kuo jih-pao pei-tao hsiang-chi" (How and why
    the *New China Daily News* in Chengtu was wrecked by hooligans),
    Kuan-ch'a 1.24:27-29 (Feb. 8, 1947). *Shen pao* (Aug. 5 and 14, 1947).

55. Ti Chi, "Chi-nan pao-t'an erh-yueh chieh-yun" (The press in Tsinan during
    February), *Hsin-wen t'ien-ti* (*Newsdom*), no. 36:24 (Mar. 16, 1948). Pu
    Yao-lien, "Shui kuan-te le wo, wo shih tai-piao" (Who can restrain me?
    I am a representative to the National Assembly), ibid., no. 39:7-8 (May 1,
    1948).

56. Ko Ssu-en, "Hsin-wen tzu-yu ti ti-ch'ao" (Freedom of the press hit a low
    tide), *Kuan-ch'a* 2.16:10 (June 14, 1947).

57. "Hsiao-hsi pan-chou-k'an t'ing-k'an ch'i-shih" (*Information Semi weekly*'s
    announcement in regard to its suspension), *Chou-pao*, no. 39:18 (June 1,
    1946). Wu Han, "Tsen-mo pan" (What to do), ibid., no. 49/50:29-31
    (Aug. 24, 1946). For a list of the 77 magazines, see Tzu Wu, "Pei-p'ing
    ti wen-hua sao-tang" (The banning and suspension of publications in

Peiping), *Wen-ts'ui,* no. 35:7-8 (June 20, 1946). See also "K'ang-i Kuo-min-tang . . ." (A protest against the KMT's atrocity in destroying civilization), *Jo-ch'ao pan-yüeh-k'an* (Hot tide semi-monthly), 1.2:2 (June 16, 1946). P'ing Hsin, "Kung-tu hsia-tu wen-kao yu-kan" (My impression on a government document), *Chou-pao,* no. 49/50:14-15.

58.   Shanghai Magazine Association's memorandum to the third party representatives of the Political Consultative Conference, in *Min-chu,* no. 53/54:1360-61 (1946); reprinted in Chang C, pp. 124-129. Cf. Cheng Chen-to, "Cheng-ch'ü min-ch'üan pao-wei min-ch'üan" (To fight for democracy and to defend democracy), *Chou-pao,* no. 49/50:32 (Aug. 24, 1946).

59.   "P'ing-t'an," *Chou-pao,* no. 42:2-3 (June 22, 1946); no. 47:2 (July 27, 1946). Chou-pao she, "Wo-men ti sheng-shu" (Our appeal), ibid., no. 12:2-3 (Nov. 24, 1945); Min Tun, "Ch'ang-shu ti hsing-hsing se-se" (Vignettes of Changshu), *Min-chu,* no. 16:420-421 (1946). T'ang T'ao and K'o Ling, *Chou-pao,* no. 49/50:2-3. "Wo-men k'ung-shu" (We accuse), ibid., pp. 4-8. "Shang-hai tsa-chih chieh . . ." (Shanghai Magazine Association's protest against the suspension of *Chou-pao*), ibid., p. 47. In this issue, three large characters reading "the last issue" were printed in red on the front cover.

60.   "Ch'ung-ch'ing cheng wen" (News from Chungking), *Kuan-ch'a* 1.17:16 (Dec. 21, 1946). "Shang-hai Cheng-yen Ta-chung erh pao ta-yang ti ku-shih" (The suspension of *Cheng-yen pao* and *Ta-chung yeh-pao* in Shanghai), *Hsin-wen tsa-chih* (News magazine), n.s. no. 11:8-9 (Nov. 1, 1948), reported the suspension of several Shanghai newspapers run by KMT members. *Cheng-yen pao* was suspended in October 1948, because its editorial on Oct. 1 indirectly involved the intraparty power struggle. *Ta-chung yeh-pao,* suspended at the same time, was said to have offended Madame Chiang Kai-shek's nephew. It resumed publication on Oct. 20, after having dismissed five editors and two reporters. According to Ho Lu-sheng, "K'un-ming hsin-wen chieh cheng-su hou" (Newspapers in Kunming), *Hsin-wen t'ien-ti,* no. 91:11-12 (Nov. 12, 1949), after nine newspapers were suppressed in Kunming on Sept. 10-11, 1949, only the *Central Daily News* and another paper still existed there.

61.   "Hsi-k'ang ti min pien i pien" (The rebellions in Sikang), *Kuan-ch'a* 2.1:22 (Mar. 1, 1947).

62.   "Chi-che t'ung-hsin," *Kuan-ch'a* 2.6:18 (Apr. 5, 1947).

63. Fan Hui, "Hsin wu-ssu yun tung" (New May Fourth Movement), *Hsin Chung-hua* (New China), n.s. 5, no. 12:46-47 (June 16, 1947). Ch'u An-p'ing, "Lun Wen-hui Hsin-min Lien-ho san pao pei-feng" (On the suspension of *Wen-hui pao, Hsin-min pao* and *Lien-ho pao*), *Kuan-ch'a* 2.14:5-6 (May 31, 1947). On July 18, 1946, *Wen-hui pao* was suspended for seven days for refusing to reveal the identity of the writers of two letters to the editor, printed on July 12, under the pseudonyms of "A Group of Policemen" and "A Police Officer in the City." The reason given on the temporary suspension order was that the paper "intended to sow dissension [among the police], spread misleading stories and destroy peace and order." See "Wen-hui pao t'ing-k'an ch'i-jih nei-mu" (An inside story of the suspension of *Wen-hui pao* for seven days), *Chou-pao,* no. 46:9 (July 20, 1946); "P'ing-t'an," ibid., p. 3; "Wen-hui pao t'ing-k'an shih-ch'ien" (The Suspension of *Wen-hui pao*), *Wen-ts'ui,* no. 40:18 (July 25, 1946). Other laws might also be invoked to suspend papers. On Aug. 16, 1947, for instance, *Chen-li wan-pao* (The truth) of Peiping was suspended because it had violated the National General Mobilization Act. See Meng Ch'iu-ch'an, "Chen-li tsai Pei-p'ing pei o-sha le" (The strangulation of the *Truth* in Peiping), *Shih yü wen* 2.1:17 (1947).

64. "T'ing-k'an kao-pieh tu-che" (A farewell to the readers), *Shih yü wen,* the last issue (Sept. 24, 1948), pp. 1-3, gives the dates and places that the confiscations occurred.

65. Huang Fei, "Hu-nan wan wan-pao pei-feng" (The suspension of the *Late Evening News* of Hunan), *Shih yü wen* 2:492 (1948).

66. T'ien Hsiao-te, "Hsin-min pao kuan-men ch'ien-hou" (The story of the suspension of *Hsin-min pao*), *Hsin-wen t'ien-ti,* no. 44:8-10 (July 17, 1948). Cf. also "Chi-che t'ung-hsin," *Kuan-ch'a* 4.22:10 (July 31, 1948); Kuo Lai-jen, "Hsin-min pao Ch'en Ming-te ssu-mien ch'u-ko" (*Hsin-min pao* and Ch'en Ming-te are in dire straits), *Hsin-wen tsa-chih,* n.s. 2, no. 12:12-13 (Mar. 20, 1949).

67. T'ien Kao, "Ch'ung-ch'ing Shang-wu jih-pao ch'uang yang huo" (The misadventure of the *Commercial Daily News* of Chungking), *Hsin-wen t'ien-ti,* no. 61:14-15 (Mar. 10, 1949).

68. Ai Fei, "Nan-ching Jen pao ti ch'a-feng" (The suspension of *Jen-pao* in Nanking), ibid., no. 58:11-12 (Feb. 16, 1949).

69. Yang Kang, "Wei Yang Tsao yuan-yü . . ." (A letter to fellow journalists
     in regard to the Yang Tsao case), *Wen-ts'ui,* no. 27:19 (Apr. 25, 1946).
     "Shang-hai hsin-wen chi-che . . ." (A protest to the government from the
     journalists in Shanghai on the death of Yang Tsao), *Chou-pao,* no. 21/22:
     40 (Jan. 26, 1946). "Fang-wen Yang Tsao fu-jen" (A visit to Mrs. Yang
     Tsao), *Ta-kung pao* (Shanghai, Mar. 29, 1946), p. 3; "Mei hsin-wen-chieh
     lai tien . . ." (American journalists' protest), ibid. (Apr. 2, 1946), p. 1.

70. Li Fu-jen, "Hu-k'ou yü sheng" (A narrow escape), *Wen-ts'ui,* no. 43:17
     (Aug. 15, 1946). Cf. also "Che-shih shen-mo shih-chieh" (What kind of
     world is this), ibid., no. 34:21 (June 13, 1946); "Tu-che t'ou shu"
     (Letters to the editor), ibid., no. 31:22 (May 23, 1946). Both reported
     that Li was dead, and the latter even gave a graphic account of how
     he was strangled around the neck with a string and shot several times in
     the chest.

71. Ch'en Lang, *STPP* 6:3842. Shen Li, "Ch'ung-ch'ing liu-yueh k'ung-pu
     chung ti chi-tuan hsiao ku-shih" (Several anecdotes during the reign of
     terror in Chungking in June 1947), *Shih yü wen* 1:370 (1947). For a
     list of the names of the arrested journalists in Chungking and the papers
     they represented, see Chiang Liu, ibid. 1.22:17. Numerous students were
     arrested too in this period for being suspected Communists. Chao Ch'ao-
     kou, "Lun cheng-fu ta p'u hsüeh-sheng" (Arresting students on a large
     scale), *Kuan-ch'a* 5.2:3-4 (Sept. 4, 1948), reported that on Aug. 19,
     1948, when the government began its "gold yuan" policy, 179 students
     in Nanking, 250 in Peiping, 63 in Shanghai, 36 in Chungking, and 3 in
     Hangchow were arrested with the warrants issued by the Special Tribunal.
     These figures were compiled from the lists of names made public by the
     government. How many more were there who were illegally arrested or
     whose names were not made public? Chao did not know.

72. "Pei-p'ing chiao-yuan . . ." (More on the arrest of teachers and students
     in Peiping), *Kuan-ch'a* 3.9:17 (Oct. 25, 1947). "Chi-che t'ung-hsin,"
     ibid. 4.1:19 (Feb. 28, 1948). Ho Ching, "Pei-p'ing ti yu-i-ch'uan sou-p'u
     shih-chien" (More arrests in Peiping), *Shih yü wen* 2.20:17-20 (Feb. 27,
     1948).

73. Pen-she t'ung-jen, "Wo-men ti tzu-wo p'i-p'ing" (Our self-criticism),
     Kuan-ch'a 6.1:3 (Nov. 1, 1949). Cf. Ch'u An-p'ing, "Hsing-ch'in, jen-nai,
     hsiang-ch'ien" (Diligence, patience, and progress), ibid. 1.24:7 (Feb. 8,
     1947).

74. "Chi-che t'ung-hsin", ibid. 2.2:17 (Mar. 8, 1947). Fu's three articles—
    "Bureaucratic Capitalism Must Be Uprooted," "T. V. Soong Must Go,"
    "The Failure of T. V. Soong"—are in ibid. 2.1:6-8, 25-26, 26 (Mar. 1,
    1947). This method of buying all available copies of an offending
    publication was not new. In sixteenth-century England, for instance,
    Cuthbert Tunstall and William Warham, the Archbishop of Canterbury,
    allegedly tried to gain control of the entire edition of the Tyndall
    Testament (printed in 1526 in Antwerp) by buying it up (Winger, p. 70).

75. "Ch'ang-sha chin-chih pen-k'an fa-hsing" (The banning of this magazine
    in Changsha), *Kuan-ch'a* 1.18:22 (Dec. 28, 1946). A government paper
    in Northwest China refused even to carry the weekly's advertisement;
    see "Pen-k'an tsai Lan-chou" (This magazine in Lanchow), ibid. 1.15:23
    (Dec. 7, 1946).

76. Ch'u An-p'ing, "Hsing-ch'in . . . ," ibid. 1.24:3-9. The weekly had 2,700
    subscribers, which was considered quite a high figure in view of the fact
    that fear of a magazine's suddenly being suspended would keep down
    the number of subscriptions. Meanwhile, the magazine was prepared for
    rainy days. In "Ko-ti t'e-yueh chi-che kung-chien" (To our special cor-
    respondents), ibid. 2.9:23 (Apr. 26, 1947) and 2.13:23 (May 24, 1947),
    it declared that those who were afraid of postal censorship in time of
    emergency might address their mail to the editor's home.

77. Ch'u An-p'ing, "P'ing P'u-li-te . . ." (On Bullitt's partial and unsound
    report on China), ibid. 3.9:3-5 (Oct. 25, 1947). William C. Bullitt's "A
    Report to the American People on China" (*Life,* [Oct. 13, 1947], pp.
    35-37) advocated immediate U.S. aid to China. Ch'u maintained that
    the problems in China could not be solved by military means.

78. Ch'u An-p'ing, "Ch'ih-chung, k'u-tou, chin-hsin" (To suffer, to struggle,
    and to do our best), *Kuan-ch'a* 4.23/24:8 (Aug. 7, 1948). For unknown
    reasons, the notice was never delivered to the magazine.

79. Tung Shih-chin, "Wo tui-yü cheng-fu ch'ü-t'i Min-Meng ti kan-hsiang"
    (On the outlawing of the Democratic League), ibid. 3.11:4-5 (Nov. 1,
    1947). "Tu-che t'ou shu," ibid. 3.18:2 (Dec. 27, 1947). Ch'u An-p'ing,
    "Ch'ih-chung . . . ," ibid. 4.23/24:8.

80. "Pen-she kung-kai chao-k'ao kung-tso jen-yuan" (Help wanted, an
    advertisement), ibid. 5.3:17 (Sept. 11, 1948). The management reserved

the right to discharge all employees "unconditionally" in case it could not continue publication due to circumstances beyond its control. The "Observer Series," which included about a dozen books written by university professors, was chiefly on the social sciences from a liberal point of view.

81.   "Tu-che t'ou-shu," *Kuan-ch'a* 5.10:16 (Oct. 30, 1948); 5.11:16 (Nov. 6, 1948). The Ministry labeled the magazine as "expressing preposterous opinions, doing propaganda for the [Communist] bandits, slandering the government, and obstructing [the government's efforts in] suppressing the rebellion."

82.   "Pien-che chin-chi pao-kao" (An urgent report by the editor), ibid. 5.12:9 (Nov. 13, 1948).

83.   When the magazine resumed publication in November 1949, under the Communist regime, it gave a detailed account of the suspension of the magazine and arrests of its staff members by the KMT government. See "Kuan-ch'a-she pei Kuo-min-tang . . ." (An account of the reactionary KMT government's persecution of the *Observer*), ibid. 6.1:3-5 (Nov. 1, 1949). The two offending articles were: Ch'u An-p'ing, "I-ch'ang lan-wu" (A great mess), ibid. 5.11:3 (Nov. 6, 1948); and "Hsü Huai chan-chü ti pien-huan" (The battle of Hwai-Hai), ibid. 5.14:8-9 (Nov. 27, 1948). The KMT troops' sudden, unannounced withdrawal from the capital dismayed the people, who had to invite the People's Liberation Army to come and maintain order in the city. I was then teaching at the University of Nanking.

84.   Cf. Hu Ti, "Pei-p'ing erh san shih" (A few incidents in Peiping), *Shih yü wen* 1:351 (1947).

85.   Chü Ts'un, "Yü pu-chang fu-jen ch'iu-liang mou-li ti mi" (The hoarding of foodstuffs for monetary gain by Mrs. Yü, wife of the Minister of Foodstuffs), *Tzu-yu lun-t'an* 3.4:5 (Apr. 1, 1948). "Tu-che chih sheng," *Shih yü wen* 1.402 (1947). Yeh Sheng-t'ao, "Pao-lu ti hsiao-kuo," *Chou-pao,* no. 15:22, complained that all exposés and criticisms could bring no desired results.

86.   "She p'ing" (An editorial), *Hsin-min pao* (Dec. 5, 1945), reprinted in *Wen-ts'ui,* no. 12:11 (Dec. 25, 1945). Yeh Sheng-t'ao, "Wo-men yung pu-yao . . ." (We will never permit the censorship of books and magazines), *Chou-pao,* no. 11:18 (Nov. 17, 1945). Chou Chien, "Wo-men

hsü-yao tsen-yang ti cheng-fu" (What kind of government do we need), *Chieh-fang chou-pao* (Liberation weekly), 1.1:5 (Oct. 1, 1945). Ch'u An-p'ing, "Cheng-fu li-jen chih-hsiang Kuan-ch'a" (The government's sharp knife is pointed at the *Observer*), *Kuan-ch'a* 4.20:3-4 (July 17, 1948).

87. This action induced the government to repeal (on Oct. 1, 1945) forty-eight wartime laws and regulations, including the prepublication censor-ship in Free China. The publishers' other demands included the abolition of news censorship in areas formerly occupied by the Japanese—a demand granted in March 1946. See "P'ing-t'an," *Chou-pao,* no. 5:2 (Oct. 6, 1945); Yü Liang, "Ta-p'o yen-lun ti chih-ku" (To shake off the manacles on the press), *Wen-ts'ui* 1.8:4-5 (Nov. 27, 1945). When news censorship was imposed again in Tientsin on June 1, 1947, *Hsin-hsing pao* decided to refuse censorship because it felt that it might as well be suspended if it could not speak its mind. See "Chi T'ien-chin . . . ," *Kuan-ch'a* 2.18:17.

88. "Nien-i-t'iao yao-ch'iu" (Twenty-one demands), *Wen-ts'ui,* no. 16:6-7 (Jan. 24, 1946). For other demands that the KMT stop its control of the press, see Sun Te-chen, "Wei yen-lun tzu-yu chin i chieh" (On free-dom of the press), *Shang-hai wen-hua,* no. 6:19 (July 1, 1946); Chang Hsiao-hu, *Shih yü wen* 2.17:6-8; Shih Fu-liang, "Wei-ta ti min-i . . ." (The great public opinion and the stupid reactionary forces), *Chou-pao,* no. 43:5 (June 29, 1946).

89. Chang C, pp. 106-132. Cf. also "Wo-men ti k'ang-i" (Our protest), *Wen-ts'ui,* no. 17:14-15 (Jan. 31, 1946). "Li-chi fei-chih wen-hua t'ung-chih cheng-ts'e" (On abolishing immediately the policy of cultural control), ibid., pp. 25-26. Chang Hui, "Ch'ung-ch'ing Tzu-yu tao pao . . ." (The banning of *Tzu-yu tao pao* in Chungking), ibid., no. 15:11-12 (Jan. 17, 1946). Li Wei-pei, "Wo-men yao yu hsin-wen tzu-yu" (We want freedom of the press), *Chou-pao,* no. 20:7-8 (Jan. 19, 1946). In October 1946, following the large-scale suspension of dissenting magazines, 39 liberals protested the KMT repression. See "Wo-men yao-ch'iu cheng-fu . . ." (We request that the government truly protect the freedom of speech and of the press), *Min-chu,* no. 51/52:1258-59 (1946). Among those who affixed their signatures to the protest were Ai Han-sung, Chang Chün-mai, Chao Ch'ao-kou, Cheng Chen-to, Hu Feng, K'o Ling, Kuo Mo-jo, Lo Lung-chi, Liu Ya-tzu, Ma Hsü-lun, Mao Tun, Pa Chin, T'ang T'ao, T'ien Han, and Yeh Sheng-t'ao.

90. "T'ing-k'an kao-pieh tu-che," *Shih yü wen,* last issue (Sept. 24, 1948), p. 2. T'ang T'ao and K'o Ling, *Chou-pao,* no. 49/50:2-3.

91. Shen Yu, *Wen-ts'ui,* no. 44:7. Yin Huai-yuan, "Cheng-fu yü yü-lun (The government and public opinion), *Ta-kung pao* (July 19, 1948), p. 1.

92. Cf. "Chi T'ien-chin . . . ," *Kuan-ch'a* 2.18:17. Ch'u An-p'ing, "Cheng-fu li-jen . . . ," ibid. 4.20:4. "Wo-men k'ung-shu," *Chou-pao,* no. 49/50:4-8. "Wo-men ti k'ang-i," *Min-chu,* no. 53/54:1306-16, esp. p. 1308.

VIII. Conclusion

1. Rex *vs.* Tutchin, *Fourteen State Trials,* p. 1095; quoted in Siebert, p. 271. This definition of seditious libel was established by Chief Justice Holt.

2. A few demands were also made for "absolute freedom" of the press after the Sino-Japanese War, although those who clamored for them did not take them seriously. All Chinese intellectuals were too busy with protesting government intervention and government corruption during these few years of confusion and disillusionment to engage in philosophical discussion.

3. *The Compassionate Samaritane* (1644), quoted in Siebert, p. 193.

4. Cf. Winger, pp. 51, 59, 60, 66, 70, 72, 109, 120, 157, 169-172, 178-179, 181-182, 198, 219; Siebert, pp. 34, 37, 41, 43-45, 49, 52, 56, 73, 150, 233, 301, 322, 338.

5. Siebert, p. 10.

6. Lü Pu-wei (290-235 B.C.), *Lü shih ch'un ch'iu* (Lü's Spring and Autumn annals; Shanghai, 1929), 15:18a-b.

BIBLIOGRAPHY

Abend, Hallett. *My Life in China, 1926-1941.* New York, Harcourt, Brace & Co., 1943.

Barth, Alan. *Government by Investigation.* New York, Viking Press, 1955.

Britton, Roswell S. *The Chinese Periodical Press, 1800-1912.* Shanghai, Kelly & Walsh, 1933.

Chafee, Zechariah. *Government and Mass Communication.* Chicago, University of Chicago Press, 1947.

––– *Free Speech in the United States.* Cambridge, Mass., Harvard University Press, 1948.

Chan-shih hsin-wen kung-tso ju-men 戰時新聞工作入門 (An introduction to wartime journalism), ed. Chung-kuo ch'ing-nien chi-che hsueh-hui 中國青年記者學會 (Young Chinese Journalists Association). Chungking, 1939.

Chang Ching-lu 張靜廬. *Tsai ch'u-pan chieh erh-shih nien* 在 出版界二十年 (Twenty years in the publishing business). Hankow, 1938.

––– *Chung-kuo hsien-tai ch'u-pan shih-liao* 中國現代出版 史料 (Source materials of the history of contemporary Chinese publishing). Peking, 1954-1959. In four series: A, B, C, D.

Chang Shih-yuan 張詩源. *Ch'u-pan fa chih li-lun yü shih-yung* 出版法之理論與實用 (The theory and practice of the publication laws). Taipei, 1957.

Chang Yun-chia 張雲家. *Yü Yu-jen chuan* 于右任傳 (Life of Yü Yu-jen). Taipei, 1958.

Ch'ang-sun Wu-chi 長孫無忌 . *T'ang lü su i* 唐律疏義 (Commentaries on laws and statutes of the T'ang dynasty). Shanghai, 1937.

Chao Chan-yuan 趙占元 . *Kuo-fang hsin-wen shih-yeh chih t'ung-chih* 國防新聞事業之統計 (The control of journalism for national defense). Shanghai, 1937.

Chao Ming-heng 趙敏恆 . *Ts'ai-fang shih-wu nien* 採訪十五年 (Fifteen years as a reporter). Chungking, 1944.

Ch'en Hsü-lu 陳旭麓 . *Tsou Jung yü Ch'en T'ien-hua ti ssu-hsiang* 鄒容與陳天華的思想. (The ideals of Tsou Jung and Ch'en T'ien-hua). Shanghai, 1957.

Ch'en pao fu-chien 晨報副鎸 . (Literary supplement to *Ch'en pao*).

Cheng lun 正論 (Righteous discourses).

Ch'eng Ch'i-heng 程其恆 and Jung Yu-ming 容又銘 , eds. *Chi-che ching-yen t'an* 記者經驗談 (Journalists' personal experiences). Kweilin, 1943.

Ch'eng She-wo 成舍我 . *Pao-hsueh tsa-chu* 報學雜著 (Notes on journalism). Taipei, 1956.

Chia ying 甲寅 (The Tiger).

Chieh-fang chou-pao 解放週報 (Liberation weekly).

Ch'ien-shao 前哨 (The outpost).

Chin-Ch'a-Chi hua-pao 晉察冀畫報 (*Chin-Cha-Chi Pictorial*).

Chin Hsiung-pai 金雄白 *Min-kuo cheng-hai sou pi* 民國政海搜祕 (Anecdotes of government officials in republican China). Hong Kong, 1964.

Ch'in-ting hsüeh-t'ang chang-ch'eng 欽定學堂章程 (Rules for the schools by imperial orders). Shanghai, 1904.

China Handbook, 1937-1943, comp. Chinese Ministry of Information. New York, Macmillan Co., 1943.

China Handbook, 1956-57, comp. China Handbook Editorial Board. Taipei, China Publishing Co., 1956.

Chinese Year Book, 1938-1939, comp. Council of International Affairs. Chungking, Commercial Press, 1939.

Chinese Year Book, 1943, comp. Council of International Affairs. Bombay, Thacker & Co., 1943.

Ching-hua jih-pao 京話日報 (Peking dialect daily).

Ch'ing-i pao 清議報 (*China Discussion*).

Ch'ing-nien ssu-ch'ao 青年思潮 (Thoughts of youths). Its probable real title: *Chung-kuo lun-t'an* 中國論壇 (China forum). Peiping.

Chou-pao 周報 (The weekly).

Chu Ch'uan-yü 朱傳譽. *Pao-jen, pao-shih, pao-hsueh* 報人報史. 報學 (Journalist, history of journalism, and journalism). Taipei, 1966.

——— *Sung-tai hsin-wen shih* 宋代新聞史 (History of journalism in the Sung dynasty). Taipei, 1967.

Ch'u-pan chieh 出版界 (The publishing world).

Chuan-chi wen-hsueh 傳記文學 (Biographical literature).

Ch'üan-kuo chung-wen ch'i-k'an lien-ho mu-lu, 1833-1949 全國中文期刊聯合目錄 (A union catalog of Chinese periodicals in China, 1833-1949), comp. Peking Library. Peking, 1961.

Ch'üan min k'ang-chan 全民抗戰 (War of resistance for all the people).

Chung-hua lun-t'an 中華論壇 (China forum).

Chung-hua-min-kuo fa-kuei hui-pien 中華民國法規彙編 (A collection of laws and regulations of the Republic of China, 1933, 1935), comp. Bureau of Compilation, Legislative Yuan. Shanghai, 1934, 1936.

Chung-hua min-kuo fa-kuei ta-ch'üan 中華民國法規大全 (A comprehensive collection of Chinese laws and regulations). Shanghai, 1936.

Chung-hua min-kuo k'ai-kuo wu-shih nien shih lun-chi 中華民國

開國五十年史論集　(A collection of essays com-memorating the fiftieth anniversary of the Republic of China). Taipei, 1964.

Chung-hua-min-kuo k'ai-kuo wu-shih nien wen-hsien 中華民國開國五十年文獻　(Documents commemorating the fiftieth anniversary of the founding of the Republic of China). Series I. Taipei, 1964.

Chung-hua nien-chien, 1948 中華年鑑 (China Yearbook). Nanking, 1949.

Chung-kuo wen-hua chien-she hsueh-hui 中國文化建設協會 (China Cultural Reconstruction Association), ed. *Shih-nien lai ti Chung-kuo* 十年來的中國　(China in the past ten years). Shanghai, 1937.

Clubb, O. Edmund. *Twentieth Century China.* New York, Columbia University Press, 1964.

De Francis, John. *Nationalism and Language Reform in China.* Princeton, N.J., Princeton University Press, 1950.

Feng Ai-ch'ün 馮愛群 . *Chung-kuo hsin-wen shih* 中國新聞史 (History of Chinese journalism). Taipei, 1967.

Feng Tzu-yu 馮自由 . *Chung-hua-min-kuo k'ai-kuo ch'ien ko-ming shih* 中華民國開國前革命史　(Revolutionary history before the founding of the Republic of China). Chung-king, 1944.

——— *Ko-ming i-shih* 革命逸事 (Anecdotal history of the 1911 revolution). Shanghai, 1947.

——— *Chung-kuo ko-ming yun-tung erh-shih-liu nien tsu-chih shih* 中國革命運動二十六年組織史　(History of the Chinese revolutionary movement, 1885-1911). Shanghai, 1948.

——— *Hua-ch'iao ko-ming tsu-chih shih-hua* 華僑革命組織史話

(History of overseas Chinese revolutionary organizations).
Taipei, 1954.

Fu-nü wen-hua 婦女文化 (Women and culture).

Gasster, Michael. *Chinese Intellectuals and the Revolution of 1911.*
Seattle, University of Washington Press, 1969.

Hsia Tsi-an. *Gate of Darkness.* Seattle, University of Washington
Press, 1968.

Hsiang-tao 嚮導 (*Guide Weekly*).

Hsien-tai ch'u-pan-chieh 現代出版界 (Contemporary publishing world).

Hsien-tai p'ing-lun 現代評論 (*Contemporary Review*).

Hsin ch'ing-nien 新青年 (*La Jeunesse*).

Hsin Chung-hua 新中華 (New China).

Hsin-hai ko-ming 辛亥革命 (The 1911 revolution), ed. Chung-
kuo shih-hsueh hui 中國史學會 (Chinese Historical
Society). Shanghai, 1957.

Hsin-hai ko-ming hui-i lu 辛亥革命回憶錄 (Recollections
of the 1911 revolution). Peking, 1962.

Hsin jen-shih 新認識 (New cognizance).

Hsin-min-hui chung-yang chih-tao-pu, tiao-ch'a-k'o 新民會中央
指導部調查科 (Central Headquarters of the New
People Bureau, Investigation Division). *Chin-chih t'u-shu mu-
lu, k'ang-jih chih pu* 禁止圖書目錄, 抗日之部
(Prohibited books—anti-Japanese section). Nanking, 1939.

——— *Kuo-min-tang kuan-hsi t'u-shu mu-lu* 國民黨關係圖
書目錄 (Prohibited books concerned with the KMT).
Nanking, 1939.

Hsin-min ts'ung-pao 新民叢報 (New citizen).

Hsin she-hui pan-yueh-k'an 新社會半月刊 (New society
semimonthly).

Hsin-sheng chou-k'an 新生週刊 (New life weekly).

Hsin wan-pao 新晚報 (*New Evening Post*).

Hsin-wen chan-hsien 新聞戰線 (News front).

Hsin-wen t'ien-ti 新聞天地 (*Newsdom*).

Hsin-wen tsa-chih 新聞雜誌 (News magazine).

Hsin-wen tu fa 新聞讀法 (How to read a newspaper). Shang-hai, n.d.

Hsin-yueh 新月 (New moon).

Hu Ch'iu-yuan 胡秋原 . *Yen-lun tzu-yu tsai Chung-kuo li-shih shang* 言論自由在中國歷史上 (Freedom of speech in Chinese history). Taipei, 1958.

Hung-ch'i 紅旗 (Red flag).

Hung-ch'i chou-pao 紅旗週報 (Red flag weekly).

Hung-shui 洪水 (The flood).

Inkeles, Alex. *Public Opinion in Soviet Russia*. Cambridge, Mass., Harvard University Press, 1950.

Jen-chien shih 人間世 (In the world).

Jen-min wen-hsueh 人民文學 (People's literature).

Jen yen 人言 (Man's words).

Jih-pao so-yin 日報索引 (Index to newspapers).

Jo-ch'ao pan-yueh-k'an 熱潮半月刊 (Hot tide semimonthly).

K'ang-chan 抗戰 (War of resistance).

Ko Kung-chen 戈公振 . *Chung-kuo pao-hsueh shih* 中國報學史 (History of Chinese journalism). Shanghai, 1935.

Ko-ming chün 革命軍 (The revolutionary army).

Kotenev, A. M. *Shanghai: Its Mixed Court and Council*. Shanghai, North China Daily News and Herald, 1925.

——— *Shanghai: Its Municipality and the Chinese*. Shanghai, North China Daily News and Herald, 1927.

Ku-chün 孤軍 (The lonely soldier). Shanghai.

Ku-chün chou-pao 孤軍週報 (The lonely soldier weekly). Peking.

Kuan-ch'a 觀察 (*The Observer*).

Kuang Wei-jan 光未然. *Chiang Chieh-shih chiao-sha wen-hua* 蔣介石絞殺文化 (Chiang Kai-shek strangulates civilization). N.p., North China New China Book Co., 1947.

Kung Te-pai 龔德柏. *Kung Te-pai hui-i lu* 龔德柏回憶錄 (Kung Te-pai's memoir). Hong Kong, 1963-1964.

Kuo-chia tang-an chü Ming Ch'ing tang-an kuan 國家檔案局明清檔案局 (National Archives—Ming-Ch'ing Bureau). *Wu-hsü pien-fa tang-an shih-liao* 戊戌變法檔案史料 (Source materials of the reform movement of 1898). Peking, 1958.

Kuo-hsin 國訊 (National news).

Kuo-min cheng-fu kung pao 國民政府公報 (Official gazette of [Wang's] National Government).

Kuo-min jih-jih pao 國民日日報 (*China National Gazette*).

Kuo-wen chou-pao 國聞週報 (*Kuowen Weekly Illustrated*).

Li Ch'eng-i 李誠毅. *San-shih nien lai chia kuo* 三十年來家國 (My country in the past thirty years). Hong Kong, 1961.

Lieh-ning ch'ing-nien 列寧青年 (Leninist youth).

Lin Lan 林蘭, ed. *Hsiao Chu-pa-chieh* 小豬八戒 (The piggy). Shanghai, 1932.

Lin Yutang. *The History of the Press and Public Opinion in China.* Chicago, University of Chicago Press, 1936.

Lo Ch'eng-lieh 羅承烈. *Hsin-min pao she-lun* 新民報社論 (Editorials of *Hsin-min pao*). Nanking, 1936.

Lo Chih-yuan 羅志淵. *Chung-kuo hsien-fa shih* 中國憲法史 (Constitutional history of China). Taipei, 1947.

Lu Hsün ch'üan-chi 魯迅全集 (Complete works of Lu Hsün), ed.

Lu Hsün hsien-sheng chi-nien wei-yuan-hui 魯迅先生紀念委員會 (Lu Hsün Memorial Committee). Shanghai, 1938.

Lu Hsün ch'üan-chi pu-i 魯迅全集補遺 (A supplement to the complete works of Lu Hsün), ed. T'ang T'ao 唐弢. Shanghai, 1948.

Lü Kuang 呂光 and P'an Hsien-mo 潘賢模. *Chung-kuo hsin-wen fa kai-lun* 中國新聞法概論 (A general survey of the press laws in China). Taipei, 1965.

Lü Pu-wei 呂不韋. *Lü shih ch'un ch'iu* 呂氏春秋 (Lü's Spring and Autumn annals). Shanghai, 1929.

Mao Tun wen-chi 茅盾文集 (Works of Mao Tun). Peking, 1958.

Mill, John Stuart. *Essay on Liberty*. New York, P. F. Collier & Sons, 1909.

Min-chu 民主 (Democracy). Shanghai.

Min-chu cheng-chih 民主政治 (Democracy).

Min-chu chou-k'an 民主週刊 (Democratic weekly). Kunming.

Min-chu shih-chieh 民主世界 (Democratic world).

Min pao 民報 (*The Minpao Magazine*).

Ming lü chi chieh fu li 明律集解附例 (Collected commentaries and precedents of the laws and statutes of the Ming dynasty). Peking, 1908.

Mu Hsin 穆欣, ed. *Tsou T'ao-fen* 鄒韜奮. Hong Kong, 1959.

Nan-hua wen-i 南華文藝 (South China literary magazine).

Nei-cheng nien-chien 內政年鑑 (Yearbook of Chinese internal affairs), comp. Nei-cheng-pu nien-chien pien-chi wei-yuan hui 內政部年鑑編輯委員會 (Yearbook of Chinese Internal Affairs Compilation Committee, Ministry of the Interior

New York Times.

North-China Daily News. *The Shanghai Sedition Trial*. Shanghai, 1904.

——— *China's Attempt to Muzzle the Foreign Press.* Shanghai, 1929.
North China Herald. Shanghai.

P'an Shu-fan 潘樹藩. *Chung-hua-min-kuo hsien-fa shih* 中華民國憲法史 (Constitutional history of the Republic of China). Shanghai, 1935.

P'an Tzu-nien 潘梓年 et al. *Hsin-hua jih-pao ti hui-i* 新華日報的回憶 (A reminiscence of the *New China Daily*). Chungking, 1960.

Pao hsueh 報學 (Journalism).

Pao-hsueh chi-k'an 報學季刊 (Journalism quarterly). Shanghai.

Pao-hsueh yueh-k'an 報學月刊 (Journalism monthly). Shanghai.

Pei-fang wen-hua 北方文化 (Culture in the north).

People's Tribune. Shanghai.

Ping-yin 丙寅 (The year of 1926).

Powell, John B. *My Twenty-Five Years in China.* New York, The Macmillan Co., 1945.

Pu-erh-sai-wei-k'o 布爾塞維克 (Bolshevik).

Quigley, Harold S. *The Far East.* Boston, World Peace Foundation, 1938.

Sa K'ung-liao 薩空了. *K'o-hsueh ti hsin-wen kai-lun* 科學的新聞概論 (A systematic study of journalism). Hong Kong, 1946.

San-shih nien-tu k'ang-chan chien-kuo kung-tso shih-chi 三十年度抗戰建國工作實蹟 (An annual report on our achievements in the war of resistance and the reconstruction of the country in the fiscal year 1941), comp. Ministry of Information. Chungking, 1942.

Sha Ch'ien-li 沙千里. *Ch'i jen chih yü* 七人之獄 (The imprisonment of the seven). Shanghai, 1937.

Shang-hai nien-chien, 1946 上海年鑑 (Yearbook of Shanghai). Shanghai, 1947.

Shang-hai shih nien-chien, 1937 上海市年鑑 (Yearbook of Shanghai). Shanghai, 1938.

Shang-hai t'ung-chih kuan ch'i-k'an 上海通志館期刊 (*Journal of the Gazette Bureau of Shanghai*).

Shang-hai wen-hua 上海文化 (Shanghai culture).

Shang-hai yen-chiu tzu-liao 上海研究資料 (Source materials on Shanghai). Shanghai, 1936.

Shanghai Municipal Council, *Report for the Year of 1919.* Shanghai, Kelly & Walsh, 1920.

――― *Report for the Year of 1921.* Shanghai, Kelly & Walsh, 1922.

Sharp, Eugene W. *The Censorship and Press Laws of Sixty Countries.* Columbia, University of Missouri Press, 1936.

Shen pao 申報 (*Shun pao*).

Shen pao nien-chien, 1936 申報年鑑 (Yearbook of *Shun pao*). Shanghai, 1937.

Shen pao yueh-k'an 申報月刊 (*Shun pao* monthly).

Sheng-huo 生活 (Life weekly).

Shih-lun fen-hsi 時論分析 (Analysis of current events).

Shih-lun ts'ung-k'an 時論叢刊 (A collection of essays on current affairs). Canton, 1933.

Shih-shih lei pien 時事類編 (Digest of current events). Chungking, Sun Yat-sen Institute for the Advancement of Culture and Education.

Shih-tai p'i-p'ing 時代批評 (*Modern Critique*). Hong Kong.

Shih yü wen 時與文 (*Time and culture*).

Siebert, Frederick Seaton. *Freedom of the Press in England, 1476-1776.* Urbana, University of Illinois Press, 1952.

Snow, Edgar. "The Ways of the Chinese Censor," *Current History* 13:381-386 (1935).

Su Ch'e 蘇轍. *Luan ch'eng chi* 欒城集. Shanghai, 1929.

Su Hsueh-lin 蘇雪林 . *Wo lun Lu Hsün* 我論魯迅 (My critique on Lu Hsün). Taipei, 1967.

Su pao 蘇報 (Kiangsu daily).

Sun Wen 孫文 . *San-min chu-i* 三民主義 (Three People's Principles). Shanghai, 1927.

Sun Yat-sen, His Political and Social Ideas, A Source Book, tr. and annotated by Leonard Shih Lien Hsü. Los Angeles, University of Southern California Press, 1933.

Sung hui-yao chi kao 宋會要輯稿 (History of institutions in the Sung dynasty). 1809 ed.

Ta-Ch'ing hui-tien shih-li 大清會典實例 (Laws and statutes of the Ch'ing dynasty). 1899.

Ta Chung-hua 大中華 (*The Great Chung Hwa Magazine*).

Ta-chung sheng-huo 大眾生活 (*Public Life*).

Ta-kung 大公 (The impartial).

Ta-kung pao 大公報 (*L'Impartial*).

T'ai-p'ing-yang kung-pao 太平洋公報 (The Pacific). Its probable real title: *T'ai-p'ing-yang ch'ih-se chiu-chi-hui kung-pao* 太平洋赤色救濟會公報 (Pacific Red Relief Association bulletin).

Tao-nien T'ao-fen 悼念韜奮 (In memory of Tsou T'ao-fen). N.p., Ch'ün-Chung Press, 1944.

T'ao-fen ti tao-lu 韜奮的道路 (The road of Tsou T'ao-fen), comp. Shang-hai T'ao-fen chi-nien-kuan 上海韜奮紀念館 (Shanghai Memorial House of Tsou T'ao-fen). Peking, 1958.

Te-tsung Ching huang-ti shih-lu 德宗景皇帝實錄 (Veritable records of the Kuang-hsü Emperor). Taipei, 1964.

T'ien Yü-chen 田玉振 . *Chan-shih hsin-wen kung-tso ti t'u-ching* 戰時新聞工作的途徑 (The path of wartime journalism). Chungking, 1944.

Times (London).

Ting Ching-t'ang 丁景唐 and Ch'ü Kuang-hsi 瞿光熙 , comps. *Tso-lien wu-lieh-shih yen-chiu tzu-liao pien-mu* 左聯五烈士研究資料編目 (A catalog of research materials on the five martyrs of the League of Left-Wing Writers). Shanghai, 1962.

Tou I 竇儀 . *Sung hsing t'ung* 宋刑統 (Penal code of the Sung dynasty). Taipei, 1964.

Tsa-chih 雜誌 (The magazine).

Tsai-sheng 再生 (Rebirth).

Ts'ai-cheng p'ing-lun 財政評論 (Finance review).

Ts'ai I 蔡儀 . *Chung-kuo hsin wen-hsueh shih chiang-hua* 中國新文學史講話 (A history of new Chinese literature). Shanghai, 1953.

Ts'an-cheng-hui yü yen-lun tzu-yu 參政會與言論自由 (Political council and the freedom of speech and the press). N.p., Shanghai Magazine Co., 1941.

Ts'ao Ya-po 曹亞伯 . *Wu-ch'ang ko-ming chen-shih* 武昌革命真史 (The true history of the 1911 revolution). Shanghai, 1928.

Ts'eng Hsü-pai 曾虛白 . *Chung-kuo hsin-wen shih* 中國新聞史 (History of Chinese journalism). Taipei, 1966.

Tso Shun-sheng 左舜生 . *Chung-kuo chin-tai shih-hua* 中國近代史話 (*Familiar talks in modern Chinese history*). Taipei, 1967.

Tsou Jung 鄒容. *Ko-ming chün* 革命軍 (The revolutionary army). Shanghai, 1958.

Tsou T'ao-fen 鄒韜奮 . *Ching-li* 經歷 (My experiences). Shanghai, 1938.

——— *K'ang-chan i-lai* 抗戰以來 (Since the outbreak of the war). 3rd ed. Shanghai, 1947.

——— *T'ao-fen wen-chi* 韜奮文集 (Collected works of Tsou T'ao-fen). Hong Kong, 1957.

Tsou Yang 鄒陽. *Kuo kung chih chien* 國共之間 (Between the KMT and the CCP). N.p., Li-shih tzu-liao kung-ying she 歷史資料供應社, 1945.

Tsui-chin chih wu-shih chi 最近之五十季 (*The past fifty years, in commemoration of the Shun Pao's Golden Jubilee*). Shanghai, 1923.

Tu-li p'ing-lun 獨立評論 (Independent review).

Tu-shu tsa-chih 讀書雜誌 (Readings).

Tu-shu yü ch'u-pan 讀書與出版 (Reading and publishing).

T'u-shu yin-shua yueh-pao 圖書印刷月報 (Book printing monthly).

Tung-fang tsa-chih 東方雜誌 (*Eastern Miscellany*).

Tzu-yu lun-t'an 自由論壇 (Freedom forum).

Tzu-yu yen-lun 自由言論 (Free speech).

Wang Chang-ling 王章陵. *Chung-kung ti wen-i cheng-feng* 中共的文藝整風 (Chinese Communists' Setting-literature-in-order movement). Taipei, 1967.

Wang Che-fu 王哲甫. *Chung-kuo hsin wen-hsueh yun-tung shih* 中國新文學運動史 (A history of the new literary movement in China). Hong Kong, 1965.

Wang Hsin-wu 王新吾. *Hsin-wen ch'üan li ssu-shih nien* 新聞圈裡四十年 (Forty years as a journalist). Taipei, 1957.

Wang Wen-pin 王文彬, ed. *Pao-jen chih lu* 報人之路 (The road of the journalists). Shanghai, 1938.

Wang, Y. C. "The *Su-pao* Case." *Monumenta Serica* 24:84-129 (1965).

Wang, Y. P. *The Rise of the Native Press in China.* Shanghai, 1924.

Wang Yao 王瑤. *Chung-kuo hsin wen-hsueh shih-kao* 中國新文學史稿 (Draft history of modern Chinese literature). Shanghai, 1951.

Wang Yun-wu 王雲五. *Shih-nien k'u-tou chi* 十年苦鬥記 (Ten years' struggle). Taipei, 1966.

Wen-hua chien-she yueh-k'an 文化建設月刊 (Cultural reconstruction monthly).

Wen-ts'ui 文萃 (*Articles digest*).

Winger, Howard W. "Regulations Relating to the Book Trade in London, from 1357 to 1586." Ph.D. dissertation, Graduate School of Library Science, University of Illinois, 1953.

Wright, Mary C., ed. *China in Revolution: The First Phase, 1900-1913.*New Haven, Yale University Press, 1968.

Wu-han jih-pao nien-chien, 1947 武漢日報年鑑 (Yearbook of the Wuhan Daily). Wuhan, 1948.

Wu-ssu ai-kuo yun-tung tzu-liao 五四愛國運動資料 (Source materials of the May Fourth Movement). Peking, 1959.

Wu Yü-chang 吳玉章 . *Hsin-hai ko-ming* 辛亥革命 (The 1911 revolution). Peking, 1961.

Yang-chou shih-jih chi 楊州十日記 (Ten days in Yangchow), ed. Chung-kuo li-shih yen-chiu she (Chinese Historical Research Society). Shanghai, [pref. 1936].

Yang Ming 楊明. *T'ao-fen hsien-sheng ti liu-wang sheng-huo* 鄒奮先生的流亡生活 (Mr. Tsou T'ao-fen in exile). N.p., Min-chu she, 1946.

Yang Shou-ch'ing 楊壽清 . *Chung-kuo ch'u-pan chieh chien-shih* 中國出版界簡史 (A short history of Chinese publishing). Shanghai, 1946.

Yang Yü-ju 楊玉如 . *Hsin-hai ko-ming hsien chu chi* 辛亥革命先著記 (The 1911 revolution). Peking, 1957.

Yao Kung-ho 姚公鶴. *Shang-hai hsien-hua* 上海閒話 (Anecdotal history of Shanghai). Shanghai, 1925.

Yin Fu hsuan-chi 殷夫選集 (Selected works of Yin Fu). Peking, 1951.

Yü-lun chou-pao 輿論週報 (Public opinion weekly).

Yü ssu 語絲 (Brief discourses).

Yuan Ch'ang-ch'ao 袁昶超 . *Chung-kuo pao-yeh hsiao-shih* 中國報業小史 (History of Chinese journalism). Hong Kong, 1957.

Yung-sheng 永生 (Eternal life).

Yung tsai chui-nien chung ti T'ao-fen hsien-sheng 永在追念中的韜奮先生 (Mr. Tsou T'ao-fen will always live in our memory). N.p., T'ao-fen Press, 1947.

GLOSSARY

Chinese characters are not provided for those persons and titles that are either widely known in English or are drawn from English language documents. In a few cases, too, the appropriate characters have not been found. Generally the Wade-Giles system of romanization has been used. There are, however, a few exceptions. For example, Chao Ming-heng appears instead of Chao Min-heng, chiefly because his articles in English, which are cited, spell his name in the former way.

A Mei 阿美
A Ying 阿英
Ah Q cheng chuan 阿Q正傳
Ai Fei 艾飛
Ai Han-sung 艾寒松
Ai-mei ti hsi-chü
　　愛美的戲劇
Ai Ssu-ch'i 艾思奇
Ai ti ch'eng nien 愛的成年
An I 安逸
Ao Chia-hsiung 敖家熊

Chan Ta-pei 詹大悲
Chang Ai-ling 張愛玲
Chang Chi 張繼
Chang Chi-luan 張季鸞
Chang Chih-han 張志韓
Chang Chih-tung 張之洞

Chang Ching-yao 張靜堯
Chang Chün-mai 張君邁
Chang Hsiao-hu 張嘯虎
Chang Hsueh-liang 張學良
Chang Hsün 張勳
Chang Hu 張弧
Chang Hui 章回
Chang I-wei 張一葦
Chang Jo-yin 張若英
Chang K'o-piao 章克標
Chang Kung 張恭
Chang Kuo-kan 張國淦
Chang Ping-lin (T'ai-yen)
　　章炳麟 (太炎)
Chang Shih-chao 章士釗
Chang Tso-lin 張作霖
Chang Tsung-ch'ang 張宗昌
Chang Tsung-hsiang 章宗祥

287

Ch'ang Chiang 長江

Ch'ang Ming Company 昌明公司

Ch'ang Sheng 倉聖

Ch'ang-yen pan-yueh-k'an 昌言半月刊

Chao Ch'ao-kou 趙超構

Chao Ching-shen 趙景深

Chao Feng 趙渢

Chao Nan-kung 趙南公

chao pao 朝報

Chao Tse-ch'eng 趙則誠

Ch'ao 潮

Che-chiang ch'ao 浙江潮

Che-hsueh chiang-hua 哲學講話

Che Tsung, Emperor 哲宗

Chen-li News Agency 真理通訊社

Chen-li wan-pao 真理晚報

Chen pao 振報

Chen-tan min pao 震旦民報

Ch'en Chi-t'ang 陳濟棠

Ch'en Ch'i-mei 陳奇美

Ch'en Chiung-ming 陳烔明

Ch'en Ch'ü-ping 陳去病

Ch'en-chung pao 晨鐘報

Ch'en Fan 陳範

Ch'en Han-sheng 陳翰笙

Ch'en-kuang pao 晨光報

Ch'en Lang 陳朗

Ch'en Meng-hsiung 陳夢熊

Ch'en Ming-te 陳銘德

Ch'en pao 晨報

Ch'en Po-ta 陳伯達

Ch'en Pu-lei 陳布雷

Ch'en Shao-pai 陳少白

Ch'en Shu-yung 陳叔永

Ch'en Ta-pei 陳大悲

Ch'en Tu-hsiu 陳獨秀

Ch'en Yi 陳毅

Cheng Chen-to 鄭振鐸

Cheng Chung Book Company 正中書局

Cheng-i pao 正義報

Cheng-yen pao 正言報

Ch'eng Fu 誠夫

Ch'eng Mai 程邁

Ch'eng Ts'ang-po 程滄波

Ch'eng-yen 誠言

Chi Lien 季廉

Chi-lin i fen-tzu 吉林一份子

Chia-ting t'u-ch'eng chi 嘉定屠城記

Chiang Chao-chi 江肇基

Chiang Hsing-yü 蔣星煜

Chiang Hsueh-k'ai 蔣學楷

Chiang Liu 江流

Chiang Monlin 蔣夢麟

Chiang Shao-yuan 江紹源

Chiang-sheng jih-pao 江聲日報

Chiang-su 江蘇

Chiang Wen-yü 江問漁

Chieh-fang jih-pao 解放日報

Chieh-fang jih-pao hsuan-k'an 解放日報選刊

Chieh-fang pao 解放報

Chieh Fu 潔笑

Chien pao 健報

Ch'ien Hsing-ts'un 錢杏邨

Ch'ien Tuan-sheng 錢端升

Chih Chien 志堅

Chih-sheng chou-k'an 直聲週刊

Chih T'ang 知堂

Ch'ih Ch'un-huan 池春還

Chin-ch'iang pao 晉強報

Chin Chung-hua 金仲華

Chin-hsiu shan-ho 錦繡山河

Chin-hua pao 進化報

Chin-hua tsa-chih 進化雜誌

Chin I 靳以

Ch'in-feng jih-pao 秦風日報

Ch'in Mu 秦牧

Ch'in Te-shun 秦德純

Ching-chi t'ung-chi 經濟統計

Ching-chung jih-pao 警鐘日報

Ching pao 京報

Ching-shih chung 警世鐘

Ch'ing-nien hsün-k'an 青年旬刊

Ch'ing-nien pan-yueh-k'an 青年半月刊

Ch'ing pao 青報

Ch'ing Seng 情僧

Ch'ing shih kao 清史稿

Chiu-kuo chou-k'an 救國週刊

Chiu-kuo jih-pao 救國日報

Chiu-kuo wu pao 救國午報

Chiu-wang ch'ing-pao 救亡情報

Ch'iu 求

Ch'iu Ssu 求思

Chou Chien 周鍵

Chou Ching-wen 周鯨文

Chou Sung-yao 周頌堯

Chou Tso-jen 周作人

Ch'ou an hui 籌安會

Chu-chang yü p'i-p'ing 主張與批評

Chu Kuang-yü 朱光宇

Chu Shen 朱諜

Chu Teh 朱德

Ch'u An-p'ing 儲安平

Ch'u-pan chieh 出版界

ch'u-pan fa 出版法
Ch'uang-tsao she 創造社
Ch'un ch'an 春蠶
Chung Ch'ih 仲篪
Chung-hua hsin pao 中華新報
Chung-hua jih-pao 中華日報
Chung-hua ko-ming-tang 中華革命黨
Chung-hua pao 中華報
Chung-hua su-wei-ai kung-ho-kuo lin-shih chung-yang cheng fu 中華蘇維埃共和國臨時中央政府
Chung Hwa Book Company 中華書局
Chung-kuo ch'ing-nien 中國青年
Chung-kuo chou-k'an 中國週刊
Chung-kuo hsin nü chieh 中國新女界
Chung-kuo jih-pao 中國日報
Chung-kuo nung-min 中國農民
Chung-kuo pai-hua pao 中國白話報
Chung-kuo wen-hua shih 中國文化史
Chung-liu 中流
Chung-mei jih-pao 中美日報

Chung Ming 重明
Chung T'ien 鐘天
Chung-wai jih-pao 中外日報
Chung-yang jih-pao 中央日報
Chung-yang she 中央社
Chung-yang ta-t'ung pao 中央大同報
Chung-yang tien hsin she 中央電訊社
Chü Cheng 居正
Chü Ts'un 菊村
Chü Yuan 巨緣
Ch'ü Ch'iu-pai 瞿秋白
Ch'ü Yuan 屈原
Ch'üan P'ing 全平
Chün-jen hsü-chih 軍人須知
Ch'ün chih hsueh she 群治學社
Ch'ün-chung 群眾

Duke Wu of Chou 周武王

Erh-hsin chi 二心集
Erh-shih shih-chi chih Chih-na 二十世紀之支那
Erh-shih shih-chi ta wu-t'ai tsa-chi 二十世紀大舞台雜誌

Fan Ch'üan 范泉
Fan Hui 范惠

Fang Ying　方瑛
Fen P'ing　棻平
Feng-t'ien tung pao 奉天東報
Feng Yu-lan　馮友蘭
Feng Yü-hsiang　馮玉祥
Fu Ssu-nien　傅斯年
Fu Tan News Agency
　　復旦通訊社

Hai-wai hu-sheng 海外呼聲
Hai-yen　海燕
Han-chih　漢幟
Han-k'ou jih-pao 漢口日報
Han Lu　泓廬
Han-sheng　漢聲
Han Tzu　泓紫
Hang Hsin-chai　杭辛齋
Ho Ching　何經
Ho Hai-ming　何海鳴
Ho Lu-sheng　何魯生
Ho Man-tzu　何滿子
Ho Shu　何恕
Hsi yu chi　西遊記
Hsiang-chiang p'ing-lun
　　湘江評論
Hsiang Kung　象恭
hsiao-ch'ou　小醜
Hsiao-hsi　消息
hsiao pao　小報
Hsien-hua Yang-chou 閒話揚州

Hsien Tai Book Company 現代書局

Hsin ch'ao　新潮
Hsin Chung-kuo chou-pao
　　新中國週報
Hsin Chung-kuo jih-pao
　　新中國日報
Hsin hsing pao　新星報
Hsin Hu-nan　新湖南
Hsin-hua jih-pao　新華日報
Hsin-hua shih-pao　新華時報
Hsin-hua shu-tien　新華書店
Hsin-lu　新路
Hsin-min pao　新民報
Hsin shan-ko　新山歌
Hsin she-hui pao　新社會報
Hsin sheng-huo　新生活
*Hsin shih-tai kuo-yü chiao-
　shou shu* 新時代國語教授書

hsin-wen fa　新聞法
Hsin-wen pao　新聞報
Hsin wen-tzu　新文字
Hsing-chi p'ing-lun　星期評論
Hsing-shih　醒獅
Hsing Su　行素
Hsiu Lu　岫廬
Hsiung Hsi-ling　熊希齡
Hsü Ching-sung　許景宋
Hsü Ch'ing-yu　徐慶譽

Hsü Hsien 徐賢
Hsü Wan-ch'eng 許晚成
Hsuan Chu 玄珠
Hsueh Fan 學范
Hu Chao 胡釗
Hu Cheng-chih 胡政之
Hu Chien-chung 胡健中
Hu Feng 胡風
Hu Han-min 胡漢民
Hu Lan-ch'eng 胡蘭成
Hu-nan kung pao 湖南公報
Hu-nan t'ung-su chiao-yü pao
　　湖南通俗教育報
Hu-pei hsueh-sheng chieh
　　湖北學生界
Hu-pei jih-pao 湖北日報
Hu Sheng 滬生
Hu Shih 胡適
Hu Shih wen-ts'un 胡適文存
Hu Tao-ching 胡道靜
Hu Ti 胡笛
Hu Yü-chih 胡愈之
Hua-hsi wan-pao 華西晚報
Hua-mei ch'en pao 華美晨報
Hua-mei wan-pao 華美晚報
Hua-pei hsin-wen 華北新聞
Hua-pei jih-pao 華北日報
Hua T'e News Agency
　　華特通訊社
Hua Wei 華威

Huai Kan 懷感
Huan Ch'eng 寰澄
Huan chou 幻洲
Huang Fei 黃非
Huang-ho wan-pao 黃河晚報
Huang Hsing 黃興
Huang K'an 黃侃
Huang Liang-meng 黃梁夢
Huang T'ien-p'eng 黃天鵬
Huang Yen-p'ei 黃炎培
Hung Ling-fei 洪靈菲
Hung Ni ku-niang yen-shih
　　紅妮姑娘艷史
Hung P'o 洪波
Huo Yen 霍燄

I Chün-tso 易君左
I Hsia 毅俠
I ku ch'ing-ch'eng 一顧傾城
I Min 逸民
I-shih pao 益世報
I Shui 易水
I Yin-ch'u 易寅初

Jen pao 人報
Jen Ssu-wei 任四維
Jen Tsung, Emperor 仁宗
Jih chih hui 日知會
Jo-hsueh jih-pao 熱血日報
Jo Yü 若愚

Kai-tsao 改造
K'ai-ming jih-pao
　　關明日報
K'ang-hsi, Emperor 康熙
K'ang Teh, Emperor 康德
K'ang Yu-wei 康有為
Kao I-han 高一涵
Kao Shih-ming 高士銘
Ko pi 戈壁
Ko Ssu-en 葛思恩
Ko Ta 戈達
K'o Ling 柯靈
K'o pao 可報
K'o Shih 克士
Ku Chu-t'ung 顧祝同
Ku K'ang-po 顧康伯
Ku Wei-chün (Wellington Koo)
　　顧維鈞
K'uai-lo chih shen 快樂之神
K'uai pao 快報
Kuang-hsü, Emperor 光緒
Kuang-hua jih-pao 光華日報
Kuang-hua pao 光華報
K'uang Hsiao-an 鄺笑蒼
Kuei-sui jih-pao 歸綏日報
Kung-ch'an chu-i ABC
　　共產主義 ABC
Kung-jen pao-chien
　　工人寶鑑
Kung-li jih-pao 公理日報

Kung-shang jih-pao 工商日報
K'ung Hsiang-hsi (H. H. Kung) 孔祥熙

Kuo-chi hsieh pao 國際協報
Kuo-chi jih-pao 國際日報
Kuo-ch'üan pao 國權報
Kuo Lai-jen 過來仁
Kuo-min hsin pao 國民新報
Kuo-min jih-pao 國民日報
Kuo-min kung pao 國民公報
Kuo-min pao 國民報
Kuo Ming 郭明
Kuo Mo-jo 郭沫若
Kuo pao 國報
Kuo Sung-ling 郭松齡
Kuo Wen News Agency 國聞通訊社

Kuo-wen pao 國聞報

Lan T'ien-wei 藍天蔚
Lao Jung 勞榮
Li Chien-hua 李劍華
Li Chu 黎澍
Li Ch'un-t'ao 李春濤
Li Chung-jen 李宗仁
Li Fu-jen 李敷仁
Li Kung-i 李恭貽
Li Kung-p'u 李公樸
Li Shu-ch'ing 李樹青
Li Ta-chao 李大釗

pu 社會科學研究初步

she-lun 社論

she-p'ing 社評

Shen Chin 沈藎

Shen-chou jih-pao 神州日報

Shen-chou kuo kuang she 神州國光社

Shen Li 沈犁

Shen P'eng 沈鵬

Shen Ts'ung-wen 沈從文

Shen Yen-ping 沈雁冰

Shen Yu 申由

Sheng-huo hsing-chi k'an 生活星期刊

Sheng-huo jih-pao 生活日報

Sheng-huo jih-pao hsing-chi k'an 生活日報星期刊

Sheng-huo she 生活社

Shih-ching 詩經

Shih Fu-liang 施復亮

Shih I 適夷

Shih Kang 師崗

Shih Liang-ts'ai 史量才

Shih-ling chi 拾零集

Shih pao 時報

Shih-shih hsin pao 時事新報

Shih-tai 時代

Shih-tai jih-pao 時代日報

Shih-tai p'ing-lun 時代評論

Shih Tai Press 時代書局

Shih Tung 史東

Shih Yen 史言

Shih-tzu hou 獅子吼

Shih-wu pao 時務報

Shih-yeh chou-pao 實業週報

Shih Yung 史永

Shui-pien 蛻變

Shun Te 順德

Shun-t'ien shih pao 順天時報

Ssu-ch'uan tsa-chih 四川雜誌

Ssu Fang 四方

Ssu Hsien 思賢

Su-lien ming ko chi 蘇聯名歌集

Su-lien yin-yueh 蘇聯音樂

Su-lien wen-i 蘇聯文藝

Su sheng 蘇聲

Sui-yuan jih-pao 綏遠日報

Sun Chia-nai 孫家鼐

Sun Ch'uan-fang 孫傳芳

Sun Han-ping 孫寒冰

Sun K'o (Sun Fo) 孫科

Sun Te-chen 孫德鎮

Sun Wen chu-i chih li-lun yü shih-chi 孫文主義之理論與實際

Sung Che-yuan 宋哲元

Sung Chiao-jen 宋教仁

Sung Tzu-wen (T. V. Soong) 宋子文

Ta-chiang jih-pao 大江日報
Ta Chung shu-chü 大中書局
Ta-chung yeh-pao 大眾夜報
Ta Han pao 大漢報
Ta-kang pao 大剛報
Ta-mei jih-pao 大美日報
Ta-mei wan-pao 大美晚報
Ta Tun 大頓
Ta T'ung Book Company 大同書局
Tai Chi-t'ao 戴季陶
T'ai-p'ing 太平
T'ai Tung Book Company 泰東圖書局
T'an Tu-kung 譚篤恭
T'ang Shao-i 唐紹儀
T'ang T'ao 唐弢
T'ang Tseng-pi 湯增壁
Tao pao 導報
T'ao Hsi-sheng 陶希聖
T'ao Hsing-chih 陶行知
T'ao Meng-ho 陶孟和
T'ao Ti-ya 陶滌亞
Teng T'e 鄧特
Teng Yen-ta 鄧演達
Ti-k'ang 抵抗
T'ieh 鐵
T'ieh-liu 鐵流
T'ien Han 田漢
T'Ien Hsiao-te 田肖德

T'ien Kao 天高
T'ien-min pao 天民報
T'ien Sheng 天生
T'ien t'ao 天討
T'ien T'ung 田桐
Ting Ching 丁靜
Ting I 丁一
Ting Ling 丁玲
T'ing Ming 汀明
T'o-huang che 拓荒者
Tou-cheng 鬥爭
Ts'ai Hui-tung 蔡惠東
Ts'ai Nai-huang 蔡乃煌
Ts'ai Shang-ssu 蔡尚思
Ts'ai Yuan-p'ei 蔡元培
"Tsao yao-shu yao-yen" 造妖書妖言
Ts'ao A-kou 曹阿狗
Ts'ao Ching-hua 曹靖華
Ts'ao Chü-jen 曹聚仁
Ts'ao Ju-lin 曹汝霖
Ts'ao K'un 曹錕
Ts'ao Yü 曹禺
Ts'en Ch'un-hsuan 岑春煊
Ts'eng Ch'i 曹琦
Tso-chia 作家
Tsou En-jun 鄒恩潤
Ts'ui-hsin pao 萃新報
Tsun Wen 尊聞
Tu Chung-yuan 杜重遠

Tu Fu　杜甫
Tu-hsiu wen-ts'un 獨秀文存
T'u Jan　徒然
Tuan Ch'i-jui　段啟瑞
Tuan Fang　端方
t'uan-chieh　團結
T'uan Wu News Agency
　　團悟通訊社
Tung Ch'iu-ssu　董秋斯
Tung-nan jih-pao 東南日報
Tung Shih-chin　董時進
Tung Ta-tsai　董達哉
Tung-t'ing p'o 洞庭波
T'ung-hai hsin pao 通海新報
t'ung-i　統一
T'ung Meng Hui　同盟會
Tzu-chi ti yuan-ti
　　自己的園地
Tzu Kang　子岡
Tzu-pen chu-i chih p'o-chieh
　　資本主義之剖解
Tzu Wu　子午
Tzu-yu hsin pao 自由新報
Tzu-yu tao pao 自由導報
Tz'u-hsi, Empress Dowager
　　慈禧太后

Wan Ch'eng　萬程
Wan wan-pao 晚晚報
Wang Ching-wei 汪精衛

Wang I-an　王易庵
Wang Po-heng　王伯衡
Wang Shih-chieh　王世杰
Wang Shui　王水
Wang Ting-ch'i　王定圻
Wang Yun-sheng　王芸生
Wei Kuang-t'ao　魏光燾
Wei Ying　蔚英
Wen-hsueh　文學
Wen-hsueh chou-pao 文學週報
Wen-hsueh tao pao 文學導報
Wen-hsueh yueh-pao 文學月報
Wen Hua　文化
Wen-hui pao　文匯報
Wen Shang　穩尚
Wen Tsai-tao　文載道
Wo-ti yu-nien 我的幼年
Wu-ch'ang pai-hua pao
　　武昌白話報
Wu ch'i　五七
Wu Chih-hui　吳稚暉
Wu Chung-hsin　吳忠信
Wu Han　吳晗
Wu-i t'e-k'an 五一特刊
Wu Ming　無明
Wu P'ei-fu　吳佩孚
Wu Shih-ch'ang　吳世昌
Wu T'ieh-ch'eng (Te-chen)
　　吳鐵城
Wu T'ieh-sheng 吳鐵聲

Wu T'ien-fang 吳天放

Ya-hsi-ya pao 亞細亞報

Yang En-p'u 楊恩溥

Yang Hsia-ch'ing 楊霞青

Yang Hsing-fo 楊杏佛

Yang I 楊昜

Yang Kang 楊剛

Yang Tsao 羊棗

Yeh Ch'u-ts'ang 葉楚傖

Yeh Chün-i 葉君宜

Yeh Ko 耶戈

Yeh Sheng-t'ao 葉聖陶

Yen Ching-yao 嚴景耀

Yen Fu 嚴復

Yen Ling-feng 嚴靈峰

Yen Tun 嚴盾

Yen Yang-ch'u (James Y. C.) 晏陽初

Yin Huai-yuan 殷懷遠

Yin-ping-shih wen-chi 飲冰室文集

Yin Yang 隱揚

Ying Hsiu-jen 應修人

Ying Wei-min 應衛民

Yung-cheng, Emperor 雍正

Yung-sheng 永生

Yü-chung News Agency 渝鐘通訊社

Yü Han-mou 余漢謀

Yü Hsueh-chung 于學忠

Yü I-ch'en 余一琛

Yü Jen 愚人

Yü Liang 玉良

Yü Ta-fu 郁達夫

Yuan I-min 袁一民

Yuan Sheng 原生

Yuan Shih-k'ai 袁世凱

Yuan Shu-hsün 袁樹勛

Yuan T'ien 源天

Yun-nan 雲南

92, 106; Central Executive
Committee, 6, 14, 17, 84, 100,
111, 115, 118-119, 198, 238;
Central Political Committee, 15;
Central Publicity Department,
15, 16, 17, 18, 19, 90, 93, 95,
101, 106, 107, 110, 120-121,
152; see also Ministry of Information
KMT-CCP alliance (1924), 14, 64,
79, 115; (1937), 19, 22, 126,
135
KMT-owned newspapers, 94, 98,
127, 133, 145, 147, 165-166,
167-169, 257, 259; see also
Central Daily News
KMT publications exempt from
censorship, 17, 244
KMT thought-control defended,
119-121, 239

Lan T'ien-wei, 29
Landlords' permission for pub-
lishers, 14, 57
Lansdowne, 5th Marquess, 34
Latinxua movement, 92, 228
Lattimore, Owen, 141
Laws and regulations concerning
publications, 7-26, 62, 84, 165,
197, 198-199, 269; see also
Publication laws; Press laws; and
other laws and regulations by
name
Lawson, Ted W. Thirty Seconds
over Tokyo, 149
League for Civil Rights, 96-97, 105,
153
League of Chinese Social Scientists, 80
League of Left-Wing Writers, 80, 82,
220, 222

Lebbe, Vincent, 210
Legislative Yuan, 177-178, 198
Lenin, Vladimir Ilyich, 239
Li Fu-jen, 179-180, 266
Li Kung-i, 180
Li Kung-p'u, 260
Li Shu-ch'ing, 143
Li Ta-chao, 65
Li Ya-tung, 42
Li Yuan-hung, 12, 50, 209
Liang Ch'i-ch'ao, 27-28, 30, 50, 56,
199, 207, 209
Liang Shih-ch'iu, 116
Ling-yu t'u-shu kung-ssu, 220
Lieh-ning ch'ing-nien, 82, 222
Lieh-ning hsuan-chi, 139
Lien Ho Book Company, 121
Lien-ho wan-pao (Shanghai), 177
Life Publishing Company, 146-147,
155-157, 252-253
Life Weekly, 88, 89, 105, 151-153,
155-157, 251-252
Lin Pai-shui, 39, 59, 60-61, 214
Lin Sen, 133
Lin Yutang, 58-59, 87, 215
Liu Shih-fu, 56
Liu Shu-tan, 96
Liu Ya-tzu, 140, 246, 269
Liu Yü-sheng, 96
Lo Lung-chi, 93, 116, 237, 269
Loans to favored publishers, 148, 167
Lou Tzu-k'uang, 100-101
Lu Hsin, 32-33
Lu Hsün, 54, 57, 80, 81-82, 87, 125,
131, 221, 228, 230-231
Lu Hsün, Mrs., see Hsü Ching-sung
Lun Chung-kuo chih ming-yün, 139
Lunacharsky, A. V., 92
Lunar calendar outlawed, 92, 228,
233

HARVARD EAST ASIAN MONOGRAPHS

18. Frank H.H. King (ed.) and Prescott Clarke, *A Research Guide to China-Coast Newspapers, 1822-1911*

19. Ellis Joffe, *Party and Army: Professionalism and Political Control in the Chinese Officer Corps, 1949-1964*

20. Toshio G. Tsukahira, *Feudal Control in Tokugawa Japan: The Sankin Kōtai System*

21. Kwang-Ching Liu, ed., *American Missionaries in China: Papers from Harvard Seminars*

22. George Moseley, *A Sino-Soviet Cultural Frontier: The Ili Kazakh Autonomous Chou*

23. Carl F. Nathan, *Plague Prevention and Politics in Manchuria, 1910-1931*

24. Adrian Arthur Bennett, *John Fryer: The Introduction of Western Science and Technology into Nineteenth-Century China*

25. Donald J. Friedman, *The Road from Isolation: The Campaign of the American Committee for Non-Participation in Japanese Aggression, 1938-1941*

26 Edward Le Fevour, *Western Enterprise in Late Ch'ing China; A selective Survey of Jardine, Matheson and Company's Operations, 1842-1895*

27. Charles Neuhauser, *Third World Politics: China and the Afro-Asian People's Solidarity Organization, 1957-1967*

28. Kungtu C. Sun, assisted by Ralph W. Huenemann, *The Economic Development of Manchuria in the First Half of the Twentieth Century*

29. Shahid Javed Burki, *A Study of Chinese Communes, 1965*

30 John Carter Vincent, *The Extraterritorial System in China: Final Phase*

31. Madeleine Chi, *China Diplomacy, 1914-1918*

32. Clifton Jackson Phillips, *Protestant America and the Pagan World: The First Half Century of the American Board of Commissioners for Foreign Missions, 1810-1860*